Palgrave Executive Essentials

Today's complex and changing business environment brings with it a number of pressing challenges. To be successful, business professionals are increasingly required to leverage and spot future trends, be masters of strategy, all while leading responsibly, inspiring others, mastering financial techniques and driving innovation.

Palgrave Executive Essentials empowers you to take your skills to the next level. Offering a suite of resources to support you on your executive journey and written by renowned experts from top business schools, the series is designed to support professionals as they embark on executive education courses, but it is equally applicable to practicing leaders and managers. Each book brings you in-depth case studies, accompanying video resources, reflective questions, practical tools and core concepts that can be easily applied to your organization, all written in an engaging, easy to read style.

Alejandro Reyes

Leading Organizational Transformation

Embracing Liberation, Vitality, and Expression to Build a Success-Capable Organization

Alejandro Reyes
Canton, MA, USA

ISSN 2731-5614　　　　　　ISSN 2731-5622　(electronic)
Palgrave Executive Essentials
ISBN 978-3-031-89762-7　　　ISBN 978-3-031-89763-4　(eBook)
https://doi.org/10.1007/978-3-031-89763-4

© The Editor(s) (if applicable) and The Author(s), under exclusive license to Springer Nature Switzerland AG 2025

This work is subject to copyright. All rights are solely and exclusively licensed by the Publisher, whether the whole or part of the material is concerned, specifically the rights of translation, reprinting, reuse of illustrations, recitation, broadcasting, reproduction on microfilms or in any other physical way, and transmission or information storage and retrieval, electronic adaptation, computer software, or by similar or dissimilar methodology now known or hereafter developed.
The use of general descriptive names, registered names, trademarks, service marks, etc. in this publication does not imply, even in the absence of a specific statement, that such names are exempt from the relevant protective laws and regulations and therefore free for general use.
The publisher, the authors and the editors are safe to assume that the advice and information in this book are believed to be true and accurate at the date of publication. Neither the publisher nor the authors or the editors give a warranty, expressed or implied, with respect to the material contained herein or for any errors or omissions that may have been made. The publisher remains neutral with regard to jurisdictional claims in published maps and institutional affiliations.

Cover illustration: Estudio Calamar

This Palgrave Macmillan imprint is published by the registered company Springer Nature Switzerland AG
The registered company address is: Gewerbestrasse 11, 6330 Cham, Switzerland

If disposing of this product, please recycle the paper.

To Rocío, my source of liberation
To Chío and Alex, my teachers of liberation and vitality
To the memory of Platón and Concepción
To the journeys of Jerónimo and Paty

Competing Interests The author has no competing interests to declare that are relevant to the content of this manuscript.

Praise for *Leading Organizational Transformation*

'I have been studying transformations for decades and never before have their success rates been so low as they are today. We have all advised leaders on the pitfalls of such large-scale change efforts with modest success by offering new processes and tools that encourage them, in my words, to 'think big, start small, and move fast.' What we have perhaps not looked at enough is the important human mindset that executives and managers approach such transformations with. I love the approach of equipping leaders with new aspirations in the service of improving their change initiative results. Furthermore, I think that Liberation, Vitality, and Expression are thought-provoking mindsets and could contribute meaningfully to the search for a better way to transform organizations. Bravo Alejandro for offering a step-by-step methodology that can improve the way all human capital experiences work in the future!'

—Sandy Ogg, *Founder, CEO.Works*

'Having had the privilege of working with Alejando at Dell Technologies on leadership development, I witnessed his rare ability to inspire transformative leadership rooted in purpose and authenticity. His book is a masterful guide to building inclusive, resilient, high-performing cultures that prioritize liberation, adaptability, and a deep commitment to shared success. As I work to cultivate a culture of results-driven accountability and collaboration at NMSDC, this book resonates deeply, offering timeless insights for any leader striving to create lasting impact in the face of complexity and change.'

—Ying McGuire, *CEO & President, National Minority Supplier Development Council*

'As most executives would attest, there are new requirements for employers to effectively manage their workforce a mindful way which requires both foresight and adaptability. In this insightful book, Alejandro draws upon his extensive experience as an HR executive, spanning 25 years of leadership across diverse industries. With a keen eye on the evolving landscape where employers must balance the power of AI against an increasing set of expectations from their employees, Alejandro expertly examines the current shifts and challenges facing organizations worldwide. Leading Success offers practical insights for harnessing talent amidst rapid technological advancements. Whether you're a seasoned HR professional or a business leader navigating change, this book promises to be an indispensable guide to shaping a resilient and forward-looking workforce strategy.'

—Leslie Nielson, *Managing Director—MAS/STS, Alvarez & Marsal, Private Equity Performance Improvement*

'How do you lead sustainable transformations in a world that is itself changing? Start here! Alejandro Reyes provides three profound, elegant, and surprising lenses, 'Liberation, Vitality and Expression.' He understands and decodes a new workforce in ways you have not seen before. Reyes brilliantly leverages his experience to blend deep thought leadership with practical methodology. He has created your GPS for the road ahead.'

—Don Jones, *President, Experience It Inc.*

'In Leading Success Alejandro Reyes enlightens us that successful companies that outperform the competition are distinct in three ways. These leaders think, act, and grow leaders differently. The blue print is passionately shared, and the value add is then up to you.'

—Steve Mostyn, *Associate Fellow Saïd Business School, University of Oxford, Honorary Professor Adam Smith Business School*

'After revolutionizing several of the world's leading companies, Alejandro Reyes, a visionary leader in HR and organizational transformation, now offers his experience and insight to C-suite leaders. Far too many corporate transformation strategies fall short in the execution. Reyes's strategic insights and profound expertise will help readers succeed.'

—Dan Fisher, *Author, Managing Partner at Contemporary Leadership Advisors*

'Alejandro is a creative and inspirational thinker and leader. 'Leading Success' sums up the lessons of his long career as an HR pace setter and puts them in the context of a contemporary world where the voices of our employees, customers, and AI play an ever-growing role.'

—Peter George, *SVP and Chief Technology Officer, Houghton Mifflin Harcourt*

Contents

Part I Mindset

1 Introduction — 3
2 Leading Success — 9
3 Leadership of Liberation — 27
4 Liberation in the Era of Purpose — 49

Part II Journey

5 The Liberation Mindset: Word vs World — 63
6 Aspiration: A Quest to Change the World — 71
7 Transformation: The History of the Future — 79
8 Commitment: Owning the Purpose — 91
9 The Vitality Mindset: The Trilogy of Success — 103
10 Culture: What We Stand for — 111
11 Talent: The Talent Economy — 127
12 Organization: Winning with Signature Processes — 157
13 The Expression Mindset: Becoming Your Purpose — 187

14	Engagement: Liberation, One Person at a Time	195
15	Expectation: Conversations for Commitment	205
16	Experience: Mastering Expression as Performance	221

Part III Outcomes

17	Business Outcomes: Transformation Success	237
18	Culture Outcomes: Smart, Profitable, and Inclusive	257
19	People Outcomes: A Renewed Mandate for HR	275
20	Legacy: Becoming a Liberator	293

Brands Index	301
Name Index	303
Index	307

List of Figures

Fig. 2.1	The future of work is forcing a revision of the road to success	16
Fig. 2.2	The three mindsets of leading success	19
Fig. 2.3	The nine disciplines of leading success	22
Fig. 2.4	The leader's choice in leading success	25
Fig. 3.1	How employees perceive liberating leadership, and how managers create the liberating environment	31
Fig. 3.2	The scope of the Liberation Mindset in Leading Success	33
Fig. 4.1	A taxonomy on the evolution of effectiveness and success paradigms across time	50
Fig. 4.2	Leading Success portfolio of Mindsets and Disciplines	59
Fig. 5.1	The foundational architecture of transformation in Leading Success	65
Fig. 5.2	The source of Aspiration: WORD versus WORLD	67
Fig. 5.3	The source of Transformation: ADAPT and DISRUPT	68
Fig. 5.4	Commitment is the driving force to scale transformation	69
Fig. 6.1	The anatomy of a liberating aspiration	74
Fig. 7.1	The anatomy of a leading success transformation articulation	84
Fig. 8.1	The critical, differentiating contribution of the commitment discipline in transformation	92
Fig. 8.2	Structure and components of conversations to create liberating commitment	96
Fig. 9.1	Vitality is the organizational infrastructure that makes the transformation become operational and *signature* (consistent with our values)	106

Fig. 9.2	The leading success trilogy, defining the map of leading success' organizational infrastructure	108
Fig. 10.1	The signature culture experience	115
Fig. 11.1	Talent Market: the winning candidate is the one who can perform the duties, fulfill the responsibilities, has the experience and the credentials	129
Fig. 11.2	Talent economy: the winning candidate can perform in a way that creates business value and deliver a return on talent for the company	130
Fig. 11.3	Example of an EVP consistent with Leading Success	135
Fig. 11.4	Framework for the Vital Talent Economy implementation	139
Fig. 11.5	Example of critical people processes for success	144
Fig. 11.6	Classification of People Processes based on Talent Economy priorities	145
Fig. 12.1	The signature business process inventory	159
Fig. 12.2	Difference between job description and position profile	168
Fig. 12.3	Example of a position profile	169
Fig. 12.4	The vital governance for leading success	178
Fig. 12.5	Generic organization review design for vitality	182
Fig. 12.6	Components of a vital enterprise governance model	183
Fig. 13.1	Becoming our transformation is how the WORD changes the WORLD	193
Fig. 14.1	The five steps to build the scalable transformational engagement	201
Fig. 14.2	Content and sequence suggested for engagement sessions	202
Fig. 15.1	What companies can do to improve execution	209
Fig. 15.2	Skill areas to define expectations for a liberating, vital expression leadership and management practice	214
Fig. 15.3	What managers can do to improve execution	215
Fig. 16.1	The essence of leading success is to ensure that our vision becomes the experience, at scale	225
Fig. 16.2	Expression and performance as the keys for signature experience	233
Fig. 17.1	Recommended implementation roadmaps per company size	238
Fig. 17.2	Implementation risk: disconnected solutions	247
Fig. 17.3	Implementation risk: oversimplified execution of transformation	250
Fig. 17.4	Implementation risk: leaders unclear of whole journey of transformation	252
Fig. 17.5	Implementation risk: investments and solutions without strategic orientation	254
Fig. 17.6	Implementation risk: Lack of transformation management infrastructure	255
Fig. 18.1	The diversity ecosystem for leading success	263

Fig. 18.2	The organic DEIB organization	265
Fig. 19.1	The evolution of the people function organization	279
Fig. 19.2	How the work in HR changes with leading success	281
Fig. 19.3	The transformation of the HR function—role perspective	287
Fig. 19.4	The people function leader for the future of work	288
Fig. 19.5	A new identify for a liberating people function	291
Fig. 20.1	Depiction of the Columns of Hercules, according to legend, with the inscription PLUS ULTRA, meaning 'There is More'	298

Part I

Mindset

1

Introduction

- A fresh perspective and a blueprint on what it will take to reset the People Function to deliver modern solutions to modern problems, even those that come to us unexpectedly.
- A way to make your company capable of significant transformation while becoming a magnet for talent for the next era, and a method to create the infrastructure to accomplish and sustain that capability.
- A new mindset for leaders to raise their awareness that our leadership is *both* the catalyst for and the limit to the organization. I.e., with great power comes great responsibility. This is much more profound that the way it reads and the foundational cornerstone of a success-ready organization.

Leading Success in the Future of Work

A few months after being fired from my first Chief People Officer role I had started writing this book. It had been in my mind for two decades, I had annotations, stories, examples, cases, and a vast reservoir of research to write something I wanted to be relevant and useful. I was under the belief I was going to write for someone else who would need to learn from my rights and wrongs, but as I learned, writing is also about the self, involving a discovery process that does not end when the book is completed. A few months into the writing journey I stumbled into a podcast from the US National Public Radio (NPR) for an interview the host Terry Gross was conducting with the laureated writer Salman Rushdie,[1] as part of her *Fresh Air* program. Rushide was talking about his latest book, *KNIFE: Meditations After an Attempted Murder*,[2] which narrated the experience of his near-death experience, being stabbed multiple times during a presentation at the Chautauqua Institution NY, in the year 2022.

I was both captivated and horrified by the story and its copious detail. My first reaction was to imagine that nobody having been on Salman's Rushdie's shoes that day would like to remember much about that event, and yet, we were listening to this gentleman who wrote an entire book about it. At some point in the interview Terry asked the question I was most interested to learn about: 'why did you write about this?'. In his answer, he said '*…I tell my students to only write the books you can't avoid writing…, there is a plenty of books already. I just could not avoid writing it*'. I immediately stopped what I was doing. Surprised that his answer was so fundamental, so internal, and honest. It took me a few moments to process the message; he had put into words exactly what I had been feeling for a long time. For years I knew I had something to say, until the point it became inevitable for me. I wanted to express something I had found, experienced, and being successful with it; something in which I had seen myself and others failing so many times and seen people unhappy, frustrated, seeing so much value not realized. I wanted to share how I had found a way.

I wrote this book with two foundational ideas in mind. First, the demonstrated experience that this content works. The content you will read is something I have implemented, very often as leader, also as a team member, most of the time as architect of the frameworks—exceptions will be noted. I have personally applied every recommended solution, tool, and approach successfully, as I learned from failure; it is not fake or invented. *Leading Organizational Transformation; Embracing Liberation, Vitality, and Expression to Create Enduring Success*—called in short for the rest of this book 'Leading Success', expands the contemporary thinking on transformation, our understanding of leadership and brings a point of view to the design of the People Function (HR), re-emerging after the pandemic but still working to find its way as the world is changing. And second, on the belief that leaders are more effective in the presence or organized thinking. There are new concepts in this book, a handful of them I would call revolutionary, but for the most part the innovation of Leading Organizational Transformation rests on how the new and the familiar concepts, tools, practices in the transformation of organizations are elegantly connected to simplify something rather complex.

I am indeed, as Isaac Newton said, standing in the shoulders of giants, who allowed me to see further: significant leaders along the way, including all the managers I have had in my career, my mentors and teachers, but also, and very prominently, the extraordinary people I have been so blessed to have in my teams, as well as great peers and customers.

One of those giants came early in my career, in one of my first jobs after college. During the onboarding session on my first day in that job a division leader had been asked to talk to our new hire cohort, and what he said that day got carved in my mind forever: 'In spite of what you may think, the truth is that you are not being paid for what you will be asked to do, but to help us find a way to make it better, to make all of this place better, to make *you* better'—he explained that making anything better, faster, smarter, or improved is the discipline of discerning and deciding the Why, the How, and the When. He then quoted Don Quixote by Miguel de Cervantes: 'You don't love things only for what they are, but for what they can become'. Those statements profoundly affected my perception of what great leadership requires.

After twenty-five years of experience in executive development and talent management, I have seen this capability in higher demand; and given our changing world, it will become one of the most critical requirements to navigate uncertainty. Over the course of my career, I have worked with more than 1,500 senior leaders, CEOs, C-suite executives, and their next line of command across the Americas, Europe, Africa, Asia, and Australia, supporting them as coach, mentor, career advisor, executive education lead. I structured their evaluations and advocated for their promotions, giving me a distinctly close understanding of how management decisions of career moves and promotions get made. Most of the above experience was lived during times of significant transformation, eras of company reinvention, identity evolution, inflection points to redefine a decade of business ahead. These environments allowed me to observe how great talent differentiates above the rest, takes and creates opportunities to unleash their organizations for growth. I have seen first-hand how the ability to lead through disruptive change is one of the most essential skills for successful leaders, and one that will only grow in importance in the future.

One of the basic management rules is that leadership requires the skill to run the day-to-day operation and also the ability to transform and evolve the business. Regardless of the organization size, industry, or territory the problem of transformation is fundamentally the same: How can we engage the right people in the right way to activate *change that endures*. In other words, how effective are we at sustaining success. The key ingredients still need to be there: business strategy, capital, a reliable supply chain, and a winning product. But vital transformations still go through people. You need the right talent in the right mindset to realize your ambitious transformation.

This is why Leading Success—a people-first approach—is essential for leaders to explore as they endeavor to reinvent their companies.

The people side of the business has changed, it is no longer a known commodity—if it ever was. The days of assuming we knew a process that worked and had the answers to most questions is over. A new era came to us almost overnight. New complexities have forced CEOs to react and respond, and to adapt their ambitions to the capacities of what the HR organizations can deliver, with their tight budgets. You read the news and understand a lot is going on with talent and society and realize your company is not shielded to any of these exploding realities. None of which were in the Business School playbook, nobody was prepared for this, but some were more ready. This book offers a perspective of how to be more ready.

In addition to the external factors of unknown disruption, the People function, Human Resources, has been itself in a soul-search journey for some time[3] and it's time for it to evolve. For a couple of decades now, as companies fight to survive competitive markets, they have implemented cost management and productivity measures, and as a result, all functional teams have sustained important cuts; very seldom, if ever, reinvestment has reached the people function. Competitive business conditions have created a generation of HR leaders who were educated for strategic impact but were pushed by business realities to solve for the immediate and most urgent priorities, leaving it to midnight time or weekends to tinker with the strategic, long-term planning and next-generation designs. It is also true that some HR leaders have become too HR-centered in the process and gained little traction and credibility with their peers as transformational business leaders. The remedy starts with HR but cannot be completed just with harder work in the function. Building a strong people brand inside and out of a company is no longer a people function's problem alone. It is the C-suite's responsibility; and primarily, the CEO, who in partnership with the CHRO, owns the design of a company to be success-ready and culturally robust to thrive in crises.

The Promise of This Book: What Will You Get from This Reading?

Here is my intended design for CEOs, leaders at the C-suite, managers at all levels, and HR executives, developing practitioners to take away from this book.

- A fresh perspective and a blueprint on what it will take to reset the People Function to deliver modern solutions to modern problems, even those that come to us unexpectedly.
- A way to make your company capable of significant transformation while becoming a magnet for talent for the next era, and a method to create the infrastructure to accomplish and sustain that capability.
- A new mindset for leaders to raise their awareness that our leadership is *both* the catalyst for and the limit to the organization. I.e., with great power comes great responsibility. This is much more profound that the way it reads and the foundational cornerstone of a success-ready organization.

I call the above *Leading Success*—a more formal definition will be explored ahead. As we set ourselves in motion to achieve it, we will be making the organization remarkably ready for success, a talent magnet, and robust against unexpected disruptions.

To be clear, there is much written about steps, models, and frameworks to define a strategy and then statements on what steps need to be performed to implementation. In this book we go beyond statements. What this reading will give you in addition, is a new perspective on how reframing your leadership can energize the organization to reach a quantum leap on performance, cultural stability, and employee desirability, critical to succeed in hyper-competitive skills and markets, and a coherent path with proven/tested actions to show how a strategy is activated at scale, from the top vision all the way to every employee in the organization.

But there is a catch: you, as CEO, must be part of, and co-own the solution. You will further discover what Leading Success means, define it strategically, then operationally for your company, and design your people agenda around it, together with your CHRO. Leading Success is not a project; is a way to run the business for success and it is only possible if you are a co-champion for it with your CHRO.

I trust you will enjoy the reading.
Alejandro Reyes
Boston, MA

Notes

1. NPR. 2024. Salman Rushide on Surviving Attempter Murder. Fresh AirEpisode aired on April 16, 2024. Retrieved from: https://www.npr.org/2024/04/16/1197964990/salman-rushdie-knife.

2. Rushide, Salman. 2024. Knife: Meditations After an Attempted Murder. Random House.
3. McCord, P. (2014, January). How Netflix reinvented HR. Harvard Business Review.

2

Leading Success

Multiple studies and researchers have correctly claimed that since the beginning of the Industrial Revolution the world is constantly changing[1] and therefore, work, employment, and workforce availability, including its cost and impact on the value chain constantly changes too. Looking back to those 250 years of history, we can see the inception of the industrial organization evolving into multiple types of teams and sophisticated forms of organizations, in particular after General Motor's invention of the global corporation. We can imagine a line of innovation, productivity, and economic yield from the 1760s to our days. This line will have smooth sections and occasional bumps in it. The pace of change and innovation is often disrupted by extraordinary breakthroughs: such as the electric motor replacing steam engines in early cars, or diesel engines replacing steam engines in trains, each bringing significant economic acceleration to industry, the economy, and society at large.

But there are other inorganic, faster, and more disruptive forces that bring accelerated changes. At the global scale, since the Industrial Revolution we have had two world wars, commercialization of aviation, the invention of the computer and then computer mobility in handhelds, the pervasiveness of industrial automation, and Artificial Intelligence acceleration happening right now, just to name the most prominent. When we say we live in constant change, we give it for granted, since most of us were born during a time when this was a given part of reality. But we can also say that some changes are different, they are more *exceptional* than others. In other words, these are events that changed the world at once, altering the consciousness of the entire world overnight. In the last two decades we have had two of these events: the

© The Author(s), under exclusive license to Springer Nature Switzerland AG 2025
A. Reyes, *Leading Organizational Transformation*, Palgrave Executive Essentials, https://doi.org/10.1007/978-3-031-89763-4_2

attacks of 9/11 and the COVID-19 global pandemic. Both are unprecedented and covered in the way of the information era; with unedited, raw access to the events and the human toll resulting after them. Even if we argue that other changes are just as consequential, we can make the case that these two, and very prominently the pandemic, were rather *exceptional* in terms of their impact to the labor force, human optimization practices and what it means to have a competitive job offer in the labor market. This is largely due to the global scale, immediacy, and synchronicity of the change experienced, when there is not enough time to think, just to act.

A very important disclaimer is pertinent at this point. This book is not about the pandemic, it is about charting a path for success in transformation and for readiness against significant disruption. However, we will discuss the events in 2020 as more than just a pandemic, this was a global social phenomenon that significantly changed everyone, with no exception, and therefore is a necessary referential for any leadership analysis for years to come.

There is a scale of disruption that goes beyond the usual. In such instances, regardless of where you are in the world, you are part of a collective crisis, and you are forced to experiment running a business in ways you never had to do it before. Such was the case with the 2020 global pandemic. Not only because of its unprecedented ferocity, and impact across nations and its duration, but also because on top of that imposing and hard to manage world, we witnessed social justice rupture taking center stage in a way it had not happened in decades. The murder of George Floyd,[2] in a very significant way reverberated across people from all backgrounds, age groups, and geographies, even internationally, in comparable ways to the social justice movements of the sixties. That unfortunate event was available on the way of the Internet: instantly global, generation-defining eleven minutes of unedited video, available for the entire planet to watch and consume from the palm of their hands. As a result, we were part of an immediate consciousness-altering experience that has been and will continue to be consequential to define what is to come in the future of work—too early to confirm how, the dust has not settled completely.

We can assert that the combination of those events was *transformative* at the level of society—globally. These disruptions changed both, how we do things and also how we think about them and what do we believe to be true—they had the power to making us revisit our assumptions, our own beliefs. But it was also *irreversible*. Such transformational and irreversible forces make it necessary to understand the impact they had in organizations—beyond the most obvious issues of remote working and cross-location effectiveness.

That conversation is the cornerstone to the Leading for Success proposition. Not only we world changed but it changed permanently—irreversibly. These changes are here to stay.

What Changed?

We may or may not believe that the world changed, that there is or there isn't such a thing as the future of work. But what we believe may be secondary to what the labor market now sees as the new reality and is responding to.[3] There is a new 'the earth is flat' crisis with a portion of leaders in many organizations who hang to known truths about people's values, perceptions, and aspirations. They are fixated on the belief that people really just need jobs, to get paid, and that they should be grateful for having one. That their company is the best in the segment and would be illogical to leave, and other thoughts like that.

For some, this still is a debate but not for much longer, evidence that a new 'wake up, the earth is round' reality is ever becoming clearer and more abundant.

This particular crisis brought to life multiple layers of need and exigency for urgent action. Among those factors, two in particular survived the immediate handling of safety and security and emerged as something else, as experiences that accentuated trends that had been there for some time and therefore became the most important factors for employees and the hardest to solve by companies worldwide. I will call them flexibility and integrity. Those have not been solved entirely, but stability has settled in most companies, with varied results, depending on the choices in their solutions so far. Decisions on these two aspects played a significant role on employee's mental health, wellbeing, and performance during the pandemic. But that is not the entire story; what has been transformational about this disruption as noted above, is how those two aspects permanently changed employee's perceptions about what success may look like for THEM. Based on their own experience, they now believe that companies have choices to make their lives better, and just as important, there are companies willing to go further on those important aspects, meaning, there is choice in the marketplace.

For business leaders this can be either a big problem or a tremendous opportunity. This book is about identifying and seizing on the opportunity to elevate the experience, the results, and the leadership capability in service of an evolved organization capable of sustained success.

CEOs and CHROs became de-facto Chief Philosophy Officers overnight, we were thrown rather suddenly into the vortex of change and the unknown, rushing to define protocols, new rules, statements, face employees who demanded sense-making answers, and responding to a more aware, more profound employee base internally, and to a polarized environment externally.

As the head of the people function, like many others in my position, I sat with my CEO looking at data, available facts arriving by the hour, with important new questions everyday to discuss and discern every new situation with excruciating detail. Then, compelled to define quickly what was the right thing to do, the path more consistent to our values, the most ethical, the one to give our people a better sense of safety, comfort, and to assure our customers we were there for them.

As we now know, teams in many companies raised to the occasion and found their own way. We did as well at Houghton Mifflin Harcourt, and thanks to the great work of our human resources teams, our executives, and all leaders, we not only survived the crisis but were able to harness the moment to move ahead, more energized, and highly focused.

How did we accomplish that? What guided us? and what did we learn in the process? In one sentence, we learned that nobody was prepared for what we experienced, but some were more ready for it. And they were more ready, because they had internalized that transformation and leadership require unique ways of clarity at all levels, but even more importantly is that everyone has to be included, not only involved; everyone has to *belong*. Some companies had explicit policies and values pointing in that direction and had work underway demonstrating that commitment. That progress and conversation worked as a credibility asset, as a moral equity that earned us the right to be heard and followed under the duress and uncertainty of those times.

Let's look at the lessons learned from the two main factors identified in our collective experience. The two areas that became most critical for managing and potentially thriving in the crisis: flexibility and integrity.

Flexibility. One of the most radical findings of the global social experiment—as it has been well documented—is remote work effectiveness.[4] With some distance from the experience, now we know the positives and negatives.[5] One of our lessons learned was that productivity was indeed achievable in remote work environments but not for all types of work or all types of situations—in other words, for a large number of office workers, a level of remote work was possible. For many, this remote configuration was entirely desirable, while for others, working at the office was an absolute necessity. We also learned that presence in co-located settings was important for speed on shared analysis and decision-making or to address certain types of major complexities. But the real outcome was not to find out just how much work can be done remotely, but instead that the regular employee now believes, based on their own experience: that their highest contribution was possible to achieve *with*, and *because* of remote work.

As a consequence, many employees adjusted their expectations that companies actually *can* accommodate, if they chose to, for a newly discovered reality: they could be effective remotely, significantly adding to their quality of life. In short, employees advocated for *more flexibility*.

Similarly, CEOs, CHROs, line managers, and team leaders were only partially ready for a remote work configuration.[6] Not all their tools and managerial practices translated to effectively deal with remote teams, or those split between on-site and remote. This experiment did not provide the assurances and the comfort to managers that the supervision, the collaboration, and critical interactions like onboarding, or mentoring process necessary to learn the business process was enough to produce the operational quality and culture they expected. In other words, many of them—but notoriously, not all of them—advocated for *less flexibility*.

Managers were confronted with competing realities bringing pressure from two ends: the need to operate effectively—pulling in the direction of back to office—and the need to retain people during this fluid period called the great resignation—where more flexibility was a currency for retention.

Practical and tactical decisions had to be made, and because disruptions arrive unannounced, there is hardly any precedent or any reliable data for 'best practice'. CEOs and CHROs had to take a position and go from there to produce guidance, policy, and protocols. Many times, looking at what others were doing was a good framework to relate to. Disruptions give you the opportunity for community learning in real time. As we emerged into the more defining stages of what was being called 'the future of work', employees expected decisions around location policy. And we knew that not everyone was going to be happy with any final decision.

In uncharted territories, leaders gather the best data available and then complete the analysis with their intuition and experience, but with that also comes a not unsignificant dose of ingrained beliefs. Hence comes the dilemma: should we follow imperfect science or strong belief? We knew conclusive studies were not ready. But policies started to be announced across companies, all of them scattered on the spectrum from more to less flexibility, and as you read them, they were phrased in terms of conviction on what the company believed was the right and best thing to do. No issue with that, but there is more to consider in that analysis. The additional variable is that not everyone involved sees the same thing and feels the same way about what is reasonable; this is, their beliefs move in a different direction. I regard this as one of the richest lessons learned in the pandemic: the ways in which our beliefs and lived experiences shape decision-making when hard data is not available. And how those decisions can lead to unexpected outcomes.

A great illustration of this dilemma comes from a relevant study from McKinsey.[7] In this study, the author's goal was to understand why people were moving in larger portions than before to find new jobs. As they looked at the data, they identified a very different way in which employees looked at reasons to join a company depending on a certain profile or 'personas' they identified. They noticed that people with a more 'traditionalist' mindset, as they called it—generationally older, motivated by status, salary, progression—looked at reasons to be in a job quite differently from those called 'non-traditionalists'—generationally younger and less concerned with advancement or status.

As you look at their findings, the group called non-traditionalists valued 'career development' and advancement as their seventh priority, while the traditionalists ranked it as number one. This is, the usual career progression, promotions, power advancement were six times less important for the non-traditionalist group. In the other hand, the dimension of 'work flexibility' was the first priority for this group, ranking it ahead of compensation and meaningful work. More traditionalist profiles designated flexibility as their fourth priority. Statistically, our senior decision-makers in most companies will likely belong in the traditionalists group, simply by career progression and hierarchy in the organization. In other words, one group will regard the 'opportunity to grow in our company' as the most important attribute for a job, while the other group values most their flexibility. In this context, decisions will require significant discussion between leaders, who need to show openness and self-awareness for companies to optimize their choices in the competitive talent market we have.

Integrity. The second aspect we need to discuss relates to the ramifications that came from the events of June 2020. As a result of the murder of George Floyd, and the unprecedented open way it was experienced in all sorts of media, globally and instantly, the world came into a collective realization that much still needed to be done to achieve the aspirations of a more equal society. That sentiment permeated all aspects of society like a storm, making the workplace a space where our people expected to have an opportunity to discuss what this meant for them and for the company. Most employees wanted to find clarity—and a level of affirmation—on what this meant for the company—what did we stand for? What we found was a variety of powerful responses, commonly voiced by CEOs issuing statements to employees, sometimes to their customers, sometimes reaching to everyone externally in support of a more just and equal society. It was palpable that there was a new level of awareness, a sense of increased urgency shared well beyond the usual advocates; now including more people in governments, almost every country, a shared concern that made companies a player, a unique contributor of this delicate change. Diversity programs, manager training, and important books and articles came to light, filled the airwaves, and found their way into boardroom meetings and leadership gatherings. Change was in motion.

In very short time, reality was putting to test our curated statements of values and beliefs at organizations of all types. Employees turned their attention to the words in our values and expected a level of consistency in actions showing integrity with those aspirations. Everyone had to dig deep, and most organizations did, proving that it is indeed possible to make a difference.

Taking a step back, in the larger scheme of things, social justice cannot be solved by companies. It is not the organization's job to solve for equality in society, but companies do have a role to play in how people live their lives inside that organization and how their customers, partners, and governments experience their leadership to bend that history's arc toward justice, not the other way around. Organizations do not own social justice problems, but they are not off the hook to be part of the community effort to achieve it. As shown in the illustration in Fig. 2.1, the pre-pandemic workplace was already in motion toward a more flexible and culturally meaningful experience,[8] providing the fertile ground for COVID-19 to raise those aspects of work even higher. This acceleration forced companies to find new ways to redesign work with different components in mind, making the reexamination of culture and purpose an inevitable gate in the path to extraordinary performance.

As a result, employees are no longer happy with pronouncements, communications, and promises. They want to see action and progress, with speed and determination, in the same way companies moved through the pandemic to sustain the business by helping their people. Paradoxically, the crisis created disruption but at the same time revealed what is possible for companies to do for their people. Employees are willing to take their chances to find that freedom somewhere else. For a large majority of employees, the world has changed. Whether we agree or not, the definition of success in the supply side of the labor market (people, talent) has evolved, and it is up to us to respond. This is precisely the challenge Leading Success is designed to solve.

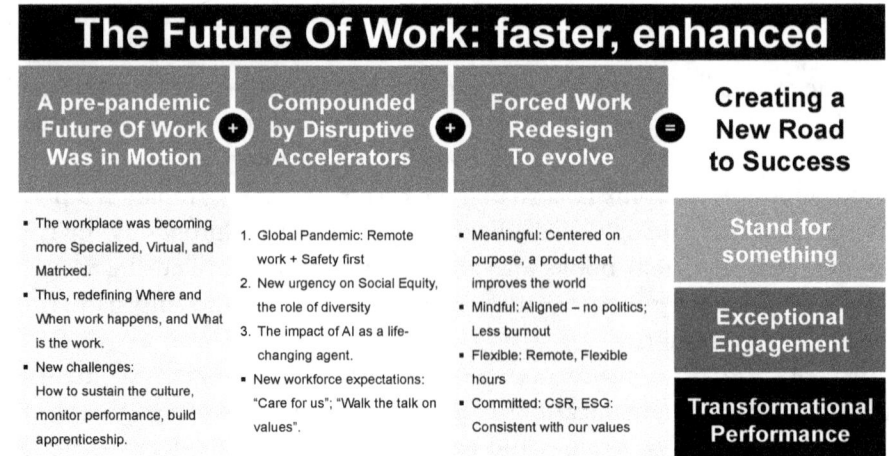

Fig. 2.1 The future of work is forcing a revision of the road to success

Defining Leading Success

One of the most important consequences of how the post-pandemic world is developing is that those new mindsets about flexibility, integrity, but also safety, leadership, and employee choice, have permeated society in general either for agreement or disagreement, and inevitably, those same thoughts and consequences have crossed the frontiers of your organizations. The impact of employee awareness, social expectations can no longer be contained to the outside of your walls. Any effort will backfire sooner or later with employees, customers, or investors. The alternative is not to tolerate or neutralize those energies, but instead to embrace them. Recognizing these irreversible changes will force you to be more prepared and therefore more powerful to harness the positive expressions they have for your business. Embracing the future of work will work best for your business; it will liberate you and your company for years to come, becoming a place where every employee aspires to work and belong. So, how do we do that?

One answer is to tighten-up a few policies and continue the work as we know it, with rather superficial, procedural adjustments. However, if we want to apply the lessons learned in this great experiment, we need to aim higher than that. We can become a disruption-resilient company. One that can withstand crises, not by accident or by sheer force as we did in the pandemic, but by design, by choice, rooted on the fortitude of our cultures. Leading Success is a way to achieve that strength.

Looking at our employees as consumers of jobs in the labor market, they are a special kind of *customers* who need to see a value proposition that works for them—like every other customer. They are asking themselves questions about beliefs and philosophy. What company do I want to work for? What are my new expectations of what companies can do for social justice and to mitigate the polarization we are suffering? Am I in the best place I can be? Am I able to be my best self and do my best work here? Does this company really care? Why should I go back to office five days a week?

These are not new questions, what has changed is the standard for the answers and the depth of expectations of meaning, truthfulness, and honesty about them, in short, they expect to be valued. Something else has changed too: the market has moved toward flexibility and social justice enough to create spaces for those seeking such environments, creating mobility. What this means for employees is that they have choices. The bar has been raised.

> **Leading Success** therefore, is a people-first business approach focused on building and sustaining the people infrastructure (talent, culture, and organization) that will accelerate the company's transformation, be remarkable, successful, resilient, and consistent to its values, while becoming a magnet to attract and retain the talent it needs, within a cost structure and growth goals. In other words, it is about building sustainable success for today's world.

We will see throughout this writing that Leading Success is about three foundational mindsets: *Liberation, Vitality,* and *Expression*. They are organizational engines that serve to amplify organizational capacity for high performance, culture affirmation, and resilience.

Leading Success Organizational Outcomes: the outcome of Leading Success is purposeful, coordinated action on people and organization for rapid execution, learning, and alignment, in ways that translates to revenue, growth, velocity, and resilience, with a primordial foundation on the companies' values.

Leading Success is about an improved ability to execute, learn fast, while building a climate of inclusiveness and belonging. These attributes sit at the intersection of two often separate capacities in companies: deep transformation and high performance. The outcome of Leading Success is the 'unicorn' organization, where the workforce and the methods align to drive change, thrive on disruption, and at the same time, perform at significantly higher levels by following its own defined values. People will find the company compelling for their careers because they can be successful here, their work is connected to customers' outcomes, and they find it fulfilling because they believe in the purpose, they belong to its culture. Customers will see a company with integrity and that reputation matters for cross generational customer acquisition, for government contracts, and for ESG metrics. Leading Success is designed to convert your operation in a solid business for the future of work.

Who Is Leading Success For?

Any company with a bold ambition, one that endeavors to become something they are *not* just yet, use their core skills and assets in radically new ways that redefines their identity, to alter their DNA to play a different game. That kind of transformation calls for more than a top-down change management approach. In these transformations, outcomes depend on qualified people wanting to be part of, and deciding to, stay in your organization. This is, companies that must connect with growing, diverse market segments for sustained growth, and with a long-term vision that depends on superior people creativity and collaboration for a differentiating value proposition in products and services.

With that said, we all know that companies can be run in many ways and, essentially speaking, no unique point of view is the only one that a company needs to be successful. Leading Success is therefore designed as an approach that will not tax the company with reinventing how they manage their business; it will reframe what we do in more powerful ways with the benefit of developing key organizational intangibles that predict success and growth in complex, highly competitive and high disruption environments. In addition, customers and employees have been moving toward a more environmental and socially aware expectations from their companies. They want to buy from and do business with organizations that care about them and their employees; and this trend is here to stay. Liberation, Vitality, and Expression have an economic value in a world where the best talent invariably correlates with customer satisfaction, highest return on capital and profit. It is now time to see what Leading Success is made of.

The Anatomy of Leading Success

Consider the following questions:

- *Why* is it imperative to lead people in a way that everyone feels *liberated*?

- *What* matters most to people to bring new *vitality* to the business, and customers?
- *How* do we create *signature expressions*—people actions, processes, products, and experiences—that embody our values, make us remarkable, successful, resilient?

Leading Success is about creating an environment where people can have 'liberating, vital, expressions' that propel the company toward sustainable success. This is achieved through three mindsets and nine disciplines.

Three Mindsets

Leading Success is built on three mindsets that work as guide for decision-making and action: liberation, vitality, and expression. See illustration in Fig. 2.2. They can be seen as pillars or guiding concepts that provide foundation to the Leading Success approach. As we progress on their definitions, we will see they interact to mutually reinforce each other. For example, the more liberating our leadership, the better the expression of people and organization. In this sense, Leading Success is founded on a liberating, vital expression.

Fig. 2.2 The three mindsets of leading success

These mindsets are focused on creating differentiating capabilities in the organization with the power to re-orient action for success and the capacity to alter the DNA of the company to be able to consistently produce what the transformation calls for.

- The first mindset is about Leadership of *liberation*, to lead the organization in ways that everyone feels faster, agile, uncontained, unrestricted, and unstuck. We will elaborate on this significant concept in the next chapter; we will only say now that people in our times are looking for ways to become their best selves at work, to be as unique as they are; to belong. Liberation leadership creates an environment that allows people to reach their full potential because they are being who they are. Only leadership can provide that focus on liberation, and only from the top. Hard as it may appear it is rather simple in definition, but profound in change. If you achieve it, you will have an enduring culture and workforce that is agile in good times and robust in times of disruption.
- The second mindset is to identify what are the sources of *vitality* for employee experience that respond to the unique needs and conditions of your business, as well as the stage of your ongoing transformation, and create a *design* for it. The main outcome we intend to create is to establish the infrastructure for enduring capacity to change and transform—hence the association with 'vital'. An intelligent self-adapting infrastructure extends the life cycle of the organization and makes success not only possible, but enduring. The vitality domains will include all aspects of talent, culture evolution, and organization effectiveness. A vitality design will demand us to build a plan to create Leading Success platforms, not only for implementation but for an adapting and evolving business reality. That is why here we define the metrics that will monitor our vitality as people do when they go at the doctor. There are vital signs and predictive health signs. In short, our focus is not going to be on being successful once, but in creating processes, metrics, and a culture that makes the company success ready and robust for the long term.
- The third mindset is what most literature identifies as execution, but I will call '*signature expression*', because it intends to produce and reinforce the behaviors for execution, customer experience, and revenue-generating actions consistent with our values to pursue that 'vital liberation' from the pillars above. This pillar is about how you imprint your company's DNA in the product, your people's experience, and in your customer's experience. Expression is inclusive of both the journey to achieve the goals and the destination. In that sense, Leading Success is not something you can

buy, it is literally earned in the hearts and minds of your people as you walk the path, as you fulfill the plan, make the investments, implement the actions, and follow through, share metrics, admit mistakes, and raise above obstacles to achieve your goals—in short, on how you show the commitment to become your purpose. Process and outcomes are indistinguishable as far as experience is concerned because they are all forms of the expression people are hungry for, becoming a voice in the expression of the company they want to belong to. In the same way a masterpiece is recognized and signed by the master artist, we will think on our signature experiences for employees and customers in the same way—recognizable and 'signed' by our unique touch. Said in different words, the way you run the business is consistent with your unique values and aspirations, in that regard it becomes your DNA, your unreplaceable *signature*. Your signature expression of success.

Leading Success, therefore, is about three pivotal concepts: Leadership of Liberation, Vitality Design, and Signature Expression. No matter how large or small, how new or how old, local or global, physical or digital your company is, all these themes are perennial and fundamental to running any operation that includes humans. It is in fact, a human centered approach.

For simplification and clarity, the path to Leading Success as far as implementation is concerned, is divided in nine differentiated units of work or segments. I call these units of work *disciplines* because they will require skill mastery and unique adaptations to your culture, so they are not to be seen as tasks but as learning processes.

There are three disciplines per pillar as explained above, illustrated in Fig. 2.3. We will dedicate the next few chapters to visit in detail those disciplines and provide clarity on meanings, methods, metrics, and implications. For a high-level orientation, here is how to read the nine disciplines.

The Nine Disciplines—A Simplified Description

In the first pillar, we will start with a discussion on leadership, on how we lead. We will make the case for liberation as the brand of leadership that yields the highest energy and deepest connection. This *Leadership of Liberation* necessitates a powerful vision, an *Aspiration* that breaks molds, goes further, that will elevate us and change us, but also change the world in some way if we achieve it, and therefore, it becomes the spiritual North Star for the organization. From that vision and with sufficient grounding on the current status

Fig. 2.3 The nine disciplines of leading success

we can define the ultimate *Transformation* we are aiming for. The proverbial 'From-To' that should be inspirational and bold but also operational, measurable. Most strategy and business books operate at this level, explaining how to make sound business choices. The 'From-To' is not just a high-level distinction. It is 100% business definition, segments, revenues, markets, growth, considers competition, industry evolution, and all the ingredients that go into a strategy. What is next is where you find much less in business literature—how we mobilize an organization, lines of command, divisions, manage and navigate through egos and territories to activate that strategy and build the success-capable company. The next six disciplines deal with this infrastructure and behavior. The path, therefore, continues with the basics: we will not go very far in the journey unless we can get our people, starting with leaders, to buy-in, to make a personal *Commitment* to the vision, and to become liberating leaders themselves. There is a wealth of elements and distinctions in this pillar, but the essence is to raise the bar in the way we lead the organization, remove the fear that liberation is something negative, loaded, the enemy of performance. I anticipate you will experience an extraordinary reframing of your own leadership story in this section.

The second pillar, *Vitality Design* is the place for designing the infrastructure that will power Leading Success for Years to come. A Vitality Design includes three main areas: Culture, Talent, and Organization. The *Culture* discipline is a voluminous space, it could cover practically everything we do in the organization, since everything adds to or subtracts from our cultural promise, there are no neutral acts on culture. This area will be dedicated to culture articulation, to the connection between culture and leadership, and ways to understand how your culture needs to evolve to adapt to the future in your vision. The *Talent* discipline will be centered on a key concept we will call 'Talent Economy'—for supply and demand considerations, which is a new way to understand talent value based on contribution to transformation, not only on duties and responsibilities. This discipline also includes the usual overall talent arc from recruiting, hiring, onboarding, and then, internal talent management all the way to end of life cycle management and beyond—alumni management. This space is extremely comprehensive, and many times is running well, but rather disconnected to the overall value proposition for the employee. We will examine in great detail this area. The *Organization* discipline will cover the notion of effectiveness, metrics, cycle planning, performance management, employee engagement, change agility, and considerations of cost structure. In this area we will cover metrics management, dashboarding, and protocols for decision-making and adjustments. The unique differentiator on this organization vitality approach will be a vital governance that collects all aspects of culture, talent, and organization to drive high quality, fast decision-making for success.

The third pillar *Signature Expression* is focused on the disciplines for implementation: Communication, Expectation, and Experience. The main discussion topic in this section will start with the choice of *'Expression'* as the name for this pillar. It is possible to consider any human activity and human outcome as a form of expression and therefore, performance, product design, customer service, and other activities are, in themselves, forms of human expression and consequently, very personal.[9] And so is our cultural heritage, ethnicity, location of birth, gender expression, and sexual orientation. In this regard, diversity is discussed in a wider context than the reductive way it normally is; namely, a program to address the company's shortcomings diversity, or as a reaction to compliance, regulation, competitive pressures. Instead, performance as a form of expression elevates the diversity discussion from being an outcome of programmatic activity, participation in events, to be an outcome of a culture of equality that emerges organically from how leaders lead. Following this logic, the emergence of a Diverse, Equitable, Inclusive and Belonging (DEIB) organization is a natural byproduct of managing with a liberation, vitality, and expression mindset. Reframing execution as expression recognizes the unique personal touch of every individual worker that is present in anything we do and makes us feel transcendent, relevant, connected to reach extraordinary levels of contribution and performance.

As far as the three disciplines in this mindset, we will start with *Engagement*, but not in the usual way that sees employee engagement as an outcome. We will introduce a new perspective of engagement, designed to be an input that affects speed, and facilitates employee disposition and commitment. The second discipline, *Expectation*, will discuss how we translate the vision into actionable tasks and roles that build a connection from vision to action. It is called expectation because it is meant to include behavioral standards, competencies as well as metrics of progression and quality analysis. And then, in the third discipline *Experience*, will be defined as the capacity to make the vision become the customer's—and employee's—experience. We will define Signature Processes as operational manifestations of our values and purpose, capable of creating the experience we are looking for.

The CEO's Choice for Leading Success

The core proposition of Leading Success is that the voice of employees matters for the success of the company, and that the role of leaders, managers of people, is a determinant factor on that voice having a contribution in the company's vitality and success. This means both, employees in the aggregate—teams, organizations—and employees as individuals. In the aggregate, as the force of transformation that powers the organization, the mobilization, and the results. As individuals, to create the commitment that moves each person to choose to engage and own the transformation; that is not a collective output. Instead, it is the outcome of a manager in conversation with their people, one person at a time. Leaders who have not come to this realization tend to see their people functions (HR) as a supplier of labor, not talent, and much less change, reinvention, or success. From that perspective, the People Function performs a necessary but non-protagonist role in the reinvention toward the future. At the same time, the HR function has been under a process of relearning and reflection over the past couple of decades,[10] resulting in more openness from HR leaders to reframe their own value, making new choices, resulting in innovative approaches to the function[11] (Fig. 2.4).

In this context, what is the choice of the CEO? The CEO's choice is to rethink the paradigm of success for the enterprise—what does success really mean? And what does it take to achieve it? With a necessary simplification at this stage of the reading, it can be summarized as follows. Choose to

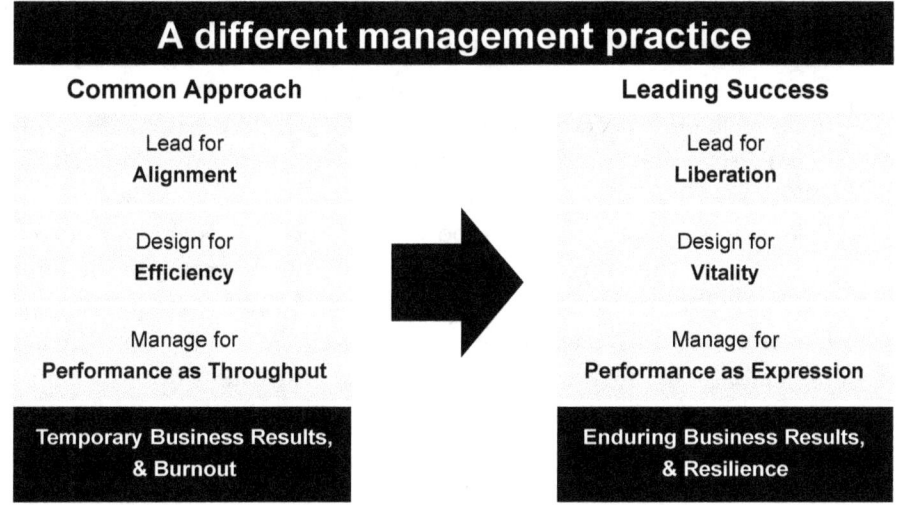

Fig. 2.4 The leader's choice in leading success

switch from a leadership predicated on alignment, where pieces are expected to fit a pre-determined pattern, to one of *liberation*, where people's superior engagement and connectivity expand possibilities and productivity. From a design that seeks to achieve efficiency—more with less—to one focused on *vitality*, where the organization has been purposefully redesigned to deliver on what the new expectations are. And, from a management culture centered on performance as output quotas, to one centered on performance as the productive expression of the highest potential of every individual. But these are not merely noble ideas for the idealized company. These are operational choices with processes and decisions, systems, metrics behind them, as you will see in the chapters dedicated to each of the nine disciplines.

These choices require one belief to develop in the CEO's mind. That the work to be performed to get to Leading Success necessitates their active work on partnering with their People Function leaders; work as a team to reinvent their way to their best version of the Future of Work.

Leading Success is a way to consistently do better for people in order to do greater for the business.

Notes

1. Ayres, R. U. (2021). The history and future of technology. Springer.

2. Samuels, R., & Olorunnipa, T. (2022). His name is George Floyd: One man's life and the struggle for racial justice. Viking.
3. Chopra, A., & Bhilare, P. (2020). Future of work: An empirical study to understand expectations of the millennials from organizations. Business Perspectives and Research, 8(1), 60–76. https://doi.org/10.1177/2278533719887457
4. Pokojski, Z., Kister, A., & Lipowski, M. (2022). Remote work efficiency from the employers' perspective—What's next? Sustainability, 14(7), 4220. https://doi.org/10.3390/su14074220
5. Grawitch, M. J., Lavigne, K. N., Koziel, R. J., & Cornelius, A. M. (2024). Remote work: More nuance and unknowns than broad generalizations. Consulting Psychology Journal: Practice and Research, 76(2), 163–183. https://doi.org/10.1037/cpb0000257
6. Kowalski, G., & Ślebarska, K. (2022). Remote working and work effectiveness: A leader perspective. International Journal of Environmental Research and Public Health, 19(22), 15,326. https://doi.org/10.3390/ijerph192215326
7. De Smet, A., Dowling, B., Mugayar-Baldocchi, M., & Schaninger, B. (2022). The great attrition is making hiring harder: Are you searching the right talent pools? McKinsey Quarterly, July 2022.
8. Malhotra, A. (2021). The post pandemic future of work. Journal of Management, 47(5), 1091–1102. https://doi.org/10.1177/01492063211000435
9. Kreuzbauer, R., & King, D. (2015). The mind in the object—Psychological valuation of materialized human expression. Journal of Experimental Psychology: General, 144(4), 764–787. https://doi.org/10.1037/xge0000096
10. McCord, P. (2014, January). How Netflix reinvented HR. Harvard Business Review.
11. Hamel, G., & Zanini, M. (2020). Humanocracy: Creating organizations as amazing as the people inside them. Harvard Business Review Press.

3

Leadership of Liberation

Leading Success is not only a methodology, it is a mindset for leaders to create success-ready organizations. Setting a new mindset is not a trivial endeavor. It is more than a message to be cascaded and explained, as mindsets are cultural markers that reflect the attitudes, the emotional tone, and the personality of the organization. For Leading Success, *leadership of liberation* is the mindset at the center of its value proposition. This chapter is dedicated to address what leadership of liberation means, how it is created, sustained, and how it works in practice.

Leadership and Its Purpose

The discussion about what leadership *is* versus what leadership *does* dominates research and literature,[1] bringing with it a rich reservoir of philosophy, definitions, points of view, and frameworks to identify and assess if someone possesses such attributes, whether a company is enabling the development of those silks, and the ways to improve on both. Most of us have read the classics on Leadership and Management; James MacGregor Burns' *Leadership*,[2] John P. Kotter's *Leading Change*,[3] Warren Bennis' *On Becoming a Leader*,[4] Henry Mintzberg's *Managers, Not BMAs*,[5] among many others. Consulting firms of industrial organizational psychologists have developed entire suites of solutions of their own, to define, assess, and develop leadership skills. Multiple generations of leaders have been educated with these models. This universal library includes serious, well researched models of competencies, development tools, and comprehensive solutions with ever smarter and useful

© The Author(s), under exclusive license to Springer Nature
Switzerland AG 2025
A. Reyes, *Leading Organizational Transformation*, Palgrave Executive Essentials,
https://doi.org/10.1007/978-3-031-89763-4_3

applications. Thanks to these efforts, leadership practice, assessment, development, and behavioral science has matured significantly in the last few decades.

Although the concept of Leadership is relatively new, its use and application has been with us all along. Every group needs a leader, either attributed by the group, or named following tradition or any form of accepted governance. This has been an anthropological reality through all of our history,[6] from nomadic stages to settlements, hunting, military, social and political activity, and more recently, businesses. The reason for this is simply the need for *intentional coordinated action*. Every human enterprise requires a level of coordination to be completed. This imperative for coordination to guarantee our subsistence, in essence, gives way to the role of a coordinator of actions and efforts, which is the foundational skill of leadership.

Leadership, as a field of study has been extraordinarily well decoded, categorized, and documented. Leading Success, however, necessitates one step further from a high-quality definition. We must go to *intent*—what leadership does, its ultimate purpose. To be clear, we are not talking about the goals of the organization, but a more foundational outcome—to unleash the organization, set it free to reach its fullest potential. And that starts with leaders who see themselves as obstacle-removers, potential-realizers, and simplifiers; in different words—as *organizational liberators*. Either by solving for group's nourishment as it was for hunters, to accomplish goals in business settings, or sending astronauts to space. In every case, a leader who identifies dysfunctional elements that stand in the way of success, and removes them, is a liberating leader.

In its most foundational core, leadership is, and it has always been about *liberation*.

Why Do We Need Leaders as Liberators?

We need leaders who are organizational liberators because every company or team, over time, becomes rigid and hostage to its own inertia. Liberation is necessary to produce breakthroughs and set a new direction, and it is the most effective and enduring way to implement organizational transformation and sustain it—particularly in the post-pandemic world. Transformations start at the strategic level and become operational in a hurry. Most of them underdeliver on their goals because of inadequate tactical execution: superficial planning, fear of making unpopular organizational changes to empower the future, wrong metrics, can't persuade the teams to follow the vision or fail to engage middle management to believe in the journey. In other words, because we failed to establish the right mindset to nurture the transformation and delegated all of it to layers below, for things to be 'resolved' down below the organization. The strategy activation portion of transformation is often overlooked. Top leaders often assume that communication is all the change management needed. According to that view, commitment comes from the quality of the explanation, checking boxes to cascade a consistent message. But there is a lot in the audiences' minds to assume that can work. Soon enough the limitations of that approach become apparent. Communication is, indeed, the core technology to reach the internalization we are looking for, but not the usual one-way, curated, corporate talk we call communication in many companies. We need something much deeper and personal than that. We need a *conversation*; something we are describing in detail in our vitality mindset.

One of the most important and honest questions any CEO may ask is the following: do we really *need* to be liberators to get our vision accomplished? After all, look at the world around us, it seems to be working well. Innovation is happening, markets are growing, and yes, we have our problems but there seems to be enough evidence that we can just go along the way we have, and things will be fine. We have technology, automation, powerful methodologies, and programs to make employees go along well.

This is not a question to be answered lightly. If we consider history as a sample for leadership, empires, and outstanding visions have been built with non-liberating leadership. In fact, it is not hard to find achievements based on oppression, slavery, and abuse. Fortunately, and in spite of occasional setbacks, a lot has been done over the last two centuries and we find ourselves in front of a stable labor market regulated by common rules, granted, there is still much to be done. We have come a long way as a society in ways that differentiating talent and competition for employment works as a balancing force. But we are not aiming for average. We are in the game of being outstanding, remarkable, consistently successful in the future of work. If that is the ambition, the usual way will not make the cut.

As the parameters of employment move toward choice, flexibility, and equality, the pre-pandemic status is going to look old for the employees you want to attract. We can't move the clock back. If you think yourself as a woman in a leading job today and we were able to transport you back in time fifty or a hundred years, same industry, same type of role, you would feel the environment completely inadequate to unfold your full potential, your voice will not carry the weight it does today, it would feel limiting, narrow and devoid of future because women were not seen as leaders, innovators, disruptors in the way we see them today. That environment would feel *oppressive* to you; not liberating at all. I say this recognizing that in some places today we are still far behind on these matters. Not just for women, but for people with disabilities, people of color, and members of the LGBTQ community.

As social consciousness evolves with time, people see new things, and also see the same things differently, with new lenses, new assumptions and beliefs, and this is exactly what just happened with the pandemic. The cultural clock moved 20 years ahead in a matter of 24 months. Rendering many companies 'old standard' very rapidly.

You need a form of liberating leadership to attract and retain the most consequential talent for your success. If you believe the world has changed, you have little choice but to initiate-or accelerate-the transformation of your organization in that direction. In the other hand, if you believe there is no 'future of work', that things remain similar to early 2020, then you will play your odds, and time will tell if you were right. I would not make that bet.

Defining Liberating Leadership

If we accept the proposition that the world has changed, then the leaders' most immediate and urgent outcome is to build an environment that compels the best and the brightest people to choose to be with us instead of being with, or going to our competitors; this is, to win the talent war of today and create the exceptional results the transformation calls for. Such strategy necessitates a reframing of what leaders do in order to achieve this crucial outcome. In essence, that means removing the organizational barriers—both mental and physical—that cause individuals and organizations to slow down, underachieve, engage in unnecessary fights, get confused or remain confused, unclear, distracted, and unfocused. In other words, elevating the probability of success and personal fulfillment of everyone in the organization. I call the above *leadership of liberation* or liberating leadership. This is one of the three pillars of Leading Success and the most consequential. It deserves to be unpacked and examined carefully.

Leadership of liberation is an employee experience, based on their objective interactions, observations, and perceptions at work, that their workplace allows them to *belong*, gives them the freedom to *be themselves*, to *be relevant* to the goals of the organization, and to have the ability to *be successful*. What this means in practical terms is shown in the illustration in Fig. 3.1. Feeling accepted, secure, included, and equal to everyone else in the team.

Be free to use their voice with the influence of their heritage and the unique experiences that define them. An environment like that makes it possible for people to use their time and creativity for work, instead of fighting chaos and dysfunction.

For leaders, it is a practice of behaviors, attitudes, and decisions, shown in the bottom part of the same Fig. 3.1, that *in aggregate, over time*, results in a liberating experience by their employees. In this sense, liberation is not a one-day thing, or a one-event thing, but it may not be a 100% of everyday thing. Managers may not always be liberating to the eyes of their employees; they are not robots, or automated entities. Liberation is the aggregate experience observable over a reasonable amount of time.

> **Definition:** Leadership of Liberation is the employee experience, resulting from behaviors, attitudes, and decisions by managers, over a period of time, that allows them to belong, to be their true selves, to have a relevant role, and to have an opportunity to be successful at work.
>
> As a result of the above, every employee has the opportunity to realize their highest-performance and become their highest-potential expression.

The above definition, consistent with Fig. 3.1, highlights three foundational interpersonal needs that are critically important for people in general, as Will Schutz described in his FIRO research.[7] First, the need to be included, to be significant, and part of the team, to have your own voice, covering the *belong* and *be myself* components in Fig. 3.1; second, the need to assert

Leadership of Liberation in Practice

	Belong	Be Myself	Be Relevant	Be Successful
Employee experience	I feel accepted, secure, included, and equal, by being part of this group	I can use my voice, my Heritage, with confidence	I am Empowered, I Own our purpose, I have a real Impact	I have clear goals, no imposed barriers, and Fair rewards
Leader behaviors	Ensure my decisions, actions and relationships create an inclusive, equal, and vital environment for everyone. • Lead purpose alignment • Build positive relationships • Lead equitable treatment	Encourage people to use their voice, positively leverage their uniqueness • Listen, no bias • Embrace new perspectives • Promote expression	Manage for empowerment, share ownership, Show the way to impact • Trust, empower, delegate • Measure outcomes • Give meaningful feedback	Remove organizational barriers, clarify what is expected, be fair on rewards • Clarify expectations • Remove systemic barriers • Reward performance

Fig. 3.1 How employees perceive liberating leadership, and how managers create the liberating environment

yourself with competence and in control, to be respected, which covers the last two components *be relevant*, and *be successful*. There is a third need according to Schutz model, *Openness*, that deals with aspects of appreciation and recognition that are explained shortly ahead.

It is too much to ask a manager to meet all these needs for their people on their own, however, that is not the job. The job of a liberating manager is to set the stage for reasonable employees to achieve these states on their own. So, the problem is not that companies can't make people feel this way. The problem is that companies neutralize their chances of people feeling that way because they create experiences that go in the opposite directions of belonging, acceptance, relevance, and success. This happens in small ways everyday by means of behaviors, attitudes, and decisions that signal to people that leadership does not care about what employees think or feel. For example, failing to remove a policy that requires people to create a report that nobody reads, that is not used to make any decision, yet consumes hours. Or choosing not to address the poor performance, or bad behavior of someone that everyone can see—and suffer for it—but the manager just looks the other way. In the worst cases, by rewarding and promoting those toxic people. These are some examples of behaviors, attitudes, and decisions that erode liberation.

Another common perception is that enough money, richer salaries, and bonuses are powerful liberating messages on their own, and that's all we really need for success. In other words, as long as our salaries are competitive, we are inoculated against losing great people and against unsustainable results. We may need to think again. For executives who interpret the ambitions of employees as purely economic, there is growing evidence[8] that employees, and not only millennials or Gen Z, but even X-Gen desire to work for companies that will not burn them out, that will give them a chance to have a life and commit to doing good in society. A common articulation for this expectation is called *Employee Value Proposition*, which will be explored later in this book. In a nutshell, this means the totality of what a person 'feels'—note that it is not about what the person 'gets'—becomes the reason why people want to join or stay. This 'feeling' therefore is the important word. We may be thinking we are giving a lot, but if it does not *feel right* for our people, it will not translate in engagement, discretionary effort, and passion.

Based on the above, what is our responsibility as companies? What can we do to establish a Liberating Leadership Style? What does it take? Our primary responsibility is to set the right environment, and that is exactly what the Leading Success Disciplines are for as we will see in Part II of this book.

The Context for Organizational Liberation

One of the most important considerations I made to name this pillar 'Liberation' was the recognition of how profound this sentiment is for all peoples from all cultures and times.[9] Liberation is one of the most perennial aspirations across all human experience. And organizations are not the exception, as convincingly illustrated by the pandemic, that the aspiration of liberation has permeated into the workplace more than ever.[10] It is to be expected; it seems inevitable that the imperatives visible at the society level will have an impact inside your organization. You will be influenced by your environment. If this is indeed inevitable, what can companies do to channel those energies in the best way possible?

The answer to this question comes from an exploration of the dimensions of influence and impact companies have as agents of liberation. In Fig. 3.2, I offer an arbitrary taxonomy of liberating domains as an illustration of areas commonly addressed by companies.

According to this taxonomy, there are three main areas of influence in the scope of most organizations to lead success and therefore act with a liberating leadership approach. Those are within the reach of actions for the vast majority of organizations: the inside of organization itself, where leaders have complete ownership of what happens. And then, there are two levels where there is influence, but not total ownership: Industry and Society. Two additional areas of liberation are represented in Fig. 3.2 as out of scope for our analysis, on domains commonly found outside of the scope of businesses in general.

Our Scope	Focus	Goal	Who benefits?
	Organizations as Agents of Liberation – an illustrative taxonomy		
In	Organization	Grow the business, develop people	Employees and their families
In	Industry	Innovate, improve life, create wealth	Customers, partners, investors
In	Society	Reduce social inequity	Community, countries, people in need
Out	Philosophy	Expand knowledge and understanding	Humanity at large
Out	Transcendence	Spiritual growth, wisdom	Vast groups of like-minded people

Fig. 3.2 The scope of the Liberation Mindset in Leading Success

First Layer in Scope: Liberating the Organization

While the word *liberating* may be unfamiliar to the workplace, its practice is not. Many leaders are naturally gifted and focused on making sure their people have essential conditions to be successful, they instinctively work to bring clarity, remove barriers, eliminate obstacles, and build environments for people to be their full selves, to ensure their voice is heard, to design the organization for roles that matter and that employees understand how they are building something beyond the 'today' and beyond themselves. But their most lasting work of liberation relates to the people they manage.

A good example is what happened to me some time ago. I was two years into my job out of college, in Dana Corporation. After a fast-track development program through rotations and accelerated learning experiences sponsored by Dana Mexico, I became the head of department at one of their several automotive manufacturing facilities in Mexico City. At the time I had two jobs to be able to afford by master's degree. I had my main role in the manufacturing company, and I was also a part-time faculty member at Monterrey Tech. My teaching schedule dictated I had to arrive two hours late to work, twice a week. I arranged with my manager to stay at work two more hours those days to ensure a fair deal with my employer. One day however, things changed after a new policy was implemented. The General Manager asked me to stop arriving two hours late to work. Even after I explained my situation, the decision was final that the company could not accept that type of exception. From my perspective at the age of 26, even though I was already married and with our first child, the completion of my degree was, to me, as important as that job. I accepted an offer for a full-time faculty position at the university where I was studying the graduate program.

The role was open at the School of Engineering, at the time under Dean Juan Lopez, one of the greatest leaders I ever came across to, and a true liberator of organizations. As I gave notice of my departure at the manufacturing company, several managers and HR met for a few hours to review my case. By the end of the day, they came up with a powerful counteroffer: a promotion to become the head of the manufacturing department (a very big deal in that company), a 25% raise, and a sign-up bonus that would be of about $10 k USD in today's terms. Honestly, I was surprised. After so much fuss over my two-hour flexible arrangement, that counteroffer almost did not make sense as a logical option from the company's perspective—this was much more expensive than just allowing me to stay with two jobs. But that offer was a potential game changer for my future; I had to consider it.

I went back to the university and told Dean Lopez what just had happened and that I would welcome any perspective to help me understand what to do, because I was unsure. Instead of giving me advise or trying to sell his job to get me to sign, he went to explain to me the FIRO-B model for human behavior.

Let me take a detour to summarize it for you. In a nutshell, FIRO B is based on a three-domain framework—inclusion, control, and affection[11]—representing the main motivators or fundamental *'needs'* developed by Will Schutz in his *Three-Dimensional Theory of Interpersonal Behavior*.[12] Inclusion represents the degree to which a person wants to include others in her or his activities and also the degree on which she/he wants to be included in the activities of others. Control indicates the desire to influence, to lead, take responsibility, and also the degree to which a person wants to control, or be under the control of others. Affection represents the desire to establish closeness, relationships, and also the extent to which someone wants to like or appreciate others, and to be liked and appreciated by others. As you may have noticed, each of these three domains has two ways to act on the person: how much the need is *expressed* and how much the need is *desired*. Expressed means that the need is about preferring to initiate the behavior; and Desired means that the need is about preferring to receive the behavior. For simplicity, each dimension can be described with a symbolic word that is a metaphor of the motivator at play. For inclusion, the expressions are to be *in* or *out* of something, a group, a vision; for *control* it is being *above* or *under* something, this is, the acceptance of having power, responsibility, and decision-making, or accepting those powers over you; and for *affection* it is to be *with* or *without* something or someone of value for you (open or close to, in the more modern version).

Relevant to our liberation discussions, the need for *Inclusion* has proven to be the primary, and the earliest force on the needs in the development of an individual, as well as the earliest on the experience of socializing in a group or organization. After inclusion is achieved, the interpersonal needs move to power and affection/openness. This critical research finding explains the innate, psychological need and importance of the (I) in DEIB. Inclusion, and therefore belonging, can take us far and fast in the journey to a liberated organization and can also significantly delay our efforts—but more on this later!

After he briefly explained this model, Dean Lopez said that the very fact that the offer was enticing to me was an indication that I was motivated by power—the capacity to do things—and he advised me to get a deeper understanding of why that was the case, what I was looking to accomplish with that power, and what was my ultimate motivation to take one job over the other. I had to make that decision by myself. He also described the job at the Engineering Division very differently from a traditional faculty member job. Instead, his vision was to hire superstars to build a department that would be a reference for many years to come. In his words 'we are building a legend here, I do not need just good teachers, I need champions who want to be part of something very special'. Part of me was wanting to hear something like this, I instinctively wanted to belong there.

This is a perfect example of leadership of liberation. Not providing the answers but showing the way, offer a liberating purpose, enhance the mindset with powerful tools of reflection to discover what I really wanted. I declined the manufacturing job and went back to the Dean to formally accept the role. He asked, 'how much would that other job pay you?' When I told him, he matched every penny of the offer. I never felt more affirmed, more empowered, and more liberated.

What Dean Juan Lopez did in that interchange falls into the examples illustrated in the bottom part of Fig. 3.1. He led with the purpose of the university, stated his north star, a bold vision to change the world. He listened to my situation and guided my thinking with the right questions, assured me that the role was not an average position but one that would be part of something unique and special. As you will see, liberating managers can be instinctual, they can just be born or develop on their own to be like that. But large-scale change that required this type of liberating leadership across layers in complex organizations cannot be left to the probability that all managers will act like this on their own. Expectations must be set, and tools must be provided as we will explore in detail in chapters ahead.

Second Layer in Scope: Influencing Liberation in the Industry

Every organization operates within the space of an industry or cluster of economic or social activity, depending on the purpose and function of the organization. Within that market or industry, companies position their products and services, they publish their research, and they are designed to act as agents of positive influence for their customers. This in turn, is beneficial for their investors and their partners.

The industry layer is quite comprehensive and consequential because the liberating impact of the company can be achieved by multiple means. The most direct impact comes with the product itself, but it is also inclusive of the technology to produce it. Vaccines are a great example of this industry liberation impact. In the development of the COVID vaccine, a new technology was tested, the mRNA (messenger RNA) technology. This technology was utilized in the development of the Pfizer-BioNTech and Moderna COVID-19 vaccines. The mRNA vaccines work by introducing a small piece of genetic material from the virus (specifically, the mRNA that codes for the spike protein found on the surface of the SARS-CoV-2 virus) into the body. This prompts the body's cells to produce the spike protein, which in turn triggers an immune response, teaching the immune system to recognize and fight the virus if it is encountered in the future. While the product itself—the COVID-19 vaccine—brings the power of an immense liberating effect, the technology used to develop the product is also a significant liberating agent on its own, since the mRNA process can be used in other vital drugs production.

Personal computers are another great example of liberation at the industry level. The product by itself brings power, with a liberating effect to anyone who can use it; gain speed, scale, accuracy. But there is another layer, the software and the microchip technologies produced in standardized ways and at scale can now create solutions outside of the original applications intended—education, industry, administration.

Software was combined with hardware to enable intelligent automation, navigation, industry optimization on multiple ways. The common denominator of the industry liberation comes in the form of *access*. A product or technology that many more people can afford and possess to make their lives better, impacting many areas of society.

Great inventions that affected millions of people live in this space. The printing press by Johannes Gutenberg, the Penicillin by Alexander Flemming, the discovery and applications of radioactivity by Marie Curie, the production line by Henry Ford, the semiconductor, the laser technology, the cellular telephony are all examples of industry creation and technology expansion, access at much larger scale, bringing with it liberation to many people, creating wealth and economic impact for investors and shareholders, suppliers, and a full array of cascaded benefits.

Third Layer in Scope: Influencing Liberation in Society

Liberating society is a quantum leap above and beyond having access to products or services. It is, in essence, access to freedom, to human rights, and to the right to live, building a world with more equality.[13] These are bigger problems than companies can solve and the only reason this layer is in scope is because there is a role companies can play to contribute, in some cases very significantly, to this social dimension. At its highest expression, this layer includes the heroic and historical work of many freedom fighters across time. There are too many to create a representative list, but a few examples will illustrate the point: Martin Luther King Jr., Simon Bolivar, Winston Churchill, George Washington, Malala Yousafzai, Joan of Arc. In a more contemporary way, this layer includes companies, institutions, and civil organizations that work outside of governments to bring this access to liberation in quite unusual and inspiring ways.

Companies often have relevant programs on Corporate Social Responsibility. More recently, based on consumer behavior, investors are demanding evidence of actions on what is called ESG, for Environmental, Social and Governance initiatives. Each one of those 'E' and 'S' are very broad spaces, encompassing emissions, waste management, energy management, water management that companies are expected to work on, and have goals for. In the social areas we have the focus on how minorities are represented in pay and in management layers, not only in the form of representation. This remains the case in many industries and companies even with varied levels of support by regulators and governments.

In addition, companies can liberate at the level of society indirectly by developing the next generation of their leaders to be more connected to social issues as part of their business, and by support the right civil organizations.

A few years ago, I attended a leadership gathering centered on the nature of leadership, and a deep reflection about *who is a leader*. The brilliant organizers, Jim Bolt,[14] and Rocky Kimball,[15] both widely recognized as gold standards in the development of executives, in association with the Women Peacemakers Fellowship at the University of San Diego[16] brought in a group of remarkable women from India. They made a presentation about their efforts to help women who had been victims of rape. Their initiative included both personal support to victims and also programs and infrastructure to prevent that crime to continue to spread. At the time it was a very serious problem in India. The session turned out to be an unforgettable experience for everyone in attendance. They shared how they were able to persuade the right power players, organize local groups, prioritize actions across multiple agendas, mobilize people for action. All of the above meant they had to put themselves at risk, with their lives on the line to save other women. They told us how they fought discrimination and status quo to even being able to be heard by the authorities—most of them men—in the first place. How they managed to be accepted as agents to negotiate agreements with law enforcement to raise government's budgets to support these efforts and increase judicial punishment for perpetrators. They described how they worked with institutions to build safe homes and how they established playbooks to educate women to limit the risk of being attacked. As we engaged in a discussion, they shared they had very limited formal education, no degrees, no MBAs, no formal training as leaders. For this audience, CEOs and HR executives this was a rather humbling and inspirational conversation that helped us remember what leadership looks like in its purest form, in action, not only to liberate people under very hard circumstances, but to have the vision to *build an infrastructure* to make those changes permanent—instinctively, they chose vitality over simple problem solving—which in this case would have been more than enough.

This session was, as you can tell, unforgettable. It was a life lesson to all of us understanding that the most important aspect of leadership is *the outcomes it serves*. These women were not concerned with 360s, skills, competencies, mentors—all of those crucially important and necessary, not to question their value—but their focus was to find a sustainable solution to an urgent problem. I cannot make justice in these few lines to the courage of these women, and what fortitude of will and determination it took to break through a problem nobody knew how to solve and that many had just chosen to look the other way. As a result of their extraordinary efforts, they gained a reputation and a space in their local government as agents of change. The whole community benefited, and their programs have prevented many crimes, helped a large number of women from being victims, and the effort spread across their country.

Companies are not here to solve social problems, but they can be a change agent, and they have a massive following that sets standards in many communities. Multiple examples of American corporations in developing countries giving scholarships, innovation competitions for women and other minorities boost their brands as model employers in ways that their reputation can be recognized for years to come.

What Liberating Leadership Is NOT

The first and most important aspect about liberating leadership is that leaders are not responsible for *liberating* their people. Liberation, realization, fulfillment, are a personal journey and a personal experience, gained from people's personal choices and attitudes. Leaders have the obligation—and the power—to change their leadership style and to change the organization, to enable those choices by enacting the policies, processes and most importantly, by removing barriers, both physical and mental, that prevent the organization from achieving its full potential and to be able to sustain their success.

Therefore, Liberating Leadership *IS NOT*:

Lack of concrete standards and results.
Absence of management, or absence of supervision.
Prioritizing style over substance: good relationships and poor performance.
Making everyone free of their responsibilities.
No hard metrics, no plans or goals.
Remove all problems for employees.
An overt focus on diversity at all costs.
A political or religious agenda.

We are not liberating people from their work, that would not be a liberating act, we are removing barriers and opening spaces for agility and velocity to give success a chance. Employees are not off the hook on finding creative solutions to problems. We will always have problems to solve. Leading Success requires a leadership with the disposition and curiosity to seek and listen for opportunities to simplify, eliminate, reframe ideas, but also to add something new that will ultimately be seen by a reasonable employee as 'liberating'. Liberating leadership is not solving problems for your people, is having the strategic courage to tackle the problems that only leadership can tackle. Remember that manager you had who knew exactly what the problem was but chose to never address it, causing many people in your department to spin their wheels, work more, achieve less, because the issue was not addressed? You were not feeling liberated.

It is important to recognize that functioning, coordinating organizations of any kind will require limits, defined spaces for operation. Liberation is not about removing quality, easing the specifications; it is about making the achievement of those specifications easier by eliminating what is in the way. And further, by revisiting the specifications themselves to validate they should be there in the first place.

What Do We Liberate from?

Liberation is about both, having a vision of what the masterpiece we have in mind looks like, and then removing what does not belong, what should not be there—just the way Michelangelo is attributed to have said in his famous quote. The implication is profound, at least at the mindset level, because liberation is not only an act of adding features, but it may also be about removing, eliminating, carving, in order to create.

Over almost three decades of work in people leadership roles and assisting executives on strategic agendas, I have found three factors that most commonly stand in the way of achievement, acceleration, belonging, passion, and commitment. While some barriers may be concrete processes, policies, physical spaces, facilities, and the like, the essential Liberation is first in the mind, the beliefs, and the emotions of our people—otherwise we would be talking about well-known process improvement techniques. The emotional-mental barriers most prevalent in organizations are classified in three main categories:

- **Lack of Clarity**: Remove anything that keeps people confused, unclear, and unfocused. Take actions to ensure everyone knows what is expected from them.
- **Lack of Future**: Get rid of the past as a guide for decisions and policies. Infuse a forward-looking approach that opens a fresh space for simplification and innovation.
- **Lack of Confidence**: Remove sources of risk intolerance and fear of failure. Creative action necessitates a fail-fast, entrepreneurial environment to flourish.

Lack of Clarity: Liberating from Confusion

There are broad sources of confusion in all walks of life. If we assume good intentions and professionalism in corporate organizations, we can agree that one of the main sources of confusion often is the very mission of the organization, its goals, what is the hill we are supposed to take? Different ideas of what is success, or even what is the current reality play a huge role on a type of confusion that is less obvious than you may think. The same is true about previous spoused values, assumptions that are no longer valid are all examples of what lies in people's minds at the center of why bold, visionary transformation fails. These perceptions and misconceptions lead to a diminished ability to coordinate and align, erosion on the shared belief that we can be successful, and shows up as breakdowns, fundamental misconceptions, or disagreements across the levels or across the segments of an organization, impairing velocity, and co-dependent work. One of the leader's most immediate tasks is to identify and then remove any wrong or limiting ideas, definitions of intent, before anything else can happen. As Peter Senge established in his celebrated *The Fifth Discipline*[17] we must have a shared mental model for the organization to be able to collectively learn—and perform. Examples typically include using inadequate metrics, allowing different parts of the organization to hold different ideas of what is success, or allowing success to be about the segments and not about the collective enterprise—those practices are much more common than some may imagine.

A good example of how to drive for clarity was the time when Michael Dell decided to move away from the 'Direct' model to a more open and diversified access to its products and services. We hired a well-known consulting firm to help us articulate what the more diversified channel array should look like. Working together with our executives, the strategy consultants facilitated the creation of a brilliant strategy. In an important part of the articulation a key term proved more nuanced that originally expected: 'flexible'. To the credit of our implementation consultants, they recommended private sessions with each c-suite executive and their core teams to probe for absolute clear understanding on what each of the key concepts meant to them in terms of priorities, operations, investment, and metrics. The section speaking to flexibility proved to be tricky as some leaders and teams read into it 'open', while others read into it 'modular', and a different group thought it meant 'scalable'. Of course, you may think we needed to be all of the above, but that may not be the case, a strategic choice may be to be flexible but remain closed—the way Apple chose to do it, with great success.

Practically speaking, the last thing you want in your implementation is for one part of the organization to work on an 'open' agenda, while another is working on a 'scalable' agenda. Keep in mind everyone was reading from the exact same document, but they were walking away with quite different interpretations of what those words actually meant. As you would expect, each leader's interpretation came from their unique history and experience. The key question to answer was not just conceptual clarity but operational clarity, the one that we can't afford to miss, or we will see dysfunction magnified as implementation propagates across the organization.

As we dug into the discussions, we forced leaders to have group conversations to explore the merits of each perspective, having the CEO to be the ultimate decision-maker about how the future of the company was best reflected at every choice and clarification. A typical strategy development exercise would have been satisfied with the quality of its articulation. But what makes strategy work is the quality of its understanding.

The biggest lesson for me was that any strategy, even when technically sound, factual, irrefutable, and brilliant as you would have expected from a robust process with a remarkable partner, will not contain sufficient clarity to drive large teams through transformation. You still need socialization, conversation that creates the commitment to the true language that makes it black and white clear what is that we mean. That is the only way to translate operationally, for the broader and deeper organization, how the new expectations of work and priorities make their work different.

Future: Liberating from the Past

Leading Success brings an unexpected paradox within. If we are to maximize success, it would seem natural to think we must continue to do whatever was that made us successful. But we all know that is only partially true. Our success is a product of a network of unique and specific interactions with markets, social expectations, interests and needs of customers and people in power, and how our product fits in that environment. As environments inevitably change, so it does success. The past, tradition, is a double-edged sword. What has worked in the past and made us who we are, both personally as individuals, and collectively as companies, will not necessarily transfer into the future. At the leader level, Marshall Goldsmith[18] discusses this risk as a key advise to executives who are promoted to levels they have never been before feeling ready to replicate playbooks from their earlier experiences, unaware that the game is different at higher levels in all organizations. Those who fail to recognize that simple fact, are destined to stall their careers. But not only individuals suffer from too much attention to the past; organizations do the same, best described by Clayton M. Christensen in his book *The Innovators' Dilemma*[19] which states that the more successful you become, the more likely you will be hesitant to change your formula for success, opening the door to disruptors who have less to lose and exploit your weak areas. When those disruptors are strong enough to be in the mix of the market, it is too late for most 'incumbent' organizations to react. This analysis is now common science, most companies know about it—and yet, we still see everyday situations that remind us that nobody is safe from disruptors and the vulnerability coming from the next technology.

What is less common however, is how this principle holds true in a smaller scale—inside the company—at the common manager level. We tend to forget that disruption is like gravitation, applies to everyone. Considering that everything you find in your first day in an organization comes from the past, part of your job is to determine which practices should evolve. Too many managers, too often stay in the past for too long. Or move to a new proposition too soon, without the conditions to lead success.

According to Christiansen, incumbent companies dominating their markets often fail to realize, in a timely manner, when to disrupt themselves instead of allowing others to do it. Similarly, as you think on the managerial level in a company, managers hold on to current or past practices for too long and they become disrupted in similar ways. Because change is hard, most companies embark in change for survival reasons more often than for visionary reasons. The same happens with managers, but in a less visible way. Liberating from the past means reviewing existing time consuming processes and activities. Eliminating day-long or week-long meetings that were critical to coordinate under earlier circumstances that have changed. At a company level, policies have enormous power to make a difference on holding people hostage to things that do not work. For example, approvals based on distrust of employees, laborious steps irrelevant to performance management with no feedback. Moving away from the past is one of the greatest value-creation tools managers possess, and the most readily available opportunity for liberation.

Confidence: Liberating from Fear

This category overlaps with the other two but deserves a segment because it represents a vast number of behaviors that cascade into leadership shortcomings that affect companies in ways that sometimes are hard to see, they are just part of the common culture. The forms of fear I see most prevalent are fear of making mistakes, intolerance to risk, and lack of trust. A good example is organization design. Over time, leaders grow familiar with certain ways of work configuration and the corresponding levels of influence and power their players have in the organizational roles. The more radical a transformation is, the more impact can be expected on the way the work is regrouped and configured, but that proves to be a monumental ask for leaders. First because they try to avoid demoting, de-scaling responsibilities, or removing the very people who have been loyal and reliable for long time, instead they often prefer delaying changes that are demonstrably hurting the speed, trust, or effectiveness in the organization. They fear destabilizing the organization by removing the people who are loyal to them in favor of people who are more competent. But also, because some organization designs give leaders the ability to operate the business more directly, giving them control of details that should reside in lower levels, such as approvals, access to discussions, and preliminary ideas to influence the course of action at various levels. Some leaders fear losing control and resist evolving their organizations to models predicated on empowerment and delegation of authority. Unfortunately, that access and influence comes at the expense of a slower operation, hierarchical decision-making, and the undermining of the leaders that should own those decisions and processes, creating dysfunction and frustration.

There are more ways for fear to disrupt organizations. Among them, micromanagement, for fear of losing control, or making decisions based on the leader's 'gut' instead of data when the analysis dictates a new, unknown, but high-potential path, because they fear a departure from the proven formulas will not be tolerated if it fails. Low risk is a culture that propagates rapidly and soon our employees will play it safe, the organization becomes a place to keep management happy, instead of driving to growth.

Liberating leaders develop a remarkable sense of fear-finding practices in their organizations and move decisively to remove them. They reinforce learning after failure and make sure teams eliminate the sources of mistakes, systematically, not just dictating it through intimidation and more fear.

Expectations for the Leader of Liberation

The ultimate test of the leader is self-liberation. Warren Bennis said that becoming a leader is synonymous of becoming yourself. It is important that you work to become your *best* self. Some leaders unfortunately give the impression of becoming their worst selves once they are in power, to the dismay of their teams and the organizations promoting them. Not for nefarious intent, but because of insufficient readiness for the job. Some people are brought for a role that looks of certain dimension, but no job stays the same; over time some areas grow too fast, or become too complex, surpassing the skill or maturity of the individual in the role. This mismatch may bring unwanted behaviors as leaders try to cope with the gap. At the center of a liberating leader is self-awareness, understanding our own limitations and biases. Even a fast-moving role can be mastered if the leader assembles a great team and is willing to learn, if she/he can liberate from fears and ego. Easier said than done but that is why we have capable coaches and capable teams to listen to.

We can become a better liberating leader. We can reach our liberating potential by listening and understanding better about ourselves. The right assessments and competent coaching are a crucial starting point. But it requires openness and disposition to actually believe what those voices have to say. I have evaluated hundreds of leaders, and one thing has been very apparent to me: many top leaders are not great at listening feedback. After all, they have found a way to be successful, some of them against all odds, through a sheer power of will, trusting themselves; so, why listening now? Their highly intelligent and skeptical minds wonder if people providing feedback may have an agenda of their own in order to neutralize her or his 'super-powers'. Feedback, introspection, and listening are the only ways to raise our leadership in order to meet the challenges of this era in which we are called to transform, to evolve organizations to their place in the future. An era of leading free people, liberated talent who are hungry for a place to belong and become their true selves. If we can do that and become success ready, disruption-proof in the process, it is worth trying.

A final word on liberating leadership as we enter the three disciplines of this pillar.

Leadership matters even more than we think. One key implication of culture and leadership, as established by Edgar Schein in his remarkable *Organizational Culture and Leadership*,[20] is that leaders must recognize dysfunctional cultures and address them, intervene to evolve their organizations to a better culture, and adapt to new realities, more sophisticated demands. But what happens if the leaders can't see, do not agree with, or even benefit from the dysfunctions? When ultimate decision-making on culture rests in the top chair, the voice of the person on that chair will dictate what the organization will do. Simply put, whatever is in the capacity of that leader to listen, to digest, accept, be tolerant of what's different, and to credibly listen to voices he/she may not like, that overall synthesis will translate into a corresponding action. Great news if the leader is open, not too great if the leader is set on her/his ways. Such conundrum represents a leadership paradox. In theory, leaders seek for input to break molds and make liberating decisions 'under the strength of the team', but in the end, very often ultimate direction comes down to the CEO's most authentic and deep beliefs, as stated by Frederic Laloux in his book *Reinventing Organizations*[21]:

> What determines which stage an organization operates from? It is the stage through which its leadership tends to look at the world. Consciously or unconsciously, leaders put in place organizational structures, practices and cultures

that make sense to them, that correspond to their way of dealing with the world. This means that an organization cannot evolve beyond its leadership's stage of development.

As a consequence, our organizations are limited by how liberated each of us are.

If we miss this opportunity, our own consciousness becomes the ceiling for the organization. It is therefore imperative to untap it and set it free.

Notes

1. Sinclair, A. (2007). Leadership for the disillusioned: Moving beyond the myths and heroes to leading that liberates. Allen & Unwin. Crows Nest, Australia.
2. Burns, J. M. (1978). Leadership. Harper & Row.
3. Kotter, J. P. (1996). Leading change. Harvard Business School Press.
4. Bennis, W. (2009). On becoming a leader. Basic Books.
5. Mintzberg, H. (2004). Managers, not MBAs. Berrett-Koehler. San Francisco.
6. Garfield, Z. H., Hubbard, R. L., & Hagen, E. H. (2019). Evolutionary models of leadership: Tests and synthesis. Human Nature, 30(1), 23–53. https://doi.org/10.1007/s12110-019-09338-4
7. Schutz, W. (1958). FIRO: A three-dimensional theory of interpersonal behavior. Holt, Rinehart and Winston.
8. Lund, S., et al. (2021). The future of work after COVID-19: The post-pandemic economy. McKinsey Global Institute.
9. Getz, I. (2009). Liberating leadership: How the initiative-freeing radical organizational form has been successfully adopted. California Management Review, 51(4), Haas School of Business, University of California, Berkeley.
10. Clifton, J., & Harter, J. (2023). Culture shock: An unstoppable force is changing how we work and live. Gallup's solution to the biggest leadership issue of our time. Gallup Press.
11. Affection was the original name for the third dimension of Schutz model as developed in 1958. A more recent evolution of the model calls this last dimension Openness.
12. Schutz, W. (1994). The human element: Productivity, self-esteem, and the bottom line. Jossey-Bass Business & Management Series.
13. Ruth, S. (2006). Leadership and liberation: A psychological approach. Routledge.

14. Bolt, Jim. 2024. Founder, Executive Development expert. Retrieved from: https://edainc.io/coaches/jim-bolt/
15. Ruth, S. (2006). Leadership and liberation: A psychological approach. Routledge.
16. Kimball, Richard. 2024. Founder, Executive Development Expert. Retrieved from: https://actionlearning.com/our-people/richard-o-kimball/
17. Women Peacemakers Fellowship. (2024). Joan B. Kroc Institute for Peace and Justice, University of San Diego. Retrieved from: https://www.sandiego.edu/peace/institute-for-peace-justice/initiatives/women-peace-security/women-peacemakers/
18. Senge, P. (1990). The fifth discipline: The art and practice of the learning organization. Currency Doubleday. New York.
19. Goldsmith, M., & Reiter, M. (2007). What got you here won't get you there: How successful people become even more successful. Hyperion.
20. Christensen, C. M. (1997). The innovator's dilemma: When new technologies cause great firms to fail. Harvard Business Review Press.
21. Schein, E. H. (2010). Organizational culture and leadership (4th ed.). Jossey-Bass.
22. Laloux, F. (2014). Reinventing organizations: A guide to creating organizations inspired by the next stage of human consciousness. Nelson Parker.

4

Liberation in the Era of Purpose

Regardless of how you believe the future of work unfolds, data and research shows that the world has changed for employees,[1] forcing companies to choose between staying the course with proven models of the past, or to allow themselves to test and try something new to adapt, to gain an edge, or to enhance their competitive advantages. This is not a theoretical choice; it is a productivity, performance, and a success choice. It has been that way historically. If we examine how companies adopt attitudes and develop capabilities to compete in their surroundings, we will identify patterns to understand how the transformation of your company may unfold in *our times*. These patterns are useful to analyze why some companies occasionally break ahead of the pack, and sometimes even reset what effectiveness, success, means at that time, defining a new era.

Searching for those insights I have developed a perspective of how those effectiveness paradigms for companies evolve over time. See illustration in Fig. 4.1. Keeping the scope of effectiveness to the early Twentieth Century (1900) to our days, I argue there have been four dominant interpretations of what effectiveness, and therefore success looks like for companies. At the turn of the past Century, the Ford Motor Company was the first to bring scale as a competitive differentiator, but with time, this capacity proved insufficient. Ford lost market leadership to General Motors, and then both of them—albeit, decades later—lost market to Toyota, powered by their remarkable new ways to produce great quality faster. Other companies, some indicated in the illustration, are emblematic of the *Industrial* era, as I identify it, with three main differentiators: capacity, repeatability, and revenue. The main outcome of an industrial paradigm is to be *Scalable*, ensure returns on

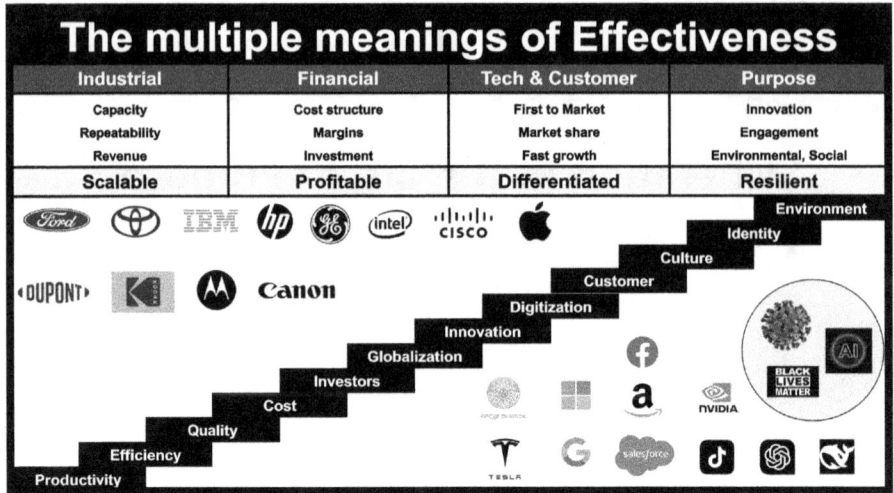

Fig. 4.1 A taxonomy on the evolution of effectiveness and success paradigms across time

capital, make the huge investments profitable. Mass production brought to us the power of the industrial revolution to consumer goods. You may argue the textile industry was the earliest to achieve and benefit from scale, and that is true, but I wanted to keep this analysis to a more contained timeframe. The textile industrialization goes another 100 years back.

An evolution over this industrial paradigm looks at the economic output of the enterprise. Effectiveness in this view is seen as profitability and market value. Being attractive to investors. Quality and productivity may not be enough; after all, both can be achieved by losing money, as it happened in 1990 to the Wallace Company (pipe and valve distribution), who became the first small service company ever to receive the Malcolm Baldrige National Quality Award; in 1992, just two short years later, it filed for Chapter 11. In the *Financial* paradigm, the next emerging interpretation of effectiveness, costs matter; the main outcome for companies in this era was to be Profitable, and we had methodologies focused on that goal, such as Michael Hammer and James Champy's book *Reengineering the Corporation: A Manifesto for Business Revolution*,[2] a book and approach that gained momentum as a forest fire. While the goal of reengineering was broader, many companies translated its principles and methodologies as a radical, fast way to reduce costs. But revenue maximization matters strategically, not only operationally. GE was the poster company of this financial paradigm. A sure bet for Wall Street, constant growth under Jack welch for over a decade, it seemed it could do no wrong. Articles and books were written about The GE Way,[3] with particular attention to their management cadence and their unwavering focus on leadership, performance, and succession, creating a generational impact in the world, in particular, managing talent, and the importance of CEO's attention to leadership. So many things were right with GE, and yet, as Jeff Immelt took over after the very successful Jack Welch, he focused on a number of innovations to rebalance the revenue portfolio toward industry and technology.[4] Globalization became a significant factor to companies and investors as a potential cost containment strategy, and also as a stabilization force to shield companies from geographical disruptions, political or natural disasters rendering earnings more predictable and consequently, a more certain forecast for financial growth. Cost, investors, and globalization worked hand in hand on this era to fuel growth and paved the road for the next era.

It is important to note these are not 'replacing' paradigms, as if for example, the Industrial perspective would not be relevant anymore, and therefore, to be replaced by the Financial perspective. These paradigms are not either/or transitions, instead they are cumulative, layered, combined. The distinction between one era and the next does not lie on their importance—they are all important—it is their influence, how their success, methods, metrics, ways of doing things are emulated, elevated by others trying to improve their game. Being the dominant concept of effectiveness prevalent at a point in time, inevitably shapes how the industry and the economy adjust and transform.

The next paradigm in my taxonomy involves a wide cluster of effectiveness drivers: innovation, digitization, and customer orientation. I clustered them together because they are intricately connected and cross-enabling. Innovation is an evolution over the financial model considering that any competitive advantage eventually erodes. After all, any product, service, technology used to fuel growth will at some point plateau and decline victims of a next version—a disruption—that is cheaper, more accessible, with more features—a phenomenon well explained by Clayton Christensen in his book *The Innovator's Dilemma*.[5] As a consequence, companies had no choice but keep innovating, keep creating the new and the next, or risk being disrupted. In this paradigm we see an explosion of technologies for digitization, enabling the mass-customization concept, the ability to use large data and connect with consumers more meaningfully. The game had changed, and the measure of success was now how digital, how much personalization any product may have. This capacity to be closer to customers, with ever more powerful analytics and also mobile devices in almost every pair of hands in the planet made it possible to use large data, real-time analytics, and faster, more targeted product development. That is why I called this era *Technology and Customer*. For those fortunate to witness this evolution over the last three decades this paradigm was a quantum departure from the past. The pivotal difference was the arrival of *accessible digitization*. Not just personal computers everywhere, but the Internet, and beyond that, the mobile device explosion. These were three colossal vectors going in the same direction, packed and experienced through a large number of key innovations, and technologies. Human centered software made the digital experience truly exceptional allowing for unprecedented capacity to be unique and different, and therefore, the main outcome on this era has been *Differentiation*.

We were well into this era, still with long ways to go on opportunities to capitalize on its promises when the world suddenly stopped on its tracks, almost literally. The COVID-19 pandemic forced everyone into a global experiment of digital life and remote contribution to keep the world running. But as we all know, that was not all of it; weeks after the world shut down operations, we had a generational social justice development in the United States, cascading across the world with protests and calls for antiracism. We still were—and perhaps we still are—recovering, adapting, and adjusting while yet another disruption hit in stride. The arrival of AI to the masses, as signified by the product Chat GPT completing a multiple-front challenge to the workplace and its effectiveness. Each one of these disruptions, on their own, would have been enough to be considered generationally defining events; but the three of them combined within a rather short period of time gave birth to something else, a new perspective altogether to be human in the world at this time. We moved from a life-threatening risk with the pandemic to a work ending risk with AI, and an increased awareness of just how much more ground there is to cover for an equal and just society. That is a lot to absorb, leaving people with an interest for knowing more about the 'why' of things. Why do we have to be back at the office? Why can't I feel that I belong in my team or organization? Why can't we do more for the environment? Why we are not listening to what our customers are saying? Will my job be replaced by Artificial Intelligence?

People in general, and employees in particular want to feel more connected to the ultimate goals and aspirations of the places where they choose to be. That is why I have called our current paradigm of effectiveness the era of *Purpose*, including the drivers of culture and identity, raising with them the material urgency to address the environment. The outcome of our era of Purpose is to be *Resilient* against disruptions.

The one hundred years arc of the evolution of effectiveness and success paradigms is completed; starting with the Industrial perspective focused on

Scale, giving place to the Financial effectiveness era, focused on Profitability, creating the innovation and funding fertile grounds for the Technology and Customer era, based on Differentiation, personalization and customization, which still is going on, but generation-defining disruptions gave place to a new era, the era of Purpose, where the imperative is to understand how we make our companies and ourselves resilient and prepared for disruption. In this environment, companies have been in trial-and-error mode, figuring out ways to be effective and win in an environment that is still fluid.

Leading Success is a navigation map and a response to the challenges of effectiveness and success in this era. One where employees care for what companies stand for, and where they can affect change in the world to make it better while we make it profitable, to make it safer and cleaner as we succeed. They look at companies as places where the intersection of our values, our achievements, and the interests of future generations can coexist. A company designed for the Purpose era—for our times. Literature has identified this trend[6] but in general, a comprehensive framework for the Purpose era is still to be created. That is the need Leading success is designed for.

Contemplating the metaphors for effectiveness and success illustrated in Fig. 4.1, there are two important points to make: first, there is no irrelevant paradigm. All of them are necessary, well, and alive. Companies need all four drivers. The question is, to our second point: which one is the priority for our company to become more effective? In short, effectiveness means different things for different companies at different stages of their own life cycle and maturity in their industries. For example, during the pandemic, the supply of vaccines was a development and production problem, reaching the scale needed to vaccinate the entire world, quite literally. These four perspectives are permanently overlapping. If we dissect out the essential contribution from each, we get to the four value propositions of effectiveness: to be scalable, profitable, differentiated, and resilient.

We started the book making the case for the post-pandemic era to drive the design of success in organizations, this is how we arrived to this paradigm and this is why Leading Success is a critical *human technology* for transforming organizations for today's world.

Leading Success rests on a number of key assumptions or principles, some of them have been identified in previous chapters, and a few more will come ahead. The principles are design parameters to identify the core tenets that will be materialized in the explanation of mindsets and disciplines as we journey through the next twelve chapters covering three mindsets and nine disciplines. The principles intend to highlight what is different, unique, and innovative about Leading Success. Let's explore.

The Ten Principles of Leading Success

1. **Success means that your customer's experience equals your vision.** In other words, what you saw, what you declared in your vision of the future is actually happening on the ground, in the world. This is the final metric that matters in transformation; evidence that your liberating, vital vision has translated to your customers, make them better, more successful, able to express their own greatness to accomplish their purposes, and therefore, you are changing the world. As a consequence, a well thought and well executed plan will bring the revenues and margins expected, along with all the metrics that mattered for your transformation. Keep in mind that a short-term high revenue model not predicated on customer success is not sustainable.
2. **Exceptional performance only comes from exceptional engagement and standing for something.** In order to get your vision in the world you will need others to help you—executives, managers, all employees, and partners. A great vision and a great conviction to make it happen is not enough when it touches only a handful of people at the top, it needs to go all across the company—you need great talent (and also vital processes) to scale that commitment. But as we are all still learning from the post-pandemic, future of work era, the best, the brightest, the difference-making talent are searching for a liberating experience at work, not just a job. There is a growing percentage of employees who are passionate for companies committed to both visionary and ambitious goals and to succeed by providing a positive, liberating, self-affirming experience to their customers and employees. This is, companies that are consistent to their purpose and values. Performance is a destination that goes through the gates of engagement and standing for something as a company.
3. **Execution, performance, and therefore, *success* are all forms of expression.** Indeed, they have always been. Achievement is an expression of power, intelligence, overcoming odds, and *becoming* something that was intended, something more, creating a legacy—it goes the same for people and organizations. In the same way singers, actors, gymnasts 'perform' their routines and their creativity on their arenas, fields, they are expressing a form or art, or a skill. Nothing is different on that sense to an office worker, a driver, a manager. Performance is built out from our expressions. It is the most fundamental evidence of life, for all organisms, and its fulfillment compares to nothing else. A liberating leadership unfolds the expression of employees and customers to its fullest potential.

4. **The fundamental job of a leader is liberation.** I have been reticent to draw a line between *managers* and *leaders*. In fact, I do not believe in that separation. Instead, I prefer to separate the moments when a particular person *leads* and when the same person *manages*. When we lead, we listen to understand, we analyze situations, and act to enable, unlock, accelerate what matters. We purposefully adopt behaviors, attitudes, and make decisions focused on an experience of liberation for our people, peers, and supervisors. Leaders do not seek to *liberate people* from their responsibilities. Instead, the focus of their leadership is on making the organization success ready by removing barriers, setting a very high bar for performance, and practice liberating leadership with employees. Committed employees will find this culture as the right environment for their own liberation. Managers optimize, leaders liberate to reach beyond optimization, renewed identity, excellence, and innovation.
5. **Creating commitment—not loyalty—is the most impactful skill of a leader during transformation and during sustained disruption.** This may sound counter-intuitive for many leaders who think, expect, and unconsciously reward loyalty behaviors toward them. People if at all, should be loyal to the purpose, the mission, not to someone in the organization. It follows that one of the leader's most critical skills is to be able to *create commitment* toward the transformation's purpose in both, big and small decisions and actions. Commitment in organizations is created through conversations, a well-known process of interaction and understanding between people. But getting to share information or to achieve alignment on an idea is different than achieving commitment. We will need leaders with the disposition to listen first, consider the input, discuss possibilities, and define actions consistent to the values, to accelerate change and results, delivering the liberating experience necessary to create commitment. This kind of leadership and this kind of communication elicit both the execution toward the goals, and just as important, a more personal conviction to accomplish the actions because of that larger picture that is liberating for the company, is also liberating for our customers and employees.
6. **Don't focus on what the organization is, but on what it is becoming.** Transformation is not a destination but a journey of constant adaptation to reach our goals. This is the case only because the world keeps changing. Very rarely a company sets a goal, then nothing changes in the market, competitors, technology, and the goal is achieved. Instead, the reality is that our goals are rather a moving target because of everyone else's interactions and ambitions. They too want to change the world,

and most likely at the expense of your share and revenues. Therefore, companies are always in a flux state. It is very important to look at metrics—often very selectively—at the end of the month, quarter, or year and feel good or bad about it. But it is even more crucial to understand how the organization is working to adapt to changes and to integrate cohesively internally to gain velocity, agility to adapt fast. You may wake up one year as the big champion of the world, just as Motorola did with the RAZR phone, but the pipeline to continue the innovation with next versions or world-changing devices was not there. Something we have to give credit to a company like Apple for example, with a relevant iPhone every year. Motorola was successful but was also *becoming* stagnant. As leaders of liberation, we must understand we really never *arrive* to our transformation, but we are always *becoming* a version of ourselves that is moving on a direction toward more or toward less capability to achieve it. Leaders must always be clear on how their actions affect what their companies are becoming.

7. **Companies are talent economies.** In essence, we always run two businesses, the external business directed to our customers, and the talent business which used to be internal, but it is no more. Supply, demand, value creation, and return on investment apply equally for our external product and our internal talent. Every job must be defined in terms of value creation, I.e., what is this role adding to the transformation's critical path? In a Talent Economy perspective, talent serves the business by ensuring the winning candidate can excel at value creation, not merely be able to complete tasks, activities, and perform duties. Therefore, we are never managing people, not even *talent* as individuals are concerned; we are managing a talent portfolio the way consulting firms manage theirs. We all live within a segment of a talent market, larger than our company who is very strongly working to take your talent assets away. You can't think on your salary bands, benefits, and variable pay just as cost structure features. They are conditions in a market to retain the very best and attract the people who will make YOU successful. People know this, and they are our new customers—our company is a product for them, and we must work just as hard to gain their loyalty as we work to retain our most treasured customers.

8. **Humans, Machines, and the reinvention of HR.** As the world looks in amazement at the prodigy of Artificial Intelligence, we wonder when—no longer if—machines will start doing part of what we do for a living. Humans will not be removed from work, at least not in a foreseeable future. Any model of AI impact you prefer to accept, indicates that the

world of the future will not be about humans alone. It will be a human–machine partnership. We are starting an accelerating transition to that stage. Broader adoption of AI in work environments will create a particular new demand, a new problem to solve in the workplace: the design of human–machine environments to produce the *synergistic partnership* between the two, something MIT's Thomas Malone calls *Superminds*.[7] What we know today as the Human Resources function, largely responsible to architect the current work environment, very soon will be a limited framework to design the future workplace. This new demand will force the HR professional to get closer to these technologies, but not just as consumers of AI packed solutions to do HR work, but as designers of the enterprise ecosystems capable to achieve the Supermind. Beyond AI, our ambitious transformations of today, our determined competitors, changing markets, and the era of Purpose, on their own, are raising the bar for HR. As a consequence, this is also the era of the HR evolution. I have included a perspective of what that may look like, based on Leading Success considerations, in Chapter Nineteen.

9. **Diversity, Equity, Inclusion and Belonging (DEIB) must be an outcome before they can be an input.** We must strive for the *organic* DEIB workplace. Salary and employment remain the strongest forces to get people to join and stay, except for the most extraordinary, value-making talent. But those spectacular individuals have choices, and they long for a comprehensive employee experience, for an opportunity to change the world, achieve their full potential while being their full selves. This is, an environment where the authentic appreciation and embracing of everyone's full self, regardless of any ethnical, historical, sexual preference or nationality, becomes a natural outcome, not only the result of a program. In other words, it is achieved organically, by the way we operate. The absence of this organic, liberating mindset reduces DEIB Programs to artificial efforts to push for something leadership is not ready to support. An authentic DEIB culture is, therefore, the necessary outcome of leading for liberation. It is only at that point, when the business can enjoy it as an input for business growth, innovation, market, and cultural relevance. As we work to get to this stage, DEIB programs are necessary to provide accountability and results as we create the liberating culture. One key element on this journey is that CEOs and CHROs must embrace the external social moment inside their companies in their journey to sustained success. Enterprise environments can no longer be cognitive and experientially divorced from society's concerns. That makes CEOs and CHROs the resident Chief Philosophy Officers. Work, more

than ever, is an extension of life. Companies, at their own premises or through their screens at people's and customers' homes, are spaces that play a role in how employees and customers experience our values and see themselves belonging. We can't elude that responsibility and therefore, we must design for it.

10. **Liberation, vitality, and signature expression in transforming organizations cannot be produced by machines**—not yet anyway! Leadership, mastering of complex changing contexts, and human interactions are still ahead and distant for AI applications, and remains to be seen to what extent leading people for liberation is something that can ever be replicated by a machine. But one thing I have learned on my studies of AI, we should never bet on something this new technology 'can't' do as next generations of AI continue to emerge. Be as it may, there is still a journey ahead, one where humans will be more identified with matters of people, than they are with execution of tasks. People will be focused on building the optimized combinations human–machine and also focused on guiding transformations of themselves, and their families, communities, and organizations to adapt successfully to a human–machine era. Cultivating liberation, vitality, and expression as a form of work and as an approach to life will serve to illuminate the discussions about the roles and the spaces for that *Supermind* we are about to create.

The promise of this book is to go beyond the declaration that a purpose-driven organization design and way of management is needed to drive transformation in the post-pandemic era. The center is now on the *how*. How exactly we build such organization? What does it take? The answer lies in a journey I have called 'The Nine Leading Success Disciplines.

Leading Success Disciplines

The goal of defining disciplines is to articulate how organizations can effectively *scale and sustain* the company's transformation and its *success*; this is, ensuring that the vision matches the experience for both customers and employees. The illustration in Fig. 4.2, identifies those Nine Disciplines and how they relate to the mindsets.

The Nine Disciplines are not a formula, or a series of steps to be followed as a recipe. If anything, the mindsets (Liberation, Vitality, Expression) would be more of a formula because I consider those to be the essential constructs for enduring success for the future. The disciplines intend to organize the

Focus of change	Mindsets	Disciplines	Outcome
Leadership		Aspiration	Liberating ambition, the 'North Star'
Reset leadership for liberation, articulate strategy and achieve commitment	**Liberation**	Transformation	Operational, concrete path for action
		Commitment	Choice for personal liberation
Infrastructure		Culture	Written, Designed, Experienced Cultures
Redesign and equip the organization for vitality, results and resilience	**Vitality**	Talent	Exceptional talent and managers
		Organization	Unleashed organization, right metrics
Execution		Engagement	Ownership, coordination, and commitment
Getting exceptional business results through a liberating, vital expression	**Expression**	Expectation	Clarity, contribution and development
		Experience	Focused execution, remarkable results

Leading Success: Three Mindsets, Nine Disciplines

Fig. 4.2 Leading Success portfolio of Mindsets and Disciplines

thinking and offer a point of view for execution inside each mindset pillar. Their content reflects my experience, prevalent research, and what has worked for multiple global companies where I have had the privilege and opportunity to implement them. Each one of the elements of Leading Success is consistent with contemporary, post-pandemic, and inclusive thinking.

With that said, while I do not advocate for formulas, any formalization of Leading Success will require a reset on the mindset, the fortification of some elements of the people infrastructure, and raising the bar on expectations for managers to drive for performance through authentic, aligned, expression, not by suppressing it. That is an implementation effort that will require consideration of which of these disciplines is necessary to address in your company. If you are new to a CEO role, you have a unique opportunity to work with your CPO and take the road depicted here. Something you will not regret doing. The mindsets and the disciplines can work however as a playbook in case anybody wants to follow the model.

Each discipline is explored in terms of why it is needed and what we get out of it. The descriptions will be detailed but only to the extent appropriate for management and leadership audiences, this is, the work, the outcomes, the value and what it takes, how it is measured, risks and do-don't perspectives. I intend to provide sufficient insight and guidance for those interested on following this path.

It is time to start the journey.

Notes

1. Lund, S., et al. (2021). The future of work after COVID-19: The post-pandemic economy. McKinsey Global Institute.
2. Hammer, M., & Champy, J. (1993). Reengineering the corporation: A manifesto for business revolution. Harper Business.
3. Slater, R. (1999). Jack Welch & the G.E. way: Management insights and leadership secrets of the legendary CEO. McGraw-Hill.
4. Immelt, J. R. (2017). How I remade GE. Harvard Business Review, September 2017. https://hbr.org/.
5. Christensen, C. M. (1997). The innovator's dilemma: When new technologies cause great firms to fail. Harvard Business Review Press.
6. Quinn, R. E., & Thakor, A. V. (2018). Creating a purpose-driven organization: How to get employees to bring their smarts and energy to work. Harvard Business Review, July 2018. https://hbr.org/.
7. Malone, T. (2018). Superminds: The surprising power of people and computers thinking together. Little, Brown and Company. New York, NY.

Part II

Journey

5

The Liberation Mindset: Word vs World

The View at a Glance

What is it?	This is the over-arching leadership philosophy at the center of Leading Success.
Why do I need it?	To reframe how you look at your role as leader, to inform how you interact with your people and the organization, to seek new ways to unleash the highest potential in both, for remarkable results.
So what?	It pays off to be a liberating leader as it delivers the transformation, sets the infrastructure for sustained success based on a people-first approach.
What's in it?	The disciplines of: Aspiration, Transformation, Commitment.

The Elevator Speech

A Liberation mindset is needed to provide the primary orientation for the role of leaders and the philosophical foundation that serves as reference for decision-making, people infrastructure, policies, practices, and expected behaviors for all employees, but primarily for managers and executives. The notion of liberation is behind every major transformation and behind every major achievement in history. The essence of small and large groups of people to mobilize for a cause is rooted in the idea of liberation as the driving force giving life to that cause.

Most c-suite and senior executives have intuitively mastered the art of storytelling to introduce their visions and to inspire people to follow. It comes as an innate ability for some individuals. It is, however, an underrated component in the skillset for transformation. Most leaders believe that, as long as a story is rational, people will follow. But the reality is that people follow for emotional reasons. This is a premise that must be recognized and designed for in transformation efforts. In addition, we have survived as a civilization by the skillful coordination of actions that are purposeful and meaningful for people. We have done that through the use of language,[1] which takes a central role in articulating the vision, the transformation, and our commitment to both.[2]

The thinking process we will use includes the following two aspects of a liberation mindset—(1) a powerful way to tell a story and, (2) the way it journeys into people's personal reasons to achieve the commitment we need to move the organization forward.

The Thinking Process

In his famous speech at the University of Rice in 1962, President Kennedy[3] established a vision that while directed to the United States as a nation, it quickly became a quest for humanity. Notwithstanding the military motivations to stay ahead of the Soviet Union in the space race, the cause was immediately understood by everyone and had the right language, the right tone, to make it a guiding star for an entire nation. Such is the power of a vision for which its time has come. The story to bring this declaration to reality offers extraordinary insights on how a vision becomes commitment for a large number of people and institutions.

Similar to President Kennedy, you have a 'quest to the moon' in your company right now. Perhaps you have been hired to drive a rather daunting transformation that many people in your own company would not imagine is even possible, or even worthy of trying. Some people at the board see this complexity and they intellectually see its challenges, but they tend to oversimplify what it will take to mobilize the large organization to achieve the expected outcomes. That's why they hired you, to figure that out.

Just how you go about this task?

Imagine we can put under the microscope a transformation effort so we can see the parts and elements that lie within. In this special microscope we will see five components, as referenced in Fig. 5.1.

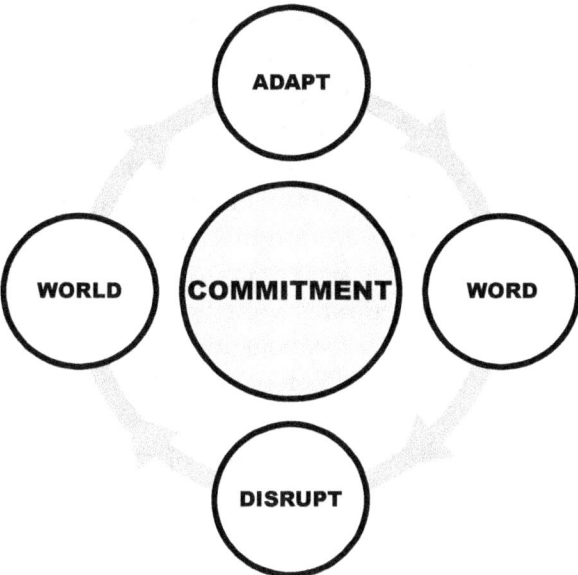

Fig. 5.1 The foundational architecture of transformation in Leading Success

Transformations can be described in terms of four main forces, shown in the periphery of this model, and one igniting energy, at the center.

Any transformation starts with a vision. That vision can be an image, a sentiment, a desire that moves someone to do something different. However, to become a transformation at the collective scale, involving others, that vision has to be articulated with language. Therefore, we call that the *WORD*. Your word as a leader.

Visions rarely come from nothing. Visions are inspired by the observation and experience of what is in front of us, what we experience, our perceived reality. Typically, we experience a gap, something missing, something that should be different. Therefore, transformations are rooted in the *WORLD*, as we see it.

In Kennedy's example, the vision was to bring a group of astronauts to the moon, land on it, and return them safe back to earth before the end of the decade—just eight years ahead. It mattered that it was President Kennedy making such statement. It mattered that it was the President's WORD. He was the leader of the nation and therefore had the authority to make that *declaration*. Some other official, in another stage would not have carried the same weight, or it would have been considered an inconsequential statement. Ambitious statements become Visions only when they are articulated by the right leader. An important part of the job of a leader is to declare visions—smaller or larger, sometimes in a week-to-week basis. Over my career in talent and succession, I have seen a very large number of executives who are unaware of their own power to establish a vision and they significantly underplay this aspect—creating a reputation of being *not transformational leaders*. They see their companies and their jobs mainly as a preservation mission to keep what is there, playing for the present, instead of making it future-ready. As President Kennedy continued on his speech, he recognized this was going to be a very difficult mission and dedicated some lines to set a foot on the reality of the time. Although there were technological components in early stages of maturity, there was no proven technology ready for this mission, no organization or infrastructure capable to achieve that vision, but that was not the reason not to commit to it. In other words, he recognized the stage of the WORLD surrounding this decision:

> We choose to go to the moon. We choose to go to the moon in this decade and do the other things, not because they are easy, but because they are hard, because that goal will serve to organize and measure the best of our energies and skills, because that challenge is one that we are willing to accept, one we are unwilling to postpone, and one which we intend to win, and the others, too.
> President John. F. Kennedy

In the same way you are expected to deliver a vision in your WORDS as the leader of your department, division, or enterprise, people will expect to see the connection between that vision and to the way they see and understand the WORLD. The last thing you want to hear is a bold vision not grounded in reality. In these moments of meaningful change, employees—and also investors, partners, suppliers—feel the need to confirm that leaders understand the issues, that their concerns are represented in the story, otherwise the vision will be dismissed as an unrealistic dream, or perceived as an imposition. Being grounded in reality does not mean you are a prisoner, a hostage, or that you are *limited by* reality; you will have to adapt to it, neutralize its effects, solve for its limitations as you defeat its odds to change it, but in that change the only limit is the capacity of leaders to think big, as we will see ahead.

These two aspects—WORD, and WORLD—provide the context and framework for the first discipline, *Aspiration*. See illustration in Fig. 5.2. In this sense, the Aspiration is about painting an understandable and worthy contrast between the current reality (WORLD) and the leaders' vision

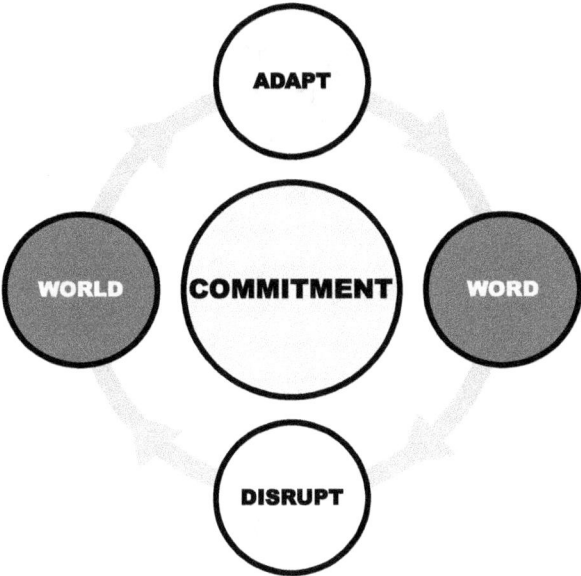

Fig. 5.2 The source of Aspiration: WORD versus WORLD

(WORD). Aspirations have to answer the question 'ultimately, why am I here for?'.

Continuing with the model, once we understand the vision and its founding reality, we work to identify what needs to continue, be enhanced, accelerated, resourced, and what needs to be modified, reduced, or be eliminated. These are the two components above and below in the model: *ADAPT* and *DISRUPT*.

These two components become the description of the *Transformation*; what we will chose to adapt to, and what we will chose to disrupt or change. See illustration in Fig. 5.3. These choices are an essential part of the liberation mindset. Our second discipline, Transformation, serves to clarify what changes and what does not change and what we are changing toward. This is, the proverbial 'From-To' articulation.

To this point in our transformation design, the four components above are concepts, they are blueprints that need to be brought to actions by people. That is the role of the fifth component at the center—*COMMITMENT*—which is our third discipline, as shown in Fig. 5.4. Achieving commitment for the vision and the transformation is absolutely essential, and it is not an 'automatic' step. This is one of the vital flaws of transformation. Leaders must overcome two common oversimplifications: (1) believing that a formalization of commitment is not necessary. In practice, commitment has to be

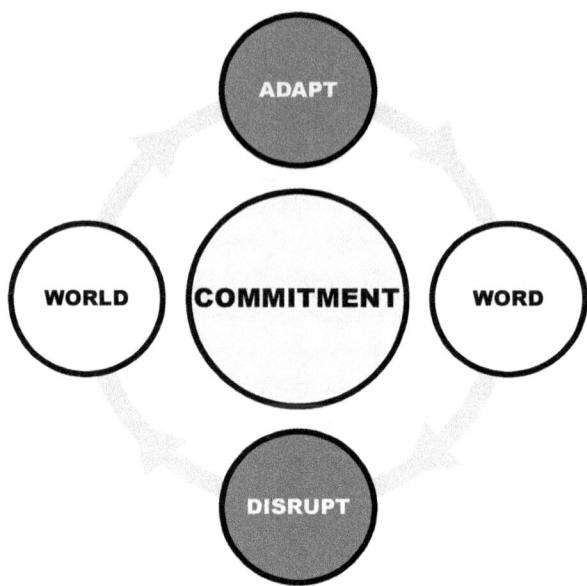

Fig. 5.3 The source of Transformation: ADAPT and DISRUPT

explicit, in the same way flight attendants ask passengers seating in emergency rows to say "yes" to their understanding that they are expected to act in case of an emergency, they don't leave it to just the message, they elicit an undistracted, articulated commitment. And (2) not understanding that *commitment is an outcome* of a journey inside the human mind, that is why some leaders confuse communication with commitment. Nothing is further from the truth and yet it is a common practice in many organizations.

When you adopt a mindset of liberation you understand that people in the organization must willingly commit to the Aspiration and the Transformation, for what they mean. This is, including their ramifications and consequences, otherwise the transformation cannot scale effectively and rapidly to its fullest potential. In the absence of commitment, you would get a diminished, delayed version of what tour transformation could be. As a consequence, your Aspiration and Transformation have to be (or feel) liberating to your employees as much as they are to your customers.

An important assumption at this point is that the CEO and the CHRO/CPO are in alignment on the direction to evolve the company toward the vision of Leading Success, or something similar, even if this is only an exploration.

This mindset or pillar consists of three distinctive outcomes that I segmented as disciplines: Aspiration, Transformation, and Commitment. It

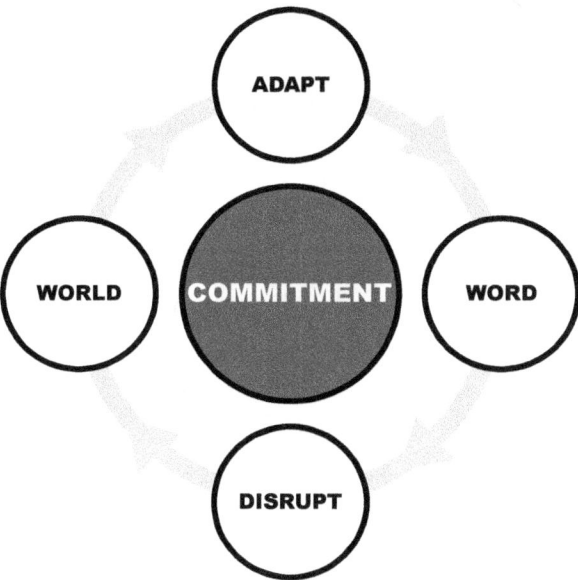

Fig. 5.4 Commitment is the driving force to scale transformation

will work best if those disciplines are followed in the particular sequence offered in this writing. Not for dogmatic reasons but merely for logic: in the end we need people choosing to commit for our transformation, and that articulation cannot be produced without a vision. It follows that we need a vision first, then the transformation articulation so we can get the commitment.

We will now dive into each of the three disciplines of the Liberation mindset: Aspiration, Transformation, and Commitment.

Notes

1. Habermas, J. (1984). The theory of communicative action: Volume one. Beacon Press. Boston, MA.
2. Habermas, J. (1987). The theory of communicative action: Volume two. Beacon Press. Boston, MA.
3. Kennedy, J. F. (1962, September 12). Address at Rice University, Houston, Texas. In Papers of John F. Kennedy. Presidential papers. President's Office files. Speech files (JFKPOF-040-001). John F. Kennedy Presidential Library and Museum, Boston, MA.

6

Aspiration: A Quest to Change the World

Aspiration is an articulation of the ultimate purpose we intend to achieve, often called Purpose or Vision. There are plenty of models, frameworks, philosophies, and methodologies to articulate the aspiration. Hubert Joly provided a useful approach to developing a purpose in his article *'Creating a Meaningful Corporate Purpose'*,[1] in which he identifies the purpose of a company to be in the intersection of four key factors: what the world needs, what the company is uniquely good at, what people at the company are passionate about, and how the company can create economic value. Jim Collins and Jerry Porras provided a model in their book *'Built to Last'*[2] called BHAG for Big, Hairy, Audacious Goal, which intends to articulate a long-term, ambitious goal that is clear and compelling, and serves as a unifying focal point of effort, acting as a catalyst for team spirit. Defining the aspiration, however, is—or can be—part of a larger discussion on strategy. While strategy is a discussion related to "how" companies will achieve their goal, the analysis for strategic articulation can influence the purpose. If, for example, a company realizes it will have access to certain technology nobody else will have for a while, that opens more ambitious spaces for the company to claim a larger purpose. The examination of the future takes central stage in the articulation of a purpose, although its roots remain centered on the ethos of the company that can be traced back to its inception, it is what lies ahead what inspires employees, customers and investors. Aspirations, therefore, are *The North Star* for the Organization, guiding the long journeys their ambitious goals demand.

A useful perspective on the role of the future on strategic planning comes from Mark W. Johnson and Josh Suskewicz, who offered a practical perspective in their book *'Lead from the Future'*[3] offering a conceptual framework and methodology to create a vision and a plan that is *future-back*, as opposed to *present-forward*, which makes the narrative very consistent with Leading Success. In their writing they see the need for the vision to be about a future that may sound unattainable or too futuristic for some audiences, but yet, it represents an answer for the way the world is changing. Future-back planning was one of the most inspiring aspects of President Kennedy's commitment to going to the moon. It illustrates how the genius of extraordinary visionaries lies in looking at the needs defined by their realities, understanding the imposing limitations of what is available today, and yet, still declaring a vision seemly unattainable at the moment, with the conviction to commit the country to develop whatever was necessary to make it happen.

A vision cannot be too immediate or too obvious or it will fail to inspire; it has to be, well, audacious and bold. And it has to be liberating too. The most powerful aspirations are the ones that move the peoples of the world to a better place, a better life, with freedoms they did not have before. Such was the case with the innovations brought by legendary figures like Henry Ford, Marie Curie, Steve Jobs, and Andy Grove. All of them envisioned new realities, with aspirations rooted on *access* to something previously limited only to the few, that is now available to the many, a value proposition that brings new freedoms and therefore, liberation.

How to Build a Liberating Aspiration Statement

There is a vast amount of literature on how to develop a vision. There are however, two main approaches used for this purpose: One is to ask constituents, stakeholders, conducting research in focus groups to get insights from direct data. With this approach you get valuable trends and clear understanding of how people may react to a particular vision or aspiration. From there your team will advance the narrative to get the content right and bring a writer to make it consumable.

Alternatively, companies can use a top-down approach. The source of the primary language is the visionary leader, sometimes called 'unreasonable leader' who insists on something others just can't see at the moment but go along with the leader persuaded by the power of the vision and the possibilities. This is the famous example of Lee Iacocca with the introduction of the minivan.[4] At that time, no consumer research study would have come up with a car with those characteristics, and yet, it was needed, it was a hit, and it was a company-savior, as demonstrated by market response.

The Anatomy of the Liberating Aspiration

I have been fortunate to participate in Purpose design and articulation several times, for global, complex companies like Dell, Laureate, and HMH. Of course it is never an easy process, it takes time and requires certain steps that can't be ignored. Purpose articulations are the highest expression of intent, with language oriented at a *contribution to humanity* level. For the most part, aspirations are less concerned with products, markets, revenues. Instead, they intend to answer the question 'what are we here for'? After you study carefully many articulations and understand their stories, you very quickly conclude there are common elements that consistently appear in most of them, giving you a sense of benchmarks to consider. The three I have most commonly found are *authenticity, universality,* and *relevance*.

Authenticity means that the purpose cannot be divorced entirely from the original intent from the company's founders, even in those cases where the company today produces completely different products and services than the founders started. As an example, IBM[5] looks significantly different from the early days when it produced tabulating machines. But as you look at their purpose, the original intent of changing the world for the better stays true. The values are consistent, the spirit of the founders, the liberation focus of the company remains. Whether you define it with a very small group of people, or you involve the whole company, the authentic nature of the aspiration must be achieved. A connection to the origins, to the source, is highly inspirational for people.

Universality is concerned with the applicability to larger problems that can be legitimately understood by many people regardless of culture, socioeconomic level, or age group. Google's mission[6] is a good example of this property "Our mission is to organize the world's information and make it universally accessible and useful". In general, you want to create statements that speak to something considered important and recognizable for many people.

Relevance intends to highlight why your existence is essential for a human need of some kind. It may sound too difficult, but most companies find a way to connect with something relevant to define why they are here. One great example of relevance is "We believe in unleashing the originality in every child" from the Crayola[7] company's brand essence. Most products or services available today serve a legitimate need. Even if you sell a product that not everyone will agree it is here to serve a legitimate need, the aspiration articulation still must identify why what we do is important.

From the key features of authenticity, universality, and relevance, I want to offer a more formal definition and guidance on how to create a Leading Success articulation for a company in transformation.

The illustration of Fig. 6.1 identifies the three elements I find most critical to keep in mind as companies and teams get closer to a final articulation of their Aspiration statements.

A worthy endeavor. The essential component of an aspiration is answering the 'why'. Why are we here? This is, identify in which ways the WORD coming from our vision and ambitions makes a change, reshapes, or improves the current situation, conditions, or limitations, visible in the WORLD. Why is the world better because of us?

Some companies' mission/purpose statements serve to illustrate this first dimension of aspiration statements, to show how the world changes because of them. Take for example Novartis'[8] *Reimagine medicine to improve and extend people's lives. Become the most valued and trusted medicines company in the world.* For Intel[9]: *We create world-changing technology that improves the life of every person on the planet.* Microsoft[10] statement is: *Our mission is to empower every person and every organization on the planet to achieve more.* A different type of organization, *NASA*[11] *explores the unknown in air and space, innovates for the benefit of humanity, and inspires the world through discovery.* Even for a very large company built from many companies like Mitsubishi Electric[12]: *We, the Mitsubishi Electric Group, will contribute to the realization*

What a Liberating Aspiration means		
Our Word changes the World	**Liberating for Customers, Employees**	**Vital change agents creating the Future**
The world is better because of our ambitions, our work, products and services	Our customers and employees grow, fulfill their aspirations and become successful	Our contributions make the company a reference for the future; an exciting place to be
ADAPT ↻ WORLD ⇄ WORD ↺ DISRUPT	Belong — Being Themselves Being Relevant — Being Successful	Purpose Customer Financial Industrial

Fig. 6.1 The anatomy of a liberating aspiration

of a vibrant and sustainable society through continuous technological innovation and ceaseless creativity.

A Liberating force for customers and employees. The next component of an aspiration is the liberation our customers will enjoy when we achieve our vision. A powerful statement speaking for customer's improvement is liberating for employees because they see an extension of themselves making the life of others better. I.e., they are working for more than just a salary.

For example, Southwest Airlines' purpose[13] is *"To connect People to what's important in their lives through friendly, reliable, and low-cost air travel. Our Vision: To be the world's most loved, most efficient, and most profitable airline"*. For Walmart[14]: *"We aim to build a better world — helping people live better and renew the planet while building thriving, resilient communities"*. In the case of Walmart, their statement gets even more specific by adding some idea of the 'how' they achieve it: *"For us, this means working to create opportunity, build a more sustainable future, advance diversity, equity and inclusion and bring communities closer together. And at the end of the day, helping our customers save more of their hard-earned money for the things they care about most. Because at Walmart, Live Better is what we do every day"*. For P&G[15]: *"We will provide branded products and services of superior quality and value that improve the lives of the world's consumers, now and for generations to come. As a result, consumers will reward us with leadership sales, profit and value creation, allowing our people, our shareholders and the communities in which we live and work to prosper"*.

Vital for our times and for the future. This component is about a vision that calls out how we want to pioneer what is to come. How we take risks and go into the adventure to go to places not everyone is willing to go. The intent here is to claim our relevance in the world to come, our presence in the future as a relevant player.

Some companies' industry and line of products lend themselves perfectly for this third dimension. Take for example Boston Dynamics[16]: *"Boston Dynamics' mission is to imagine and create exceptional robots that enrich people's lives. We see this work as the next step in the evolution of machines that reduce the danger, repetition, and physically difficult aspects of work. Our Vision: We are driven to create robots that will fit seamlessly into our lives and expand our potential. Boston Dynamics has just begun to scratch the surface of what robots can do, and we are excited to be building the future for today, tomorrow, and beyond"*. For Partnership on AI[17]: *"Our Vision: A future where Artificial Intelligence empowers humanity by contributing to a more just, equitable, and prosperous world. Our Mission: Bringing diverse voices together across global sectors, disciplines, and demographics so developments in AI advance positive outcomes for people and society*". Taiwan Semiconductor Manufacturing Company (TSMC)[18]: "*Our vision is to be the most advanced and largest technology and foundry services provider to fabless companies and IDMs, and in partnership with them, to forge a powerful competitive force in the semiconductor industry. To realize our vision, we must have a trinity of strengths: Be a technology leader, competitive with the leading IDMs. Be the manufacturing leader. Be the most reputable, service-oriented and maximum-total-benefits silicon foundry. Mission: Our mission is to be the trusted technology and capacity provider of the global logic IC [semiconductor] industry for years to come*".

Do we need all three elements? Ideally, yes, we want a statement that can encapsulate all three elements because that gives us the highest level of affirmation to current and prospective employees, customers, and investors. However, there are no strict rules on these statements. As you can see in the examples, the variation is substantial in how many words, how much detail is shared. Leading success necessitates that the 'North Star' is clear in terms of the 'why' following the three components of liberation in Fig. 6.1: How is the world better, how are customers and employees more liberated, and how do we build a more desirable future?

President Kennedy's aspiration to reach the moon provided absolute focus and then some, by defining specifications for success—landing a crew on the surface of the moon and returning them safely back to earth before the end of the decade. It was a liberating moment for the entire human race, not just at the time of the statement time alone, but especially when the vision was fulfilled live on TV. It was a shared achievement for humanity, and it left. A legacy in many forms: global technological aerospace technology, military applications, research, materials, propulsion, instrumentation, global cooperation.

Your company is not too different. You as leader own the responsibility to coordinate a team to get an aspiration statement done. Some companies enjoy a unique privilege to have a founder's statement from the time of their creation. These statements are typically fresh, ambitious, and reflective of a time when a unique need was completely out of the box for its time, and yet, it continues to be visionary and liberating. One well known example is Johnson & Johnson's Credo,[19] which has stood generations of changes and remains relevant to this day.

In the end, your Aspiration is the ultimate reference point for the next decade or more, the anchor for all efforts, decisions, investments, and actions driving your company. I have never seen a leader who does not understand the importance and power of their aspirations, in the form of vision and mission, but I have seen many of them not using it. I have seen actions, projects initiatives not connected to these foundational principles. Furthermore, I have seen leadership teams convinced that their aspirations are dated, relevant for other times, missing something to speak for the future, and yet, remain tied to those articulations. My word of advice is to take a long, deep look and discuss about it with the right people to determine if your transformation necessitates a revision of the North Star. Markets radically change, technology makes previously unthinkable things possible, customer bases erode and new are created. While it is important to preserve a connection to our origins, it is crucially important to know where we are going in a changing world. Do not hesitate to reset your North Star.

Notes

1. Joly, H. (2021, October 28). Creating a meaningful corporate purpose. Harvard Business Review.
2. Collins, J., & Porras, J. I. (1994). Built to last: Successful habits of visionary companies. Harper Business.
3. Johnson, M. W., & Suskewicz, J. (2020). Lead from the future: How to turn visionary thinking into breakthrough growth. Harvard Business Review Press.
4. Iacocca, L., & Novak, W. (1984). Iacocca: An autobiography. Bantam Books.
5. IBM Corporation. (2024). IBM History. Retrieved from: https://www.ibm.com/history/ctr-and-ibm.
6. Google. (2024). About Google—Mission. Retrieved from: https://about.google/intl/ALL_us/.
7. Crayola. (2024). About Crayola—Brand Essence. Retrieved from: https://www.crayola.com/about-us/company/brand-essence/.
8. Novartis. (2024). About Novartis—Purpose. Retrieved from https://www.novartis.com/about.
9. Intel. (2024). Company Overview-Purpose. Retrieved from https://www.intel.com/content/www/us/en/company-overview/company-overview.html.
10. Microsoft. (2024). About Microsoft—Mission. Retrieved from: https://www.microsoft.com/en-us/about.
11. NASA. (2024). About NASA—Mission. Retrieved from: https://www.nasa.gov/about/.

12. Mitsubishi Electric. (2024). About Mitsubishi—Purpose. Retrieved from: https://www.mitsubishielectric.com/en/about/purpose/index.html.
13. Southwest Airlines. (2024). About Southwest—Purpose and Vision. Retrieved from: https://www.southwest.com/about-southwest/.
14. Walmart. (2024). Corporate Walmart—Purpose. Retrieved from: https://corporate.walmart.com/purpose.
15. P&G. (2024). P&G Policies and Practices -Purpose, Values, Principles. Retrieved from: https://us.pg.com/policies-and-practices/purpose-values-and-principles/.
16. Boston Dynamics. (2024). About Boston Dynamics—Mission, Vision. Retrieved from: https://bostondynamics.com/about/
17. Partnership on AI. (2024). About Partnership on AI—Mission, Vision, Values. Retrieved from: https://partnershiponai.org/about/#mission.
18. TSMC. (2024). About TSMC—Vision, Mission. Retrieved from: https://www.tsmc.com/english/aboutTSMC/mission.
19. Johnson & Johnson. (2024). J&J Credo. Retrieved from: https://www.jnj.com/our-credo.

7

Transformation: The History of the Future

Transformation is the articulation of what it will take to achieve the aspiration. This is, the identification of specific aspects of the business and organization that must change in order to see the vision come true, and it must be defined in business outcomes language: financial indicators, market growth, product development, customer satisfaction against competitors, and also in terms of people, talent growth, cultural resilience; any operational dimension of the business that would be a direct consequence of what has been set forth in the vision. While transformations must be inspirational, their highest value for Leading Success lies in the clarity to convey what is changing, and what is not changing. It must be quantitative and identifiable. Typically, a transformation consists of a succinct, yet powerful "From—To" articulation. Depending on what business or industry you are, a few lines can tell a very ambitious story. One that would require a complete new set of skills, new geographies, the acquisition of new assets, mergers, access to a different type of investors. The characterization of the "To", which is the identification and specification of the destination place is directly connected to the corporate strategy, or in some cases, their business model innovation. Strategy is much more than a "From-To" chart, it is a deep analytical endeavor requiring a significant number of resources—mostly time, but for many companies, also implies external support from expert consultants. Over time, a number of approaches have proved useful and powerful to guide a discussion about strategic choices and business model innovations. Some of the most notable include Michael Porter in his book *Competitive Advantage* [1] still widely used as an essential reference for strategy. Another well researched framework was offered by Adrian Slywotzky in his book *Value Migration*,[2] which was centrally focused on the idea of business model innovation. This book came at a time when the transition from the financial to the customer era was starting—per our analysis depicted by Fig. 4.1. In a similar category of relevance, W. Chan Kim and Renée Mauborgne brought an extraordinary framework in their *Blue Ocean Strategy*,[3] providing conceptual innovation to both the definition of a winning aspiration and to business model innovation. More recently Mark W. Johnson and Josh Suskewicz offered a practical perspective in their book *Lead from the Future*[4] offering thought process and a methodology to create a vision and a plan that is *future-back*, as opposed to *present-forward*, which makes the narrative very consistent with Leading Success. These four methodologies are guiding references to illustrate how strategy informs the transformation Two different things that often are confused as one. A *strategy* indicates how we will play the game but does not explain what needs to change—*transform*—in the existing way we play it for us to be successful. For example, if the strategy is that we are going to focus on one specific segment of the market to command premium price with deep specialization and quality, that does not answer the question of what needs to be different *from* the way we do things today *to* a new way of doing things capable to produce the new outcomes we want. This is, the 'From-To' articulation. In the example above, perhaps now we need more marketing talent, a different approach to pricing, remove a product line, even if it is considered legendary and a 'sacred cow', to be able to focus on the new products. These are all transformations in the business that need a story of winning for customers and employees, a story of legacy and a new identity that go with it. These methodologies, and perhaps many others you can find, answer the strategy question in ways that facilitate the understanding of the transformation as a liberating, vital endeavor.

Porter's Competitive Advantage—Industry Perspective

For Porter, Competitive Advantage is the ability to outperform rivals by delivering superior value or by operating more efficiently. He concluded there are three generic strategies companies can adopt. First is Cost Leadership. This is, achieving the lowest operational costs in the industry by optimizing the value chain. Second is Differentiation, centered on offering unique products/services that command premium prices through innovation, quality, and branding. The third is Focus. In this generic strategy the company will target a specific market niche by focusing on a combination of cost and differentiation focus. Some interpret Peters' three generic strategies as only two—cost and differentiation[5]—, considering the Focus strategy as a special case of those two. In order to sustain the company's competitive advantage management must commit to a continuous improvement and innovation process, and in fortifying the areas of competitive strength to discourage new entrants by raising the barriers to imitation. Porter's model included a thorough industry analysis containing five components he called forces: Threat of New Entrants, Bargaining Power of Suppliers, Bargaining Power of Buyers, Threat of Substitute Products or Services, and Industry Rivalry, that would illuminate areas of relative strength, weakness, opportunity, and risk or threat. A key element for Porter was Market Segmentation, which would allow the company to carve a space where strengths and opportunities are maximized and threats and weaknesses are neutralized.

Value Migration—Business Model Innovation

Adrian J. Slywotzky explores the concept of value migration, where value-creating forces, driven by customer preferences, or enabling technologies would cause a shift from obsolete business models to new, more effective ones that meet evolving customer priorities. The book outlines three stages of value migration: inflow, stability, and outflow. It identifies the causes of value migration as changes in customer preferences, technological advancements, and innovations in business models.

For Slywotzky, everything starts by understanding customer priorities through market research and data analytics, continuously informing changes to the business model, and in this effort elevating business model innovation to one of the most important areas of effectiveness for a business. Value migration represents a version of Porter's competitive advantage when considered dynamically as forces shift over time. Slywotzky untapped the potential of business model innovation that continued in subsequent approaches in which the market and industry are modeled using specific competitive parameters to optimize against our intrinsic capabilities. No longer a static perspective, the beginnings of analytics led to more sophisticated models, like Blue Ocean Strategy.

Blue Ocean—Making Competition Irrelevant

Blue Ocean Strategy is an influential business strategy book published in 2005 by W. Chan Kim and Renée Mauborgne, professors at INSEAD. The book introduces a novel approach to strategy that focuses on creating new market spaces, or "Blue Oceans", rather than competing in existing industries, or "Red Oceans". The core principle of Blue Ocean strategy is the concept of Value Innovation which involves delivering high value to customers—something they can't find in other competitors but solves an important need that is going unattended—while simultaneously reducing costs, thereby opening up new and uncontested market space and most importantly, making the competition irrelevant. Blue Ocean brings with it a remarkably good methodology. There are useful tools and analytical frameworks to guide your thinking at every stage of the process. For example, the Strategy Canvas is a visual representation of relevant industry features and their analytics that maps the current state of play relative to competitors. It helps identify the factors on which the industry competes, illuminating areas of potential incursion that nobody is addressing. A lot of insight is gained by using the tools. The Four Actions Framework asks teams to identify categories of product features that must be changed in four areas: (1) What to eliminate: features that the industry takes for granted; (2) What to reduce: which factors should be reduced below the industry's standard, because they are not differentiating; (3) What should be raised: which features should be raised well above the industry's standard; and (4) Is there anything that should be created: which new features should be created that the industry has never offered. On its external perspective, the methodology includes The Six Paths Framework, which is about looking across alternative industries, strategic groups, buyer groups, complementary product and service offerings to discover new ideas that could lead to blue oceans.

The Blue Ocean strategy calls out the core transformations that must occur mainly in the four actions framework and the canvas. The direct analysis of those areas facilitates the identification of the 'from-to' factors and the visualization of a story that connects those changes to link purpose with strategy and change. The notion to go into a blue ocean is a metaphor with great liberating potential.

Lead from the Future—Mapping Back from the North Star

Lead from the Future by Mark W. Johnson and Josh Suskewicz presents a strategic approach to innovation called 'future-back' thinking. The authors argue that traditional 'present-forward' strategies are insufficient to deal with rapid technological changes and evolving market conditions. Instead, leaders should envision a compelling future to plot a path with that end in mind, to create the strategies that can make the envisioned future a reality. I have seen several future-oriented methodologies, all of them persuasive and insightful. The Future-Back thinking process outlines a systematic process that facilitates the identification of what must change, including defining a vision, exploring potential future scenarios, and developing strategic pathways. In terms of Leading Success approaches, the authors emphasize the importance of aligning the organization's culture, resources, and processes with the envisioned future, provide practical tools and frameworks to help leaders implement this approach. Lead from the Future serves transformation because the method is centered on innovation, agility, and long-term thinking. The key point is to remove the immediate pressures of the short-term constraints of the business to concentrate on an unrestricted version of the future. Lead From the Future directly identifies the elements of change that become the transformation. Its methodology takes into account the importance of leadership and culture.

The right approach is for each company to decide. Most large companies bring consultants with their own models on strategy articulation. There are only so many questions to answer, as Porter indicated. Regardless of the methodology, a transformation needs two components for success at this discipline: the right strategy and a powerful story to share with employees. In the era of Purpose, you will need both.

How to Build a Liberating Transformation Statement

Transformation articulation is not new. Almost every business manager has been part of a strategic definition process, and most leaders have gone through it in multiple companies. The technology on how to do that is available. I will focus our attention on the outcomes and the unique differentiators that matter for a Leading Success approach, which basically means, how liberating, how vital, and how *signatured* it is. See the illustration on Fig. 7.1.

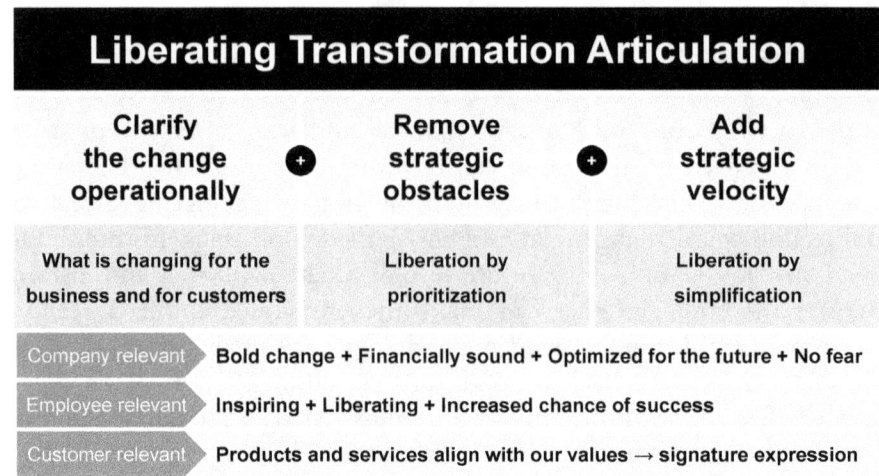

Fig. 7.1 The anatomy of a leading success transformation articulation

Clarify the change operationally. First, the basics. As any transformation articulation, we must answer first what *is* changing and what *is not* changing for every relevant group of stakeholders: managers, employees, strategic partners—and customers. It must be operational, grounded, and specific to cover the full message of what is changing. Do not leave important things to interpretation. Change Management methodologies will provide the right tools for a comprehensive description of the steps to follow. However, in its essence, we are particularly interested on a handful of metrics, a few operational descriptors that will signal the true nature of the change in play. For example: from analog to digital, from 5 to 40% market share, from six stores to three hundred stores—these are the things people remember and serve to paint the scale of change in ways that make it easier to appreciate what it will take to accomplish. In President Kennedy's speech in Rice University, discussed earlier, he is painting the picture of what it will take to bring a crew to the Moon—and back, safely to Earth— that it will be expensive, and that it will require the invention of materials and technologies the United States did not have at the time. Otherwise, the journey could be fully appreciated. These are very important messages to signal to our leaders, to our employees at large, and in some cases to a few select external partners. The most critical groups of people need to understand what is the scale and shape of the vision. Keep in mind that most meaningful changes imply doing things never done before, and embracing beliefs that may go counter to the identity and culture spoused for a long time.

Every transformation is about moving away from something and going closer to something else. It is a departure for the right reasons. Be explicit on what those reasons are, but go beyond revenues, market shares, and financial metrics—the company reasons; identify why customers get more choice, more affirmation, more freedoms, and a better life. Describe how employees win with the change, how the effort extends to voice the internal challenges to solve. That is why we need the two other aspects of the articulation in Fig 7.1.

Remove strategic obstacles. This is, removing sources of energy dissipation. Strategic obstacles to the desired future may include decisions to move away from areas with adequate revenue but limited relevance in the future. An area with those attributes consumes energy and resources, delaying the building of new capabilities. It is not easy to make the leap, in part because the company may not be tooled, skilled, or ready for what is next. Transformational leaders recognize that is the only way to meaningfully participate in the future. Under a certain point of view, and particularly in some industries, those changes are inevitable if the company wants to have a shot to stay in the game. Very often the Netflix case is called out as an example of these difficult choices: being dominant in a certain area and technology, just to risk it all to have an opportunity to be relevant in the next digital era. Removing a belief, such as Dell did to expand from their Dell Direct model to retail. A declaration to go to the moon before the end of the decade. Those are huge bets with formidable liberating power that unleash a wave of energy across the company or country, energizing people toward decisive prioritization and focus.

Add strategic velocity. This is, creating capabilities that accelerate and optimize your future. All companies have ways to add speed and agility to what they do. Sometimes it is a matter of investing on certain tools, or adopting practices such as Agile, Six Sigma, Process Improvement. But also means ways to unleash decision-making and empowerment across the ranks. The liberating effect of changes that add velocity cannot be underestimated. Simplification, in terms of strategic articulation will mean things related to product, going to market, serving customers. Areas more related to employees and management are clustered in the Culture Discipline on Chapter Nine ahead. However, strategic velocity goes beyond finding ways to do the same things faster. It means finding new ways; game-changing ways to 'cheat' the physics of your current status quo. In today's economics, few companies can afford building capabilities on their own, so they choose a partner, a joint venture, an acquisition to add instant capabilities that equate to a time-travel forward of years, if they had to do it on their own. Choosing to participate on a new segment, (from computers to enterprise solutions), or to add a segment of the supply chain (google acquiring Motorola's cellular technology patents to build its own devices), expanding to an adjacent business (Amazon going from digital retail to enterprise data systems) are all great examples of strategic acceleration, liberation, and discovery.

Your Outcomes with the Transformation Statement

Clarity. Clarity is never overrated, keep in mind that in Leading Success, this clarity will further evolve into commitment. It is in our best interest therefore, to ensure an acute sense of precision when selecting the vital few changes to include in the articulation. This is important for customers, investors, and suppliers, but it is existential for employees. At the level of external audiences when Apple made the bet for the iPhone, the choice was not about devices alone, the vision called for the creation of a whole ecosystem: with the iTunes music purchasing and lists creation site being the visible part of it, but not the only one. Storage, software, partner developers, deals with artists, musicians. The device was only a platform for a complete remaking of what Apple would become. This change was clear in Steve Jobs' speech at introduction day for the iPhone[6] *"we have created a phone, which is an internet device, which is an iPod"*—calls, internet, music. Later on, video functionality was added extending the revenue stream to movies, and over-the-air functionality allowed the iPhone to detach from a Mac for updates making it truly mobile for updates and data manipulation. That clarity, in three words, signaled a whole set of new expectations that still today reverberate in their business model and product development.

Internally, the message should be equally clear. If you realize that the future value proposition is migrating away from your existing configuration, that your future vision calls for a realignment of how you think of yourself differently, that is exactly what you should say. One thing is to define operational changes, but another is to clarify *mindset changes*. Your ambitions may require that the center of gravitation of your company moves from manufacturing to design, or from product to services, from product delivery to customer success. This is, you need to think of yourself differently. Your FROM-TO must spell out those words. Big changes should not be left for people to deduct, to guess, to find out later. No surprises.

Prioritization. Setting priorities is liberating, empowering, and assertive. Making the choice to remove clutter, proliferation of options, and get the organization to focus. Distractions can be of many kinds, mental, physical, previously committed deals, platforms, or any kind of roadblocks, practices, or strategies that make roads longer. This dimension of liberation is one of the most important features to gain real credibility with our employees. Some of us will remember the full spectrum of the cellular telephony since its inception and we can picture in our minds the many incarnations of these devices. From the first 'brick' phone, the Motorola DynaTAC back in 1973, then the flip-flop StarTAC, the Razr, the iDEN two-way radio, and the well documented Iridium platform. Each of them was a story of unprecedented success at their time. And all of them created by the same company. But success is not easy to sustain in technology. Rapid innovation caught up to Motorolas' capabilities. Not in product innovation, but concept, platform, business model, and organization innovation. Success can be deceiving and make you ignore data. Entrants in the industry were hungry, nimble companies rooted in analytical consideration of trends, options, and radical prioritization. With such a large organization, it proved hard for Motorola to select one path forward instead of many and it is hard to carry a large portfolio on a market that was shifting away from technology toward cost. Having multiple capabilities, platforms, software interfaces hurts you in that transition. Prioritization is hard for all innovators.

Simplification. In many ways, simplification is a derivative of prioritization, but not always. There is also redesign. Simplification in redesign comes from looking at how the work gets done and find new ways to make it more accurate, faster, easier. The metaphor I commonly use is that we can master the driving around a dangerous mountain in a curvy road, but we can create a tunnel instead, so we do not have to spend time solving the wrong problems. Some skill sets are there because the context we have designed dictates we need them. Adding velocity may require investing in tools but it also may be all about processes and internal policies. How many reviewers a quality process needs? How many interviewers a hiring process needs? Are there ways to automate segments of those processes to get our people focused on higher order issues? Leonardo DaVinci is believed to have said that simplification is the ultimate sophistication, because differentiating simplification is never about 'over-simplification', reduction, elimination, or removal—alone. It is about unpacking a complex situation or product to reimagine it with a fresh perspective on the value it brings as outcomes and customer experience. For those who remember the unbelievable experience to see the first Mac Computer, with a mouse, completely designed for user experience, it was such a departure from the available personal computers at the time that required you to be a technology enthusiast to be able to use them. That simplification changed the world.

Relevance. The ultimate test of a transformation is the understanding and articulation of how much better will the company be after we complete what we intend to transform? Everyone involved will want to know if the transformation is worthy of the effort. Whether they have a say on it or not, everyone needs to buy-in to gain momentum company-wide. It follows that a transformation that does not speak to managers, to employees, to customers, and investors is going to have a harder time taking off the ground. In the illustration shown in Fig. 7.1, we call out a few identifiers of relevance for those constituents. For the company and businesses, this transformation has to be financially attractive, even for those non-for-profit organizations, their measure of success may equate to revenue, number of users, number of branches, quality of service, and the like. Additionally, and significantly, relevance is to be judged in terms of the future. Not the past. In most cases that means a decisive call out of what is not included or a bold move to pursue segments, territories that require a real stretch. For employees, relevance will mean how desirable will it be to be part of this journey. How much learning will they get, how much the transformation recognizes their pain: tools, organization, skills, or simply, more people. If there is no mention of any aspect of the people's voice, that is going to be a very distracting message. I recall some years ago being in a strategy-reveal meeting with all executives, some 200 people in the room, with the CEO and the complete c-level executives in the stage. I was less than three months in the company, so it was such a great time for me to be able to attend the downing of the new era, the next version of this company. The strategy was basically incapsulated in one page, but very notoriously—at least for me—it said absolutely nothing about people, not one word. To this day I still regret being the one asking the question, but I could not resist listening to the rationale, as we would have to go and explain that to our teams. Such an omission was not going to go unnoticed. We were up to something when, after I stated my question, everyone in the stage instantly reacted by looking at the CEO. As we heard the CEO give his answer, it reminded me of another time that I heard exactly the same argument, almost word by word: "people are so crucially important that we don't even have to write it. It goes without saying it". Nobody in the room bought that one, neither would the people outside that room. An omission can steal the energy of the people reading it, we must consider what relevance means for all our audiences. Finally, relevance for customers is only measured in terms of their success working with your offerings and dealing with your company—not only on how your products or services performed.

Customer success has become a mature field of study, a science on its own, and one key aspect of consumers if you are B2C but even if you are B2B, is how connected, how visible are your products to your values and societal aspirations.[7] To what degree your products and your brand build a positive reputation for your customers gaining for them access and credibility. This means, how 'signature' are your products and customer experiences as reflective of your aspirations? How liberated they feel when they use your product and when they interact with you; how liberating your offerings are.

Brevity is an asset, clarity on operational expressions of your transformation is the currency at this stage in the journey. One aspect I would underline is the future optimization of everything your transformation speaks about. I think in this sense, the one thing not to overlook is the potential reactions your own people and your own customers may get from a truly visionary transformation. Be prepared to discover that the bolder the vision, the harder it will be to digest for a group of people who built the successful past and who are convinced that the world has not changed enough to warrant us to change with it, or that is going in the wrong direction. Hopefully, that does not include your c-suite executives or your team members. Never underestimate that the power of a visionary transformation may not be for everyone. That is why leading success includes an additional discipline in this mindset—*commitment*.

Notes

1. Porter, M. E. (1985). Competitive advantage: Creating and sustaining superior performance. The Free Press. New York.
2. Slywotzky, A. J. (1996). Value migration: How to think several moves ahead of the competition. Harvard Business School Press. Boston, MA.
3. Kim, W. C., & Mauborgne, R. (2015). Blue ocean strategy: How to create uncontested market space and make competition irrelevant (Expanded ed.). Harvard Business Review Press. Boston, MA.
4. Johnson, M. W., & Suskewicz, J. (2020). Lead from the future: How to turn visionary thinking into breakthrough growth. Harvard Business Review Press.
5. Martin, Roger L. (2015). There Are Still Only Two Ways to Compete. Harvard Business Review. Digital Article Apr 21, 2015.
6. Apple (2007). Apple Reinvents the Phone with iPhone. Retrieves from https://www.apple.com/newsroom/2007/01/09Apple-Reinvents-the-Phone-with-iPhone/

7. Metha, N., & Pickens, A. (2020). The customer success economy: Why every aspect of your business model needs a paradigm shift. Wiley. New Jersey.

8

Commitment: Owning the Purpose

We have established that Leading Success is a business approach that elevates performance by raising agency, engagement, and authenticity by way of a liberating leadership mindset. The implementation of these foundational mindsets—liberation, vitality, and expression—depends, at the core, on a simple human act that cannot be overestimated: *commitment*. This is the third discipline of Leading Success.

Commitment gets less than its fair share in business strategy literature but that has been changing as of lately.[1] It is not that its obvious importance is overlooked, it is rather how our tradition of management automatically checks the commitment box along with the communication box. Commitment includes communication, but not the other way around. In other words, the management playbook does not have *plays* for creating commitment, it does have plays for communicating expectations—clearly, passionately, authentically—but mostly intellectually, and mostly in 'one to many' forums. Our standard playbooks do not unpack the human interaction necessary to arrive to a committal act, required for agency and ownership—vital in transformation and in operation. This commitment-building play—or to be more accurate, *process*—is not uniquely relevant for multi-year transformations,[2] it is also crucial in the operation journey, year to year, quarter to quarter and day to day.[3]

In order to define the Commitment Discipline and introduce the process that governs it let's consider why it is so crucially important. As depicted in the illustration of Fig. 8.1, most transformations don't fail in the Aspiration or Transformation articulation phases, but in the ways those visions and

Fig. 8.1 The critical, differentiating contribution of the commitment discipline in transformation

expectations are deployed through the ranks. The missing point? A foundational human capability called *conversation*. As we will see, not just any conversation, but the kind that is capable of creating commitment.

Senior executives are instinctively wired for speed and simplification, and they consider everyone is wired in the same way. Similar to a marathon race, at the moment of the starting shot, the front runners (executives, c-suite) start running fast with information they have discussed probably for months at the time the first changes are announced broadly to employees. In a way, the CEO and her/his closest collaborators are "done" with that information, psychologically exhausted and with a feeling of 'achievement'; they are now running as fast as they can to what is next. Minutes after the shot was fired in the marathon, the middle of the pack runners start to move. That is your middle management ranks. It will take another few minutes before whole pack is finally running. Front runners may already be in the third mile before the last runner starts to move, creating a gap that gets little attention at the top but not at the bottom. People see management running fast and they still can't answer how that transformation affects *them*. It may have been 'communicated', but it has not been understood; it was presented, explained, but it never was discussed, internalized. This is, it was not *committed* to.

The illusion of communication as commitment is pervasive because it feels right. It feels rational, it is programmable, transactional, traceable, we have metrics, and it is an undeniably important milestone. We tell ourselves "…well, people are adults; if they have questions, they are welcome to ask, if they don't ask, then silence is agreement". Except, we are not asking for agreement, that is a very low bar for transformation; we are asking for commitment. In the heat of schedules and results, everybody is busy trying to remove things from the schedule. Unless we create—and force—a space to have those rich *conversations capable to create a liberating commitment*, managers in general will tend to 'delegate up' the transformation story to anything the corporate communication event included and very likely will not take it to themselves to 'walk the last mile' to a *liberating commitment*. The reason? They have not internalized it themselves. The process was not designed for that. Getting from communication to commitment is a much higher bar and yes, it is a time-consuming process, but the benefits multiply many times over when the transformation is ongoing.

Leading Success, therefore, depends on a pivotal human technology, necessary to be mastered by managers, across levels, functions, divisions, to achieve authentic, robust collaboration. That technology is the ability to have *conversations that create liberating commitment*.

How to Build a Liberating Commitment Conversation?

At the time a reputable consulting firm had provided Michael Dell with the final report document containing the strategy definition, the future direction was clear, and it had been discussed many hours by the senior team, the board, and other key people in the organization. A few sections earlier in this book I explained how some nuance in terminology had to be polished to confirm all senior executives would read and translate the narrative in the same way.

Part of my job was to activate the strategy to the one hundred thousand people at Dell. We were a formidable team including HR, Communications, Strategy, and Marketing. We were ably aided by the team at Stone Yamashita Partners in San Francisco, and we were ready to implement. The strategy was to ask leaders, and all managers subsequently, to be the "teachers" for their teams in explaining the strategy by answering three fundamental questions:

- What is the strategy and why this is the best future for Dell?
- What does the strategy mean for our customers and for our employees?
- What do we expect from you, as leaders?

We called this 'The Leadership Imperative', following a tradition started years earlier at the company. The process included a "train the trainer" session for all 700 top executives in the company. All in one place. We gave everyone the high-level strategy narrative but not a lengthy PowerPoint. The briefing was clear enough for that level of leaders to realize what was being decided and the implications. As part of the formidable experience to provide them with the tools, we had a session called "honest questions". This was staged in breakouts of small groups of executives, facilitated by C-suite leaders. The idea was simple: a Q&A about the strategy, but a very special one. We asked every group to work for a few minutes to come up with the questions that should be answered before leaving that room. The task was to start with the regular clarifying questions, and then to go further. We wanted to hear it all, the conventional questions and the less conventional, the most politically incorrect, the most purely skeptical and soul-searching questions. We created a safe place to voice authentic disagreement, to voice emotional biases and disbelief—if there was any of that. Our goal was to put all the noise in the open, to have a real conversation about the strategy, not for debate, but for deeper understanding. This was not about relitigating the strategy but instead, to have the opportunity to explain what illuminated the decisions, what was weighted in the balance, the judgments and assumptions that were made, what risks were considered. There were only two rules for the breakout facilitators (the c-suite): (1) no question is too far off, therefore, no judgment; and (2) if we don't have the answer, we will not invent one, we will say "I don't know, but we will find out".

The designed outcome was to land in a place where executives would have the opportunity to use their voice, for the c-suite to listen before they talk, and together, discuss first-hand what were the answers to the questions those teaching executives would probably get and have to respond themselves.

I walked into the sessions with some trepidation for the boldness and unpredictability of the design, but after walking around the breakouts all I could see was leaders taking the opportunity to voice really hard questions and get honest answers, intelligent answers. Those were not easy interactions. As experience designers, we had an idea of the likely areas of concern, but once you open the dialogue you got to be prepared to listen actively and intently.

The result? In a word: commitment. Executives reached a level of comfort with the strategy far beyond 'agreement', or 'understanding'. We needed belief, commitment, resilience for the long journey. Not because we had all the answers, or because we created an amazing presentation to tell, convince, or explain, but because we trusted the leadership's judgment, we tested the robustness of the overall proposition, unpacking the 'why' and explored the possible cracks. We designed a space to be vulnerable as a group. As a result of this conversation, our leaders embraced the future and got attuned with the emotional part of the strategy. We abandoned the assumption that more detail would be more clarifying or convincing. We got the leader's trust and disposition to pursue that dream—we got their commitment. We also removed a big weight from their backs. Now they had answers for their most authentic and rebellious questions; *now they believed*—they felt *liberated*.

What had just happened? We did not call it this way, but in essence we had built a *conversation to create liberating commitment*.

Defining a Conversation to Create Liberating Commitment

In its simplest form, a conversation to create commitment is one in which the outcome is a formal declaration of commitment from all parts involved. A mode detailed definition is the following:

> A Conversation to Create Liberating Commitment is a special type of conversation structured to deliver an authentic personal commitment to a particular ask or request, grounded on, and necessary to the transformation of the organization. The immediate outcome of this conversation is *coordinated action for success*. But the broader outcome is much more than that. When we look at these conversations in the aggregate, as an organizational discipline across all levels and areas, these conversations build a fabric of connections and commitments across individuals and teams that contributes to organizational alignment, velocity, resilience, a renewed identity, and confidence, therefore, elevating success from a short-lived event to a sustainable capability. Culturally, these conversations make every employee an *owner* of the success of the company and become a source for managers and employees to feel relevant, included, engaged, and therefore *liberated*.

It may sound complicated, but it is not. The structure is simple: an opening with a proposition or idea stating what is the intended outcome, followed by a discussion to engage in a clarifying interaction to achieve as much clarity and understanding as possible, to finally close with a commitment.

Open: Where are we going. Why it matters for us.
Discuss: What is it going to take. What is expected of you.

Close: People choose to make (or decline to make) a liberating commitment.

This is the fundamental structure of conversations to create liberating commitment, where the liberation component appears in all three segments in different ways. In the opening, it is about the vision; in the discussion, it focuses on what is changing and how that change is liberating for both customers and employees; and finally, in the closing, liberation comes as a choice. In the story about Dell's transformation, allowing leaders to ask real questions, and sharing honest answers made leaders feel included, able to understand why it was strategically and emotionally sound getting behind something so relevant. In other words, it felt liberating; and therefore, leaders chose to make it their part of their own journey. Commitment is not necessarily immediate, automatic, very few things in life are. It is a mental and emotional process that, depending on what the change involves, it may take minutes, hours, or days before people can get to an authentic commitment stage. For some individuals, it never comes, and we will discuss about that in a later section. For enterprise-wide transformations it will be important to highlight key components and pre-requisites that will facilitate larger groups of people going through these conversations. We need a scalable process for a commitment building conversation. See the illustration in Fig. 8.2.

In large-scale transformations, before a conversation about change and commitment can get started it is highly recommended to conduct several

Conversations To Create Liberating Commitment		
Open	**Discuss**	**Close**
Where are we going and why	What it is going to take What is expected of you	People choose to make a Liberating Commitment
WORLD **Affirm** How the context is changing Why now is the time	**ADAPT | DISRUPT** **Make Meaning** What is the change **Liberating** for the company	**Ask for Commitment** Allow time and space for people to **Understand**, Accept intellectually
WORD **Declare** The liberating vision **Liberating** for customers	**Define Success** What success looks like **Liberating** for YOU	**Adopt**, Embrace emotionally **COMMIT** Own

Fig. 8.2 Structure and components of conversations to create liberating commitment

listening sessions or surveys. A preliminary step called Consultation. Conversations to create commitment cannot come across as top-down mandates, unless unique circumstances dictate it should be, for example in an emergency such as the pandemic: sending everybody home, requesting the use of face masks during recovery time. For transformation environments it is important to set the context right by including research, valid data, meaningful analytics as sources of insight and validation.

The opening is a proposition, a description of the direction—what we are going to do—and why it is important and urgent, why now is the time and not later. As illustrated in Fig. 8.2, this first element, opening has two components: WORLD and WORD.

The WORLD is about describing the existing situation, the realities that ground our need to act—the burning platform—that must be addressed, highlighting both risks and opportunities. This articulation typically includes current-state *affirmations*, where are we now, what is the competitive landscape, market, and technology context.

The WORD is about the articulation of what the company will do to modify the observed reality to address the challenges and the opportunities. This articulation typically includes future-state *declarations*, the solution, the vision, the bigger dream, using our leadership voice to define how the WOLRD will change because we are in it.

At this stage it is crucial to indicate how this proposition is good, empowering, and therefore, *liberating for our customers*. A successful opening to a conversation for commitment requires clarity around purpose and goals. In other words, a connection with the aspiration in a way that is relevant to all and each level of the organization. In our Dell example, this proposition was contained in the strategy content itself, the CEO contextualized why this direction was urgent and important for Dell to remain relevant in the evolution of the industry. He also provided clarity on the path to success and explained why this would be liberating for our customers, as technology was shifting in a different direction—they would be able to do more of what they wanted. The aspiration component was clear. At every level, managers were asked to do something similar. As managers connected with their people to talk about the aspirations for the company, they also talked about the aspirations for their unit or team, sharing their views on the evolution of the department, function, or team. In this case, to connect better, to make things simpler and more agile to the benefit of everyone internally, liberating from constraints, friction, and other distractions. In Chapter Fourteen, Engagement, we elaborate on how this conversation is implemented at scale.

The discussion is an interchange of ideas. This is determinant to achieve a high-quality commitment; one in which people clearly understand what they are signing up for, no surprises, whether by negligence or by design. In this discussion the point is to share what is changing and what will be expected from the team, and from the person we are speaking with.

Making Meaning. The discussion component starts with answering the question 'what is going to change?'. This is about clarifying what is changing in the company, processes, priorities in order to fulfill the vision. In most cases, we will use the 'From-To' articulation created in the Transformation Discipline, along with a story that explains why the change is good for both the company and the team. Managers make meaning by sharing the rationale top management used to define the path, and allowing for discussion to develop. It takes an interchange of ideas to fully make meaning of change.

Defining Success. The next step is to make sure employees understand they are in it too, that they were thought and prioritized in the vision and how the entire proposition is consistent with the Purpose and values. Our goal is to achieve engagement being rational and real, not to over-sell, paint it too good to be true. If the vision is liberating on its own, we will not have to over-sell, people are hungry for bold, liberating visions where they are part of the story. We must keep in mind that not all Transformations are happy stories for everyone, sometimes they bring some pain in the process. It is imperative for employees to understand the rationale, our intent and principles, how values play out in the change, and our chief assumptions, for them to find it liberating and worth pursuing passionately. The discussion brings clarity on what we are going to ADAPT to, and what we are going to DISRUPT. Managers should focus on both, the headlines and the small font, no surprises. In my previous story, the session to openly discuss difficult questions was the quintessential definition of dialogue. A structured, respectful, authentic interchange of concerns with honest answers. This environment gave us a chance to be heard, to get the leader's attention to make sense, of key questions: Why was this the best option among many alternatives? Why did we choose one path over another? But we also used it to define the expectation that this should be led by each one of them in the room. We made the case that this approach was the most liberating for them as it would position every leader as the storyteller and presenter of the future. At all levels, managers must allow for honest questions and be ready to provide honest answers. In significant change initiatives managers should be equipped with key points to remember, we need authentic answers but with a level of alignment.

The closure is a place of arrival for the discussion. Some managers would expect to hear immediately from every employee a "yes, I do" answer. We must keep in mind that commitment for some people is a process, not a switch to flip on. When the changes include important modifications to the work people do, or the status they currently hold, their sense of power, identity, and their perceived future in the organization, the conversations are not easy. Even for people whose roles stay the same, they may experience a level of rejection to the new vision product of a long-held belief of what this company or team *'was about'*. Managers must be ok with a few days of digesting the changes as indicated in the visual, for people to move from intellectual understanding to an emotional embracing that leads to a sense of ownership for the change, which is the test of authentic COMMITMENT.

An invaluable byproduct of a conversation that creates liberating commitment is trust. Those executives came out from the sessions with affirmation that their leaders respect them, that their leaders were authentic, and that any conversation can be had without retaliation or suspicion.

Your Outcomes in the Commitment Conversation

Authentic engagement. The reference point to answer the question 'why are we doing this?' is no longer external, it is now personal. People are engaged with the company's purpose and actions—the why and the what—because they find them worthwhile and also liberating. They see how these actions connect with their own aspirations.

The fabric of connections. Companies capable of managing commitment at the level of every employee are like a bullet-proof vest. If you think about a bullet as a risk moving in our direction, you do not want a vest with only a few thick bars of protection, with a lot of space in between those bars. That would be the case with an organization where only the top management is fully committed to the transformation. Everyone else is following along, doing their best, but risks will not be dealt with the immediacy, effectiveness, collaboration, and expediency to be mitigated—the bullet passes through. Instead, we need a vest with a resilient fabric, one that fills every spot across the chest with thick and thin bars including the whole organization. In other words, we need all employees, not only top managers fully in the game. This is what happens when managers use conversations that create liberating commitments. Risks do not penetrate to the organization, they are detected, identified, and dealt with, preventing them from disrupting the pace of the organization toward success. We need a company-wide fabric of connections, purpose, and commitment in order to pull out significant complexities where we need the company to be 'different', respond different, and behave different than before—a company with a modified DNA. That is not going to happen by commanding it, it will only happen by personal conviction and commitment by every person (or by a large critical mass).

Positive disposition for execution. Change management is always important, but it should not be the only reason why we keep moving. In the absence of commitment, managing change becomes indispensable for operation and we find ourselves relitigating goals, managing objections, appeasing big players, neutralizing power struggles. An authentic commitment removes a layer of resistance and spins the organization in a positive mindset about liberation and pursuit of a worthy aspiration we all share. This brings velocity, agility, and learning to the organization.

What You Should Avoid

If you have been in organizations even for a few years, going over change projects, you have seen this big issue we will identify as the enemy number one for transformation, and the one thing we should avoid with all our means: the sense and feeling of have been in a misleading conversation, been lied to. At the collective level is disheartening. For example, saying there will be no exits, when we well know there will be. Granted, sometimes we cannot anticipate this news until there is more substance to it, but the language should be honest nonetheless, saying that we are learning if any layoffs may be necessary and that we will come transparent as soon as we confirm. Similarly, at the person-to-person level, manager to employee, something that feels misleading has serious effects. The golden rule is to be honest and respectful. People will find out if we were sharing only half-truths, or if we missed something really important that should have been shared, if we kept them in the dark purposefully, and they had to discover the truth later, probably with a degree of surprise and humiliation. It is hard to recover from those episodes. Keep in mind we are dealing with emotions, people's futures, and professional ambitions. Even for those employees who are not affected the impact may still be negative because trust in leadership erodes, delaying—if not negating—a true level of engagement. Stay true, be courageous in those moments.

Understanding the Leadership of Liberation Mindset

You can't skip any of these first three disciplines: Aspiration, Transformation, Commitment. Even if you are hired to 'press the easy button', there is so much hiding behind the nuances of the organization, that the most perfect aspiration will have to be at the very least validated for language relevance, terminology, communicability, if not for a more substantial change. No CEO is hired to preserve a status quo, nor any executive for that matter. So, regardless of what level of executive or manager you are, you will have to express an ambition, your WORD to your team. Depending on your level in the organization, you will have a chance to redefine what that ambition is. Sometimes it will be every three or five years, for other managers it is one to three years. In addition, you will have to translate operationally what that means for the team. In very senior positions that will be a formidable task of clarity and verification of numbers, standards, benchmarks, to make the gap to the future visible, palpable. Large and small operations, long standing or startup operations are all in the same need to understand what the vision means for them. And finally—so far in the journey—a space for dialogue and opportunity for confirmation of commitment to pursue and get to the aspiration. While the two first elements on the Liberation mindset are more commonplace in business literature—aspiration/vision, and transformation—this third element is a key feature of Leading success. There is no way to expect sustainable progress without a *commitment*, but this is an informed commitment. Executives, team members need to understand what they are signing up for—no surprises is a first great step for trust and a foundational milestone in the fortification of our cultures.

Notes

1. Hamel, G., & Zanini, M. (2020). Humanocracy: Creating organizations as amazing as the people inside them. Harvard Business Review Press.
2. Habermas, J. (1984). The theory of communicative action: Volume one. Beacon Press. Boston, MA.
3. Habermas, J. (1987). The theory of communicative action: Volume two. Beacon Press. Boston, MA.

9

The Vitality Mindset: The Trilogy of Success

The View at a Glance

What is it?	This mindset is the liberating *design* for the organization; the design that makes it vital for its people. Liberation should move from a feeling, an idea, to a material experience. The Vitality mindset guides the organization design to be consistent with the ambitions of the transformation
Why do I need it?	In one word: sustainability. To build a differentiating infrastructure—processes, practices, policies, metrics—that will change how the organization works to be able to produce the transformation we seek. A vital design for sustainable success
So what?	We walk the talk to achieve the engagement and performance our transformation needs. Our processes speak the language of our transformation and values. Employees and customers feel validated on their choice to be with us as they start to see evidence that we mean what we say, and that it works for their success
What's in it?	The disciplines of: Culture, Talent, Organization

The Elevator Speech

Transformations are meant to bring new life to organizations, and they usually do. The expectation and excitement of a new journey for the right reasons, and perspectives of improvement come all together in times of definitions, announcements, installation of changes. The challenge however is to sustain the excitement beyond the initial burst, to make the everyday in the organization to feel just as lively and exciting. This is, we want to infuse our organization with a vital employee experience.

> **vitality**[1]
> Vital force, power, or principle as possessed or manifested by living things the principle of life; animation.
> The ability or capacity on the part of something of continuing to exist or to perform its functions; power of enduring or continuing.
> Active force or power; mental or physical vigor; activity, animation, liveliness.

Vitality is necessary for a fulfilling life, including work life. There is no great achievement without it, individual or collective. People tends to gravitate toward places that feel dynamic, energizing, robust, and enduring. It makes everyone feel more alive. Vitality follows liberation; it cannot live under an oppressive form of leadership, such as micromanagement, or an overly hierarchical environment. A vital organization is rarely a matter of chance, it must be designed. Vitality in organizations is most commonly associated with startups; however, it gradually fades away as companies must become 'big' in their journey through success as brilliantly described by Chris Zook and James Allen in their book *The Founders Mentality*.[2]

The essence of a vital design is to re-write the code, alter the DNA of the organization by redesigning how people lives in it: processes, policies, practices, values. Think on a modernization project for a city; vitality design would not be just paving the same old roads, adding traffic lights, paint jobs; it would be instead, creating new streets in the city, connecting neighborhoods, adding highways, tunnels, bridges in places where people had to go around obstacles spending energy and time. The city becomes a different place in the same historical grounds and tradition, preserving its core symbols but removing old structures. A vital design would make your company feel 'interactive', connected, easier to deal with. In other words, liberating *by design*. As a consequence, working in such organization feels energizing, empowering, nurturing.

Defining Organizational Vitality

Vitality can be understood as the energy and passion employees bring to and absorb from their company's environment. Vitality is an outcome from the experience people live as they journey through the everyday, the methods, managers, policies, and state of mind of leaders. Vitality is the emotional, psychological, and biological outcome employees experience as a result of their interaction with an organization where all the employee points of contact with the company are such that they manifest the company's values in a way that shows a capacity for survival, endurance, and meaning. A vital organization is not only energizing, but also purposeful and intelligent. There are however, energizing companies that are more schizophrenic than focused. Energy alone can be disorienting if we lack an intentional focus, a cadence, a smart flow of communication, access, commitments, and execution. A vital design comes from liberation, not from agitation.

Leading Success recognizes that the ambitious aspirations necessary for the transformation of the company will require changing the way the company and its people work. Leaders in general dedicate most of their energy and time to the definition of the transformation, that covers only one third of our framework—disciplines 1, 2, and 3. A vitality design requires companies to spend time *changing the culture*, the ways they see and connect with their talent and how they redefine the organization for simplification and effectiveness. Those are the disciplines 4, 5, and 6 in the model; called the Infrastructure for People Success.

Vitality, therefore, needs to be imagined, designed for, and infused in the norms of work of the company—its operating system—in a way that they are 'hardwired' in policies, processes, metrics, rewards systems, and governance. Exhortations can only go so far, we need to re-code the organization to alter how it works to make it capable to achieve and sustain success. In the illustration shown in Fig. 9.1, the fundamental model for transformation shows vitality as the nervous system, represented as circular arrows, connecting the WORD, WORLD, ADAPT, and DISRUPT domains, bringing information, feedback, and also harmony, alignment, simplification.

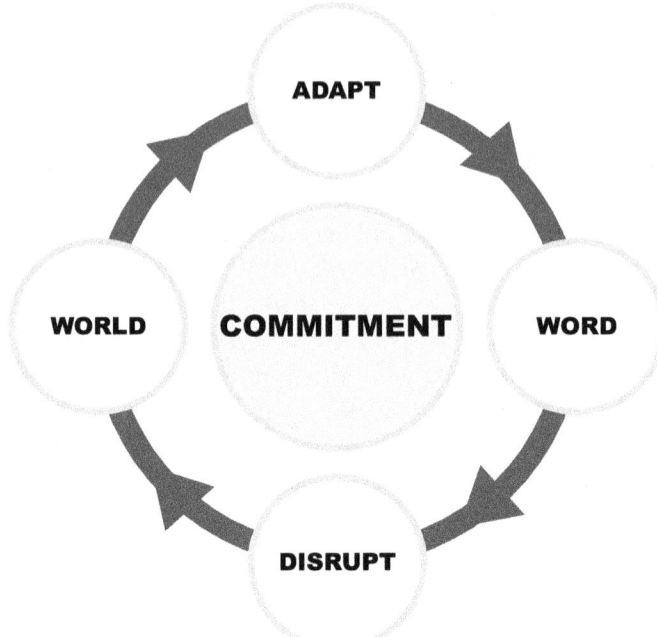

Fig. 9.1 Vitality is the organizational infrastructure that makes the transformation become operational and *signature* (consistent with our values)

The Thinking Process

The operational way to describe vitality for an organization is to examine how its processes work. No matter how well defined and committed our outcomes are, if our processes are designed and oriented to something else, that 'else' will be the natural outcome we will see. Getting to different results is a discovery and intervention process to redesign or replace systems, processes, policies that were designed for different priorities, for a different time. In those cases, the employee and customer experiences are contrived, forced, not consistent or replicable and people spend time, energy, calories rowing against the flow. No wonder why we see all the burnout creeping in our companies. Infusing vitality is akin to rejuvenating the organization to the time when it was created, with a sense of ownership and passion that is shared by management and employees, with little status difference between them—as it is was at startup. Those early teams come together solving problems creatively every day, more concerned about the problem than their roles, sleeves up, and sharing ideas as equals. They team up to climb organizational mountains constantly, arriving to the top and celebrating an achievement they owned. A very satisfying, liberating feeling.

We wonder if there is a way to replicate those states of mind and engagement at scale, in such a way that the team develops a similar bond and passion about the journey and the destination. As you look and study transformations, more often than not the strategy itself and the organizational goals are clear, but as companies move to implementation leaders just push the ball to managers with little preparation, and sometimes little understanding of the changes necessary for success. In other words, there is no playbook to translate vision into implementation, coordination, new priorities, and new metrics. Without this understanding actions will be carried out according to whomever is in charge at the various levels and segments of the organization. The likelihood of contradictory approaches, confusion, and misunderstandings in high. Teams revert to what they know how to do, and the transformation becomes slow, transactional, generating friction, and uninspiring.

Happily, there is a playbook. One of the main reasons I wanted to write this book is precisely to share this methodology. The way to scale the nine disciplines for Leading Success and produce a liberating, vital expression to every person in the organization exists. I have applied it in several global companies, and it is called **The Trilogy**.

Activating the Vitality Design Mindset

The Leading Success Trilogy

Achieving a Signature Expression necessitates a scalable method for organizations to organically produce the outcomes they need. Leading Success works on the principle that ultimate exceptional performance is predicated in superior engagement and consistency to the declared values; this is, standing for something and doing it. The Trilogy is a method that delivers on this capability and creates a sustainable infrastructure to operate in the new way—changing the DNA of the company to alter its potential and capacity to create the new, while organically delivering an innovative, diverse, belonging, and inclusive work environment.

The Trilogy comes, not surprisingly, in three parts as identified in the illustration shown in Fig. 9.2, using a metaphor of a cinematic journey that is built in three stories that extend over a larger arc of time and also meaning, to create a more robust and rich expression.

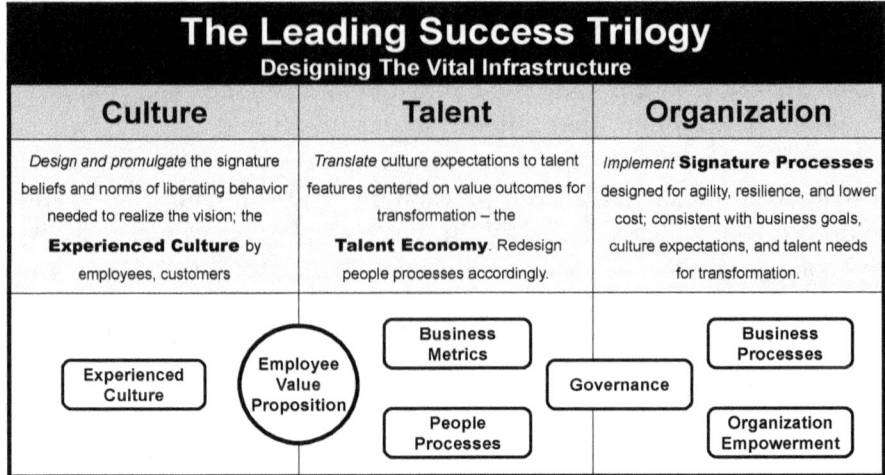

Fig. 9.2 The leading success trilogy, defining the map of leading success' organizational infrastructure

- **Part 1: Culture.** The journey starts with a first step, the *first movie* focused on clarity of purpose, well-defined business goals, and the principles and values we will follow. Typically, this is how we communicate and build commitment around the company's purpose, values, mission, strategic goals, markets, and customer ambitions. Our goal with this first step is to communicate the "North Star", purpose, values, and any other directive principles with the intent to get the emotional commitment of our people to pursue the goals, explain and make people and customers relate to the vision. The main outcome of this first part of the trilogy is to achieve understanding and establish the Culture we want our customers and employees to experience with us; that's why I called it *Experienced Culture*.
- **Part 2: Talent.** The second step, or second *movie* is about the translation of those ambitions into the content of the work people do, the standards by which people plan and are evaluated against. To accomplish this goal, we focus on a concept called *Talent Economy* to examine how the value to the transformation is being created at the job level; value sits above job description. A pivotal design in this second part of the trilogy is the *Employee Value Proposition*, a construct that serves to build a bridge between culture and the operation, illuminating how the company should be experienced by our best employees at the operational level. This segment goes to identify the most critical People Processes that should be redesigned for vitality and offers recommendations for a liberating vital experience on each.

- **Part 3: Organization.** The third step, or third *movie* is about a comprehensive examination of an end-to-end *organization design*, not to be confused with an organization 'chart'. With this in mind, talent and organization are discussed as a combined segment of infrastructure for a vital experience. After all, people processes are embedded in every aspect of the organization that it would be quite unnatural to design them too independently apart from each other. Organization vitality infrastructure covers five distinct areas of design: people processes, business processes, organization empowerment (structure), business metrics, and finally governance, acting as an aggregator and center of decision effectiveness and accountability. The main outcome of this Part 3 of the Trilogy is to arrive to processes that are capable to produce the outcomes the business and talent necessitates for success in a way that is consistent with our signature culture and values, thus called *Signature Processes*, borrowing from Linda Gratton's reflections in *Beyond Best Practice*.[3] If we accomplish that redesign, we have 'rewired' the enterprise to naturally, organically, achieve our highest ambitions, consistently, naturally.

The illustration in Fig. 9.2 shows the seven areas of infrastructure design according to the description above, setting the stage to look into our three disciplines: Culture, Talent, and Organization. Experienced Culture, Employee Value Proposition, Business Metrics, People Processes, Business Processes, Organization Empowerment—also known as structure—and Governance.

The next three chapters are dedicated to each of the corresponding Disciplines responsible for the infrastructure for vitality: Culture, Talent, and Organization.

Notes

1. Oxford English Dictionary. (2024). Vitality definition. Retrieved from: https://www.oed.com/dictionary/vitality_n?tab=meaning_and_use
2. Zook, C., & Allen, J. (2016). The founder's mentality: How to overcome the predictable crises of growth. Harvard Business Review Press.
3. Gratton, L., & Ghoshal, S. (2005). Beyond best practice. MIT Sloan Management Review, 46(3), 49–57.

10

Culture: What We Stand for

The first part of our Leading Success Trilogy is to design and promulgate the signature beliefs and norms of liberating behavior needed to realize the vision, the *Experienced Culture* by employees and customers.

Culture is the one topic everyone you know feels she/he is an expert. In some ways they are right, everyone has always been—since the day they can remember being alive—immersed in a culture: family, school, friends, clubs, teams, church, and of course, work environments. Cultures are inevitable. As long as human behavior is involved, cultures will emerge and cannot be avoided. They are nurtured by our behavior, decisions, priorities, and by the people we chose to include in any group.

Our goal in this discipline is to prevent our organizational cultures to emerge on their own, by happenstance, and instead, to design for them to grow the closest possible to what we intend to have as a culture. The inevitability of cultures naturally emerging in groups of people comes with a hard consequence: we can't hide it; everyone can feel it, everyone can see it, and permeates every aspect of people's involvement in the organization. Cultures connect people with the organization and its purpose.

Designing the organization for vitality starts with an intentional design for the culture we need. This culture articulation is translated to behavioral expectations and ultimately into process and policies, as discussed in The Trilogy. The Culture discipline comes after the Aspiration, Transformation, and Commitment disciplines are completed, and it works as the link connecting the strategic intent with the organizational design. In other words, strategy precedes culture, and therefore, the company's culture should be designed to fit the strategy and not the other way around. There may be a few exceptional situations when the existing culture conditions or directs strategic choices. Perhaps in the public sector, in policies for nations or cities. In most business applications however, it is the business North Star, the strategic opportunity to gain competitive differentiation, and the impetus to extend the business opportunity that defines what the culture needs to be in order to accomplish such endeavor. If the existing culture is dysfunctional or inadequate for the future imperatives, then we have the opportunity to redefine it at this stage, in this very Discipline.

As a starter, it is important to have a formal definition that illuminates our discussion in this discipline. Edgar Schein is one of the most recognized thinkers on organizational culture. His book *Organizational Culture and Leadership* [1] is one of the foundational readings every manager needs. His definition of culture still is the benchmark of the industry:

Definition of Culture

> The culture of a group can be defined as a pattern of shared basic assumptions learned by a group as it solved its problems of external adaptation and internal integration, which has worked well enough to be considered valid and, therefore, to be taught to new members as the correct way to perceive, think and feel in relation to those problems.
> Edgar Schein

An example of external adaptation is how new competitors often expose unaddressed weaknesses in established companies' business models or in their operations, forcing them—usually via bad financial and market results—to think radically different on their choices. Leaders of these disrupted companies move to implement changes that may go against their traditional history, but they have to take their chances. The history of mobile devices and intelligent phones offers many examples. Motorola, with the largest market share in mobile telephony in the late nineties and early 2000s saw a determined, efficient Nokia moving along gradually and strongly behind them, until a point when they became the first in market share. The decisions, the strategic responses to keep Motorola relevant created behaviors and perceptions that changed the culture. Once determined to continue centered on analog radio technology, the company moved fast to digital; once focused on engineering, quality, and reliability, the company started to pay attention to design and fashion, as phones clearly became more than just reliable radio-communication boxes. Those were not the historical cultural attributes at Motorola, but now they had to be, in order to survive.

Internal integration refers to how the groups and people within the company relate to one another. Any group, for example a family, has a balance between their members. But sometimes that balance gets destabilized by family events such as the addition or subtraction of members. Your aunt from overseas comes visiting for a couple of weeks; a divorce, a marriage with children; all of these events change the group dynamics of the family. The same happens in organizations. Stability gets unbalanced by organizational events such as mergers and acquisitions, the hiring of a new CEO, aggregating several functions previously operating as independent units, the acquisition of a brand that elevates the profile of the company to a future-looking direction, as illustrated by CVS moving from "CVS Pharmacies" to "CVS Health" and their bold acquisition of Aetna in a $69 USD Billion transaction.[2] Any of these changes alters the culture because in every case the expected behavior, the decision-making criteria, and the power dynamics change. Private equity-based companies live through these dynamics most of the time as they are expected to grow acquiring differentiating capabilities and integrating them fast. These inflection points require us to define new parameters: how decisions are made, who will be in power, how will we address markets and competitions; what projects, markets, products, investments will no longer be relevant, and how we make sense of the above to employees as a liberating, vital proposition. As decisions are made to implement synergies, scaling capabilities, and the way management handles them will also affect the culture. How companies deal with reductions in force, with power struggles, the elevation or the diminishing of functions is always compared against the company's values and how people were shown respect in the process. Internal integration can destroy a company much faster than external adaptation. It may be less visible, but never goes unnoticed.

External adaptation and internal integration, both require the ability to connect with employees. Companies get very excited about Wall Street's understanding of success but take for granted their own people's understanding of success and actions to get there. Most transformation efforts march with alignment at the very top but poor alignment below. Imagine an army marching to battle where generals ask their troops for coordinated motions, but troops are uncapable to follow because they were not trained, not read into the strategies. Leading Success requires commitment, as stated earlier, the phase where we connect with the entire organization, manager by manager to discuss with employees why the path to follow is not only liberating for customers, but also indispensable for their results, and how it is liberating for employees as we are a great organization to be part of, that stands for something.

CEOs thinking about their cultures will benefit from the following operational insights, collected from my years of work in culture renewal:

The Five Principles of Culture as a Discipline

1. **Cultures are inevitable.** Like a garden, cultural life forms will come out, you need to cultivate the seeds of the culture you want for the offspring of the desired tree to grow. Culture is not the kind of problem you can just throw money at it to solve.
2. **There will be more than one culture in any organization.** But all organizations must find its core, ONE culture at the center. The more global and complex the organization, the more cultures will exist. Nested organizational cultures must be harmonized and have elements all recognize as the ONE core culture.
3. **Cultures must be designed**; built by choice, never left to chance. Organizations must be designed to serve the strategy and reinforce the culture. Cultures are like a train on its tracks. If you want a different destination, you can't achieve it unless you create a new track to that new direction, otherwise the train will follow the *inertia track* that exists today. As the say goes 'your culture will eat your strategy for lunch.
4. **Cultures are rooted in our heritage, our true selves, but aim for the future.** Cultures should reflect aspects of the original founder's intent at its more fundamental core, but not be hostage to our past. Cultures can radically change, even if it takes some time. Cultures should reflect the desired future in remarkable ways.
5. **Organizational gravitation always wins;** culture will follow leaders and practices. People will identify cultural markers based on what they see happening in small and big decisions, how the processes work, what leaders do in times of conflict and pressure. In culture matters, what we do is who we are.

The Anatomy of a Liberating Culture Discipline

There are three foundational elements to the culture in a group, and a fourth element that emerges from the three. Very often, leaders plan for culture evolution with the belief that all they need to do is to explain the culture we want, and that managers, employees will take it from there. For most companies, that is not what happens. It is possible that a small group of committed people may be able to translate culture to operation on their own, but even in those cases, implementation would take many forms, even contradictory forms, created with good intentions but little guidance, and we may end up creating many versions of "the truth" we wanted to elevate. The mechanics of culture are like the mechanics of stellar objects: gravitation always wins. People will gravitate toward the culture we want if the ways to operate, what we measure, the ways to get recognition and growth, progression, are all connected in unmistakable, unambiguous ways to the expected culture we want. The three foundational elements of an organizational culture are shown in the illustration in Fig. 10.1.

Written culture. This is the official, curated, and formal articulation of our culture. This is what you will find in brochures, books, posters, and websites. Culture authors differ on terminology and number of components, but there are mainly three clusters of content: The first is always Purpose and Values, some versions include Mission and Vision; a common second

Fig. 10.1 The signature culture experience

element is Principles, or any articulation of expectations, norms of behavior; and finally, Diversity, which may be included in the above, but we will make an special segmentation and exploration of this element in Chapter 18, due to its relevance to the future of work and the premise of Liberating Leadership.

A written culture is the first step toward intentionally building a culture by choice. We need *the one source of truth* for cultural guidance, philosophical reference, which is critical in every organization, but it is even more crucial for complex, global, multi-industry organizations at the intersection of very different regions, products, customers, and businesses. A culture 'at the center' is an important factor for cohesion and unity even in the presence of significant variation. In the end, people want to know they are part of something larger than their particular segments or business units.

Most culture articles and literature address the process to come up with a written culture. Methodologies, consultants, books are dedicated to this first element.

In Leading Success and Liberating Leadership we see the culture articulation playing three key roles: first, as the *aspiration* that explains who we are, what we are all about, and what we stand for. We also see it as an *expectation* to reset the measuring bar for everyone in the organization, and very specially for its leaders. A written culture also highlights the *choices* we have made in our ambition and determination to become something else; it must describe the new DNA necessary to develop within the organization to succeed in that ambitious future we are about to create. Written cultures are the most prevalent in organizations.

Designed culture. In general, a less discussed aspect in culture articulation efforts. The Designed Culture is the way in which those statements of values, norms of behavior, expectations are 'hardwired' into organizational process. For example, if we say we care about hiring more people of diverse backgrounds, and we do not change how we recruit, what we measure, how managers interview diverse people, we will find out that we will not be able to achieve that element of our culture; organizational gravitation 'the way we do things here' will win. If something is not required, necessary for the work to be accomplished, it will not happen, or it will be left to employees to remember, to come up with ways to do their best to fulfill our culture. A much more effective way is to redesign the process to make it simpler for people to achieve. Granted, not everything is a process, and we can't codify everything that happens in an organization, but leaving the big blocks of activity untouched is a tacit recognition that we are leaving culture implementation to chance: that new employees will learn it, and that existing employees will remember what we meant.

This concept of 'process-proof' is not new. Back in the 60s the manufacturer Toyota came up with a concept called 'poka yoke' which means 'error-proof' and it revolutionized quality in manufacturing by creating mechanisms that would only work when workers did the work in the right way.[3] Good examples in everyday life are those bookshelf or tables assemblies we buy in furniture stores that will not fit unless the pieces are correctly placed. While no design can guarantee cultural alignment, some processes—and systems—can go a long way on prevention and guidance. This goes the same for marketing, product development, or people processes. We will deep dive on this are in Chapter Twelve, Organization.

A Designed Culture means we have redesigned our most important processes and policies, implemented programs that directly reflect our cultural values, updated our metrics and recognition systems to align with the new norms of behavior. For example, adding an incentive component of cultural improvement (with validated, unbiased metrics) in the variable payment calculations for managers; these actions draw people's attention that the company 'really means' what they say. Our goal in Designed Culture is to affect how work gets done in ways that are consistent with the Written Culture to be perceived by employees—ideally everyday—or at the very least in critical milestones, in ways that our written values are visible in their recruitment, onboarding, goal setting, feedback, assessment, promotion, bonus, and how they see leaders conducting themselves. In short, they can see how culture is experienced in action, not just communicated in words. This is, our people processes are now 'Signature Processes'. It is very compelling for employees to see the organization prioritizing things they value and that feeds the feeling of affirmation for their decision to stay with us or joining us. Those in remote locations will feel in harmony with the larger, central organization and will see the line of sight from activity to culture, putting their everyday action as the reason culture is real. Signature processes do not have to be only for people processes, they should also be for customer processes.

Experienced Culture. One thing is to write our aspirations, expectations, values, and purpose, another thing entirely is how employees *experience* that culture. A key part of making that experience happen is coding our values into our processes and policies. All of the above still is written paper, exhortations, process, and workflows. Sometimes systems will help people follow the right path. However, in general, people still need to commit to follow with fidelity the new processes and make a conscious effort to implement them. This means, we need the managers. In the end, how employees actually experience our aspirations, expectations, values, and purpose depends on how their immediate manager and line of command commits verbally, and in actions, with consistency, to create the work environment for that experience to naturally emerge. Because the experienced culture depends on the managers, that experience may vary significantly within the same company, division, or department, adding a highly impactful, highly variable factor into the culture equation. The most successful companies find resources to reduce the variation on management experience by defining expectations and implementing programs, using high standards for developing future managers; not everyone gets the privilege to manage others.

Manager Culture. Based on the above, there is a Manager Culture component. Managers represent the 'last mile' of the culture power grid. Corporate messaging fades away if employees do not perceive their immediate leaders buying in. I have had significant conversations with leaders who have their valid reasons to resist the culture change; they have embraced their own cultural artifacts for long time, sometimes they have been role models of their own subcultures, within their own organizational divisions. The more successful a segment of a company is at creating an independent local culture, the more fragmented the culture of the total organization becomes. Quite a paradox for some leaders. They feel punished for creating a great local culture—the problem is that those cultures often are disconnected, if not contradictory, to the aims of the larger organization, thus becoming a local success at the expense of the total company. It is not uncommon that successful, charismatic leaders quickly develop a following, and start creating distinct language for their teams insisting they are different, and so on and so forth. The goal, therefore, is to find a common ground. People get profound on their beliefs on cultural evolution, and, as many find out, a discussion on future culture is a conversation to create commitment, where we have to deconstruct in order to build something new—in other words, someone will have to let go of the past, and that is an imperative of liberating leadership to do in a respectful and appreciating way. These are deeply philosophical conversations and great venues where a competent HR leader works as a broker between the many universes of frameworks, visions, truths, and personalities. We must avoid making culture definition a power play, but we must recognize, sometimes a final decision from the top is the only way to unlock a stagnated discussion. This is not an anomaly, in fact is a feature of mature decision-making organizations where decision rights are defined and used.[4] We will discuss further on this capability in Chapter Sixteen, Experience.

Leaders, as a consequence of their reactions—consciously not—can *amplify* positively or negatively the culture message and with that, their subordinates' perceptions, and attitudes. When amplifying positively, they work to 'make sense' of things, to *make meaning* for their people. They purposefully work to reinforce the story of success and elevate the morale of teams by pointing at the possibilities and the importance of raising performance to achieve the transformation. They are consistent with the story of how employees, their specific employees, win as the company wins. When changes are hard on people, such as reductions in force, projects that must be terminated, significant cost reductions, leaders are expected to be honest, and always in alignment to the appropriate legal guidance. Bad news are hard, but they can be much worse if people believe we are purposefully hiding something from them. Truth, even hard truth is liberating. Positive amplifiers explain the 'why' with authenticity; they are not propagandists of a future that does not exist.

On the other hand, leaders can amplify cultures negatively—diminish the culture—by criticizing the new ideas of change and cultural evolution. Most commonly, this happens when they fail to show commitment with the new direction, they visibly don't like it and do not echo the merits of the future vision, and, by omission, they send the message that they really are not enthusiastic, they are not buying it, and the tacit message is that their teams shouldn't either. Silence in transformation is one of the most powerful forces that works to diminish vitality. People must hear it from their leaders that they are fully *in*, that they can see the light and the end of the transformation, and that the light is liberating for them. When a leader is negative on culture it rarely goes unnoticed, people are smart and can read between the lines, can listen through the silence; CEOs must act decisively on these circumstances by reinforcing the right message and by engaging with her/his leaders to unlock their resistance. Amplifying leaders are liberating leaders and work for the connections between the pieces, the teams, and the people, not only for control and ownership; this is easier said than done. Much goes into transformations with leaders' personal aspirations and career goals of their own. It is an art form to coalesce and concede for the greater good and to give a different future a chance.

Where does the manager culture come from? Managers create cultures based on their personalities by consciously and unconsciously elevating or suppressing aspects of work life they happen to value very high or very low. Among the best personality assessments available today, the Hogan Assessment[5] provides great insight into the culture leaders are likely to create. By identifying what leaders 'value' at work, the assessment illuminates areas of unconscious behavior that may go unnoticed by the leader but not by their subordinates. Thus, sending a message of 'what matters here' with the inevitable consequence of altering the culture of the place. For example, a leader with a low score on 'recognition' will not consider recognition is important, will not seek recognition, and will not give it either. This manager will reject the notion that others should get recognized. Sooner or later employees will tend to extinguish that element in their work life and the place will gain the reputation that people are not recognized there.

The local culture created by the local leader is very strong and can amplify or neutralize the written culture and create friction for the designed culture. Therefore, it is supremely important for leaders to recognize their values, biases, unconscious preferences, and how those affect their teams. They may be the reason why the culture needs to change under them. This is why choosing who will manage others matters significantly in the ability of organizations to be successful consistently, methodically, and resiliently.

Changing the culture is the ultimate commitment of a leader in transformation.

Edgar Schein illuminates this point very pointedly.

> …culture and leadership are two sides of the same coin in that leaders first start the process of culture creation when they create groups and organizations. After cultures exist, they determine the criteria for leadership and thus determine who will or will not be a leader. But if elements of the culture become dysfunctional, it is the unique function of leadership to perceive the functional and dysfunctional elements of the existing culture and to manage cultural evolution and change in such a way that the group can survive in a changing environment.
> The bottom line for leaders is that if they do not become conscious of the cultures in which they are embedded, those cultures will manage them. Cultural understanding is desirable for all of us, but it is essential to leaders if they are to lead.
> Edgar Schein

Building a Liberating Culture Discipline

The effort necessary to develop a culture articulation for an organization is demanding and voluminous, not to mention that it is extremely relevant, highly discussed, and with a lot of visibility. Not an easy project. Below I offer a few considerations for CEOs and CHROs as they plan to execute on those projects.

Ensure clear governance. These projects are complex and relatively long. Nonetheless, they always find an audience, people who have been waiting for something like this to emerge will jump to the opportunity full of enthusiasm and willingness to participate. We need to remember that these projects can become 'political' in the sense that everyone wants to be leading them or direct them toward certain language or approach. Therefore, clarity on governance is indispensable. From the beginning a few things should be clear: first, who makes final decision at every step, who is running the project, what roles are defined for key players—the c-suite in particular. Culture articulations inform marketing, communications, government relations, but that does not mean those areas *own* the narrative. Ownership of the narrative is a prerogative of the senior-most executive committee, those in direct line of report to the CEO or an expanded team as some organizations have it in their designs. Ideally, the governance process names a group as steward of this content. That solves for ownership, but we also need a driver, a champion that will do the work and convene the governance process. Based on experience, culture is a people function area and should be led by the HR leader and sponsored by the CEO. The final product is a formal product on the way ISO documents work. Revision control will have to be defined and kept with formality. I have seen vast works completed just to see how departments feel allowed to change words, amend without telling others. This is a very important aspect to keep in mind for consistency.

Plan for strategic timing. Culture narratives are major milestones in the life of an organization—or they should be, anyway. A full project may take an entire year to complete if not more. These articulations are based on a process called *discovery* via broad consultation efforts and must go over multiple revisions. Depending on the size, global scale, and complexities of the organization the time could be no less than nine and go up to eighteen months. It will be important to follow a schedule tied to the cadence of the company. I.e., plan for big decisions and revisions to align with major meetings and milestones in the annual planning of the company. If you intend to announce a new articulation at some leadership summit, or at some board meeting, then plan backwards from that date to make sure you don't land in the wrong month and miss an entire cycle. Getting out of synchrony with the natural governance cadence of the company and the Board will cause a loss of momentum that will require a restart later in the cycle.

Plan for internal and external consultation. Culture articulations should look forward but must be rooted in the origins of the company, not necessarily 'the past', but 'the source'—the founder's original intent and vision. For example, on IBM's 100th anniversary the company published an article to reflect on their first century,[6] masterfully stating the fact that today they are a very different company than the creator even envisioned, but they identified the guiding values that originally inspired Tom Watson at that time to create the company to make an elegant, well-founded connection to who they are today and how they see themselves going in to the future. To this day, that is one of the most inspiring pieces of cultural stories ever produced. Cultures are mostly—but not uniquely—a discovery process. They require a layered understanding of the founder's intent in order to become spiritual forces going forward. Getting to that point, or anything close to it takes a lot of input and dialogue in a process we call *consultation*. The typical consultation will include your employees and that would be enough in most cases. Some companies also include their customers and some also include key stakeholders. In the education industry, for example, is common to add parents and alumni. The main change management outcome with consultations is that everyone should feel they had an opportunity to participate—*everyone*. That does not mean everyone has to participate in the same way. You can have an all-employees survey and organize focus groups with fewer employees. Consultation is a conversation to create commitment in the sense that once people are involved, they expect to remain involved. Therefore, regular updates to those involved will be very important.

External consultation is also necessary as a validating reference. We will look at competitors' articulations, industry benchmarks and see what trends are dominating the market. Remember that this articulation is not only for internal consumption. It is the basis for social media, website visits, and an important feed for new customers, new employees, new advocates, and evidence that you had the vision to see something in a particular way. Documents get created fast and there are many of them. Project leaders must plan carefully for version control, controlled distribution, and knowledge management repositories to keep one source of truth.

Remarkable. Culture articulations are meant to elicit our highest aspirations, to speak to our elevated, most adventurous, and timeless selves. This is not a technical document, but there may be a room for a technical expression that implies a monumental aspiration; great examples would be: zero emissions, zero defects, no children living under the poverty line, 99.999% reliability. Culture narratives are an emotional, transcendent writing intended to clarify what is our vision, our ambition for the future, and the role we will play to shape it. For the right people, our intended audience, the narrative must feel almost irresistible. What this means is that executives will need assistance to fuse all the input into a coherent, inspiring narrative.

Short-term and long-term plans. Culture work is never about just the writing. There are multiple steps to follow in order to install the culture across the company and to create ways to embed our values and principles in processes and metrics—to convert those in *signature processes*. The most critical aspect for this complete journey to happen is to identify the journey on its entirety, not just the writing part, in the plans shared with leaders from the very beginning. Otherwise, we risk sending the message that 'here it comes another project' to implement the culture. You can't afford executive disengagement resulting in culture implementation being now the job of HR. It is the CEO's and the CPO's job to clarify to executives and managers from the beginning that they will be signing up for a multi-year journey. If not presented that way, implementation will feel like a different project, something 'after the fact', something 'not essential' and they will interpret that work as unnecessary attention being put on the culture work.

The Anatomy of Failure in Culture Work

Two Worlds

Like many other things in life, Culture does not mean the same thing for everyone in the organization, and that includes the CEO and the most influential leaders in the organization. Intellectually, everyone agrees that culture is the most important ingredient to produce change, but in practice some will see a line of demarcation as to what culture is really about. For starters, some leaders expect culture implementation to be an HR responsibility, or even further, they see culture as something to use for employee talk, external engagements, documents, but not really for business alignment.

To many of those leaders' surprise, once the words are out, they take life of their own in the actions of the whole organization, people chose to believe and expect consistency.

Sometimes influential leaders, see two worlds; they box culture as something that must be done for hygienic purposes, but not for broader use. Culture is a term that may have baggage from previous companies and these leaders may just be reacting to their experience. It is not uncommon to find companies living in two worlds. One world is built of official channels, broader communications, and another of decision-making, prioritization, funding. CEOs and leaders intending to live in two worlds soon realize people can see through that ambivalence and will find their cultures become sterile.

Inconsistency

Cultures emerge, they do not wait for launch dates or implementation schedules; they materialize like drops in humidity. Culture emerges from everyday human activity, behavior, decisions, and reactions. A *designed culture*—the one in our policies, process, and priorities—that aligns with the *written culture*—the one in our statements, values, documents—is never by accident. Companies work very hard to keep that alignment. If left to its own devices, after we announce a culture narrative, people will fine-tune their eyes and ears to test for alignment. When no effort has been made to translate what that culture means to employees in their everyday life, and what it means to customers and the implications to our product design, the culture becomes inconsistent with the experience. A brand new articulation that falls into inconsistency, is worse than not have done any culture work at all.

On the other hand, a well known case of culture consistency is Netflix. Their culture implementation is one of the best examples of how embedding your principles and values in the ways you run the company makes the difference between just talking 'the culture talk' versus walking 'the culture walk'. Netflix designed their culture deliberately to make their values actionable in regular employee processes while enabling their business philosophy and model. A great description of that culture model and its design across the company can be found on Reed Hastings' book *No Rules Rules*.[7] Consistency does not mean right or wrong culture; it means that you operate in accordance with your stated beliefs. Some may disagree with Netflix stance on measuring performance or will claim that paying top of band is not affordable for many companies, that their model is not for everyone. Well, that is precisely the point. Your culture must work for *you*. The main point is that they actually manage their people following their beliefs. Inconsistency begets skepticism and distrust. Great talent is looking for a higher standard on culture.

In its book *Personality and the Fate of Organizations* Robert Hogan[8], creator of the Hogan Assessment, demonstrates how the leader's personality decisively impacts organizations—and countries—much more than we may have expected. The weight of the leader, who that person is, what that person values is too significant to ignore or to overcome by their direct reports without a conscious effort by the leader to neutralize her/his tendencies. This explains the significant weight of the manager in how employees experience the company's culture.

This disproportionate manager impact is a bigger reason to work on the other two factors in Fig. 10.1—Written Culture, and Designed Culture. But there is another factor that is to be considered: *who* is selected to lead matters a lot. So, in creating a culture, choosing the right leaders will bridge the last mile in the culture implementation power grid, as amplifiers for positive outcomes. Reed Hastings called it *talent density*. The better the people you hire, the less you have to worry about them doing the wrong thing.

That is why our next discipline is Talent.

Notes

1. Schein, E. H. (2010). Organizational culture and leadership (4th ed.). Jossey-Bass.
2. Troussaint, J. S. (2017, December 6). What the CVS-Aetna deal means for the delivery of US health care. Harvard Business Review. Retrieved from https://hbr.org.
3. Ohno, T. (1988). Toyota production system: Beyond large scale production. CRC Press.
4. Bienko, M. W., & Rogers, P. (2006). Who has the D? How clear decision roles enhance organizational performance. Harvard Business Review.
5. Hogan, R., Hogan, J. Warrenfeltz, R. (2007). The Hogan Guide. Interpretation and Use of Hogan Inventories. Hogan Press.
6. IBM Corporation. (2011, June 16). IBM 100-year anniversary [Insert]. The Wall Street Journal.
7. Hastings, R., & Meyer, E. (2020). No rules rules: Netflix and the culture of reinvention. Penguin.
8. Hogan, R. (2007). Personality and the fate of organizations. Psychology Press.

11

Talent: The Talent Economy

The talent field of study and its practice are vast and extremely consequential for organizations. As we visit this discipline, we will not be able to cover all the territory. We will concentrate on aspects that make talent management a liberating, vital force in the organization. I will introduce a perspective on talent I have called *Talent Economy*, centered on enterprise value and actions that will make a difference toward a liberating, vital, environment.

While culture emerges from talent—people and their interactions—the Leading Success model suggests that the Talent discipline comes after the Culture discipline because we believe cultures must be designed, instead of becoming only an emergence from behavior. Talent, in this view, purposefully nurtures a desired culture, by design. It is assumed, therefore, that C-suite leaders, facilitated by the CEO and the CHRO have worked together to discern and articulate what they want for a culture that generates the outcomes the transformation is requiring.

A Broader Understanding of Talent in Organizations

A common view on talent is to consider it a 'market'. There is demand and there is supply. There are costs and prices and there are regulations, transactions, categories. On that perspective, the primary mission for the talent function is to meet the talent demand with talent supply. Because talent are people, companies put 99% of their energies in the supply side of the talent market equation, perhaps to a fault. For both, internal (promotion, succession) and external (regular recruiting and hiring) sources, the bulk of the attention goes to *the person* and less to *the job*. While this may sound counterintuitive, it explains a large number of failures in hiring, creating a material risk in transformation environments. Namely, hiring highly qualified, expensive talent for a job that was poorly defined; often described in aspirational terms not useful for discriminating with precision between potential candidates. Exceptional candidates in the pipeline read those specifications, go through interviews, and potentially sign up for a job that in practice does not look like the one the candidate interviewed for. To be clear, this is not intentional. Companies hire in a hurry, often without sufficient understanding and reflection on how the future state redefines the job they are hiring for. Managers therefore, tend to over index the present needs, pressed by urgency and responding to what is proven, what works, the old priorities. Understanding the demand side of the talent market—the job—is more important than ever as we are looking to address a multi-year change that will alter the DNA of the company. The demand question is very simple: what is really the job requirement, *considering the journey we are embarked on?* Hiring managers spend some time on it, but not enough to be able to break down the nuances of skill, experience, perspective, how the role is intended to change, what are the non-technical challenges, situational circumstances expected now and in the future, and also, intending to contribute to a particular culture. In short, we risk hiring for what we need now instead of hiring for what we need to *become*.

What makes it hard? In general, leaders prefer candidates—internal and external—that can solve the urgent problems and look and think like them. But meaningful transformation will require hiring for a future vision; one that may require different people, different skills that come from different trajectories, different cultural and managerial traditions. This is, hire people most leaders will naturally feel less comfortable with. As a consequence, organizations focus on the more tactical and operational aspect, which is filling open positions, instead of loading the organization for future success. A second factor in talent effectiveness is what happens after those capable employees have been hired. Beyond onboarding, the key point is how to define for them what is *success*. What does it mean to 'win' in their job. The talent market perspective largely ignores what happens to the recently hired talent once they are in the company. The Talent Market view is 'business neutral', is transactional. In other words, the task is completed as the position is filled, as shown in Fig. 11.1. Under this view, the common metrics are speed to hire,

Fig. 11.1 Talent Market: the winning candidate is the one who can perform the duties, fulfill the responsibilities, has the experience and the credentials

cost of hire, percentage of open positions. All HR centric, not about business transformation.

Talent inside the company becomes a closed-door environment: the definition of success is based on internal past achievement and affirmation of what is known to work. But transforming companies can't afford to hire for the past.

Even though the market view on talent is mostly transactional—filling open positions as fast as possible—the story does not end with the hiring. Our talent continues to *be in the market*. First internally, as anybody entering the organization becomes a potential candidate for other jobs, but also for external markets. Other companies keep track of your best and brightest, they continue to follow them, continue to be in contact, they see how you are investing on their development, and they will know—probably better than you will know—when they are feeling stagnated and ready for a change. That is possible because of networking, professional associations, and social media with specialized applications for labor market. All of that makes it all too easy for everyone to permanently be 'in the market' even if they do not intend to be, or even notice that they are. Our people are constantly tested on their resolve to stay in our companies. If we have a questionable track record on the things employees value to stay, we will see people leaving, and we never lose the least talented people first, we lose the brightest and highest potential talent.

Because of this larger interaction with the talent market at large, and the growing impact talent has in the economic value of the business, every company is not only an internal market, but it is a small *talent economy*.

What you do with your talent translates in economic value, in capital valuation, and market value growth. Therefore, the game only starts at hiring, and paradoxically, it is when many managers think they completed the task. In a Talent Economy perspective, talent serves the business by ensuring the winning candidate can *excel at value creation*, not merely because they are able to complete tasks, activities, perform the duties in a job description. For transformation to pay off, for a liberating, vital expression to materialize, there is a larger set of interactions that will impact the economic plan forecasted in your transformation.

Talent, therefore, is an *economy*, not only a *market* and that is the way Leading Success frames it for enduring success. What does an economy view of talent include?

In a Talent Economy perspective there still is a demand and a supply for talent—see Fig. 11.2—but fulfillment (filling the demand for an open job) has been replaced by value creation (accelerating transformation) and return on talent (building results and infrastructure) as the ultimate measures of success. Instead of a job description, there is a Position Profile, describing what is success for this position—more on this in the following sections. The measure of adequacy for the role is not only capacity to perform duties and responsibilities, but the unique abilities to create a high-performance environment, create capabilities not in place today, and reinforce the desired culture.

Fig. 11.2 Talent economy: the winning candidate can perform in a way that creates business value and deliver a return on talent for the company

How to Build an Economy-Based, Liberating Talent Discipline?

Building the talent discipline under a Talent Economy mindset will necessitate a coordinated design between the three disciplines of Vitality: this is, Culture, Talent, and Organization, as it was described in Chapter Nine, referencing Fig. 9.2. It is possible for companies to have great culture articulations, superb investments in talent, learning, development, and solid, efficient systems and process, but in ways that they function relatively independent from each other. There is no common theme connecting those resources and people goes through them as different aspects of the company experience. Vitality requires mutual reinforcement across all the people and process infrastructure. What does this mean?

It means, deliberate infrastructure design: a defined culture, sustained by talent that aligns with its principles and values, and processes that reinforce, do not contradict, what we say we care about. As we unpack the talent component, the Talent Economy identifies three main areas for value to manifest—see the center of Fig. 11.2: the first milestone is an employee perspective of what success means for *them*; we call that an Employee Value Proposition or (EVP). In the second milestone, we focus on fine-tunning the ways in which we interact with people for all aspects of their life cycle with the company. This is, how we manage talent for engagement and performance, consistent with the EVP, to create the liberating, vital experience that will bring the value. And finally, in the third milestone, we redesign our people and customer processes for signature experience—the one that is a manifestation of our values and aspirations.

The next three sections in this chapter will cover these areas as if they were part of a roadmap, the one you may need to follow for implementation of the Talent Economy. A couple of important assumptions must be clarified before we embark on those rich conversations:

- The first three disciplines are covered. This means that your Leadership of Liberation outcomes are completed: there is a formal aspiration for where the company is going, clarity on what is the transformation we look for, and commitment in the c-suite.
- The fourth discipline is completed. An Enterprise Culture Narrative is completed: the purpose, values, principles that will serve as north star for vitality design are documented and agreed upon.

Talent Economy Roadmap Milestone 1

Define an Employee Value Proposition for Your Company

Over the last couple of decades, the term Employee Value Proposition (EVP) has been used to describe what people are trying to find in their jobs. Seminal research on people's motivations at work was first developed by Abraham H. Maslow[1]. In his article *A Theory of Human Motivation*, published in 1943, he introduced the model or hierarchy of human needs. The model identifies five levels of needs people seek to fulfill in their lives: (1) Psychological, (2) Safety, (3) Love and Belonging, (4) Esteem, and (5) Self-actualization. A progression from the most indispensable to the most fulfilling. The model has endured as a basic construct to understand the mechanics of the human fulfillment path and also serves as a context to understand employee (worker) value propositions over time. It is to be expected that in times of relative abundance more workers will have the psychological and safety needs fulfilled, and a larger proportion of the workforce would be experiencing the higher levels in the model. Similarly, in times of crisis, war, economic depressions, more workers will not be employed and thus unable to fulfill safety, housing, and food consistently. For example, the mere fact that people had paid work, fulfilling their basic needs, seemed to work well as a value proposition at some points in history; early in the industrial age as many people migrated from farms to cities, the great depression, some hard unemployment times such as recessions. But merely having a job, collecting a salary, may not be sufficient in the global economy of today. It should be acknowledged however, that even to this day there are places where basic needs are not fulfilled for people and having a job with a salary would be indeed a huge value proposition.

More recent studies, in particular from Gallup[2] and Gartner[3] illuminate the modern look at employee expectations. This new research indicates that while a fair compensation is a critical factor and remains one of the top reasons for career decisions, it does not guarantee the access to, and the retention of the most critical talent, and it does not guarantee that people already in the company will be fully engaged either[4]. Creating value in a job requires the employee's full engagement, full energy, and focus on the purpose and on the plans. But since that is a personal choice, it means we need to do our homework first to create an environment where that can happen.

> **Employee Value Proposition, Definition**
> An Employee Value Proposition (EVP) is the perception by employees of how valuable, how worthy, and how liberating is for them to be in a company, based on multiple employment factors, time horizons, their everyday, and their aggregate experience, and how they feel overall about being at the company.

A few things to understand about any Employee Value Proposition:

- Is not a scientific number or a hard metric. However, we can quantify elements of the EVP using validated instruments.
- It is a perception from the employee standpoint. It is not an expression of what the company sees, wants, or offers.
- Value takes different forms to different people. That is why the aggregate experience is so important in measurements.

A differentiating Employee Value Proposition (EVP) for the Future of Work:

- **EVPs must be materially valuable**—at least—industry standard rewards (base salary, commissions, benefits, pensions, equity). People should not feel they are being taken advantage of.
- **EVPs most feel worthy** for people dedicating part of their lives to the company (high aspirations on purpose and values, ethical leadership, ESG oriented, competent management, developmental, chance to grow)
- **EVPs must feel liberating** for people to stay (offer flexibility, fair treatment on performance and advancement, equality, able to be themselves, can do their best work, they belong to a nurturing environment, legacy)

The main distinction between a traditional versus a future of work Employee Value Proposition comes from its outcomes on employee's *perceptions* and *feelings* instead on the intrinsic offering the company provides. That may sound counterintuitive. For years an EVP was expressed in terms of what was made available, what was offered to employees. A fair compensation, benefits, the possibility to grow. Language directed to 'the worker' in all of us, not to the whole person we all are in our many versions: the happy newly married, the single parent, the diverse individual, the incapacitated employee. Therefore, the understanding of 'value' was all about a richer offering. But two factors made this perspective insufficient. First, as society grew more socially aware, employees expected more from their employers in terms of socially responsible actions and equity, diversity, environmentalism. Second, the pandemic demonstrated that it was possible to perform, get results remotely[5]. In addition, the pandemic also worked as an accelerator of digital business models from the very small (order sandwiches online) to the very large (managing large-scale contracts and services). As a consequence, enterprise value creation moved further and faster from physical products to customer experience elevating digital skills, software, and customer experience design as something prominent, not optional for a company's survival. Tech skills, customer experience, software in general are grounds in which employees' attitudes and engagement have a larger impact on value creation than they do in physical products alone. It makes sense to evolve the value proposition to meet those expectations.

The evolution for EVPs is the result of considering *the whole person*, the understanding that the frontiers between work life and personal life are blurred or simply disappeared and with that, the concept of value for employees is now more about how they feel working for the company than the richness of what is offered.

Based on these findings, our opportunity is to design organizations to match what people value as we move into the future. According to the research from Gallup and Gartner, there are visible trends to consider[6]. First, employees want to be seen as *whole persons*, not just as workforce, cost structure, overhead, or simply a collection of skills. The second aspect is to remove the artificial disconnection between work and life. Family, personal time, and worktime are intertwined; technology makes it possible with ever growing speed and convenience. Finally, how people *feels* may be seen as an unfair approach. After all, how anybody feels in a job responds to a lifetime of experiences and circumstances, impossible to design for. But a reasonable employee will not expect to work in a paradise; employees are smart, and they will know the comparative differences across the industry. In that sense, it is possible to make people feel great working for a company versus another. That is the whole premise of the vitality design.

How Does an EVP Look Like, in Practice?

Companies need explicit EVP models in order to identify the main drivers of employee value that will be prioritized. These drivers of value act as statements of commitment from the company to existing employees and also as a promise or 'brand' for how the company wants to be perceived by potential

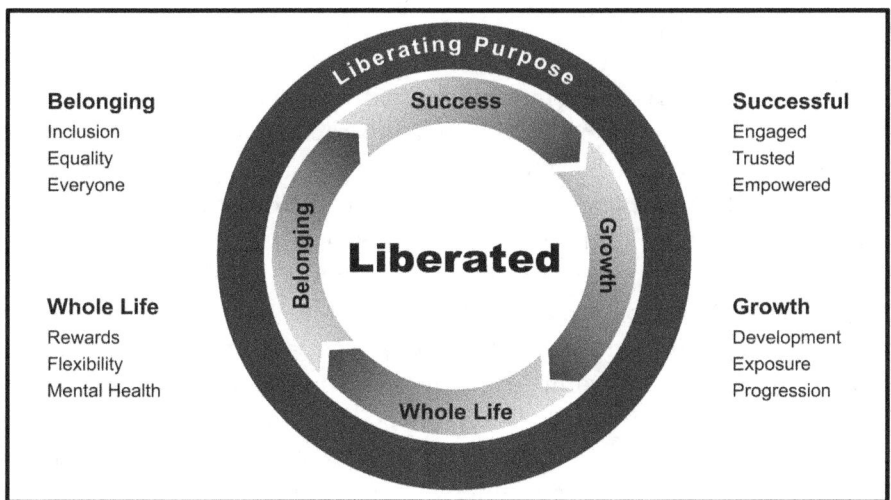

Fig. 11.3 Example of an EVP consistent with Leading Success

employees. The illustration on Fig. 11.3 shows an example of how an EVP, consistent with Leading Success, may look like for a company.

The right EVP will be the intersection of employee's interests and the philosophy of the company, with comparable priority. This is an operational design to ensure talent and organization processes reflect that balance. The EVP is shown in between the disciplines of Culture and Talent in Fig. 9.2 for a reason. It is a bridge between our aspirations and the employee experience, but it also is *committed language.* Both the culture narrative and the EVP are documents people will read with more interest than ever before in the history of modern corporations. People wants to see what we stand for, will take our word for it, and hold us accountable. No leadership group I have ever been part of takes this lightly, however, on occasion, leaders feel varying degrees of freedom to deviate or ignore their own words when convenient. In the past, people will notice and look the other way, with the only consequence being the company losing credibility to their eyes. Today things have changed. People will ask direct questions and express their frustration very directly. These deviations from our own words are also powerful reasons why trust in leadership erodes, skepticism grows and suddenly, without even noticing, employees become more transactional in their approach to work; their spirit is no longer in it. No team wins championships with a transactional attitude. Losing the hearts of our people is a big risk and we must ensure we declare in our culture the things we intend to do and live it for real, not for the document, or for the photograph moment.

Developing Your EVP

Writing the EVP starts with your Culture narrative. Once that articulation is final, the purpose, values, and any statements therein will serve as a foundation for the EVP. It may be as simple as gathering a group of multi-function and multi-level, diverse team to propose an articulation or it may take a more formalized effort with professional consultants to support its writing. Some may argue that a comprehensive culture narrative is sufficient to express our commitment to employees, that we may want to keep it simple and not issue an EVP. I believe the answer lies in the culture of trust—or no trust— already prevailing in the company. In general, however, the new generation of workers will want more specificity; for too long, they have heard that they should not worry, that they are covered by our values, that people are the most important aspect of the business, only to realize that there is no *operational commitment* stated anywhere, no process, no metrics, or any specific translation in policies or programs of what that culture means for them. A formal EVP is all of that and it is increasingly important for employees to understand us better and in the best cases this articulation will serve to validate that we are the right company for them, or not. And that is better for all parties.

An EVP normally is a five to ten pages document, with a visualization as the one shown in Fig. 11.3, with a few statements and commitments highlighting the areas or dimensions included.

I Have My EVP, What Should I Do Now?

Make it known! And most importantly, make it understood. EVPs are best positioned as a direct consequence of our commitment to activate the culture narrative in concrete forms, observable and accessible to all employees. Its ideal timing is to come a few months after a cultural articulation, but it does not have to be only at that time. EVPs can be a way to reenergize the company's commitment to a culture that is still relevant but has been in the back burner for a while. EVPs signal to employees we are doing our part as company, we are listening and making efforts to walk the talk, that we are creating infrastructure to make our cultural aspiration real. Culture, talent, and organization are linked to one another the way proteins are linked to the DNA helix. On their own they are interesting but not vital. Only a culture that is visible in the organization and management practices, in the everyday of things, will make the strategic differentiation we are looking for in both transformation and sustained performance. With the above said, the short answer for a successful implementation of an EVP is *the manager*. The one and only way to install an EVP is ensuring two things happen: something must change in policies, programs, or investments in a way that it sends a message to people, a statement of commitment to show we are putting our money where our mouth is; and second, all managers are trained to understand what their role is in making the EVP real in their small or large teams. Left to communication only, or to large corporate policies alone, the EVP is not going to elevate the vitality of the organization. We will dedicate a segment to managers in Chapter Fifteen, Expectation, where we will elaborate on this indispensable component of Leading Success.

Talent Economy Roadmap Milestone 2

Reset Talent Management on Value and Vitality

Talent Management has always been one of the most strategic actions a company performs. No different that it is for professional sports teams, we need the best players in the most important positions on the field. But it is more than collecting players; in the end, we want to win games and championships. We want economic value for everyone involved (investors, customers, employees, and the community—via our CSR actions), in short, we want *success*. Counter to what many may think, not always the teams with the best players win the big games and championships. Ultimate success comes down to the aggregate outcomes the team achieves while playing together with the direction from coaches and managers; the proverbial 1 + 1 = 3. Each player, however, brings a unique contribution to those outcomes. Professional sports have developed sophisticated metrics to master the understanding of the value players have in team's success. Baseball statistics showed that a player being able to get on base was more valuable for team performance measured by wins and losses, than a player that aims for home runs, measured by the variable *on-base percentage*, portrayed in the movie *Moneyball*, based on Michael Lewis's book of the same name[7]. Similarly, for Basketball, the metric Plus/Minus points differential for a player indicates how many more or less points the team scores when a particular player is on versus off the court. It is not enough to attract and sign a great Baseball or a great Basketball player, but to understand where the value comes from in that particular position.

Companies are not that different. For their key positions managers go out of their way on efforts to recruit and attract, to pay above the media, to add signup bonuses to bring star players to their roster but unlike professional sports teams, they do much less effort to understand where the value really comes from in each position and to ensure the potential value materializes.

Talent Economy is an approach to make the above happen. It can be seen as an amplification of the good practices most companies already have in searching and bringing good talent, now extended to include actions to make it possible for people to do their best work, get their best results (value) while being who they are. For championship winning teams it comes down to team identity, great players, and great coaches that are able to bring together said team. They embrace their identity, excel at their understanding of the game (positions and schemes) and understanding of the competition (competitive differentiating factors).

For your peace of mind Talent Economy is not a program or an initiative, not even a project. It is a change of mind, a fresh perspective that will demand additional documentation and conversations to elevate the existing talent management process in companies. It can be seen as a realignment of the components around talent that are already highly valuable on their own but still with opportunity for a deeper connection to the business transformation.

As Fig. 11.4 illustrates, talent management for vitality can be represented by three clusters of activities, to be performed by managers: manage the demand, understand the supply, and increase the return on talent value. Here is the succinct breakdown for each of them:

- **Manage the demand**. Managers define what clusters of work—jobs—are in the team, engineer roles to maximize performance and development opportunities as much as possible. Then go one step further, define what is the value each of those positions brings to what the transformation needs. That information will be documented in *Position Profiles*.
- **Understand the supply**. Managers know their people and enhance their capabilities constantly. This comes with three key actions. Identify who are the true best talent for the future, then *connect* with them, not just 'manage them'. But they also have to know and identify people outside their team as part of the portfolio of talent for the future. No talent managers should be confined to only their team, but the entire universe of possible talent.
- **Increase the Return on Talent Value**. For coaches/managers of sports teams, the concept of *return on talent value* is easy to understand: win championships with the personnel you have; or go as far as you can in the tournament. That can only happen if 1) the coach is an expert on the

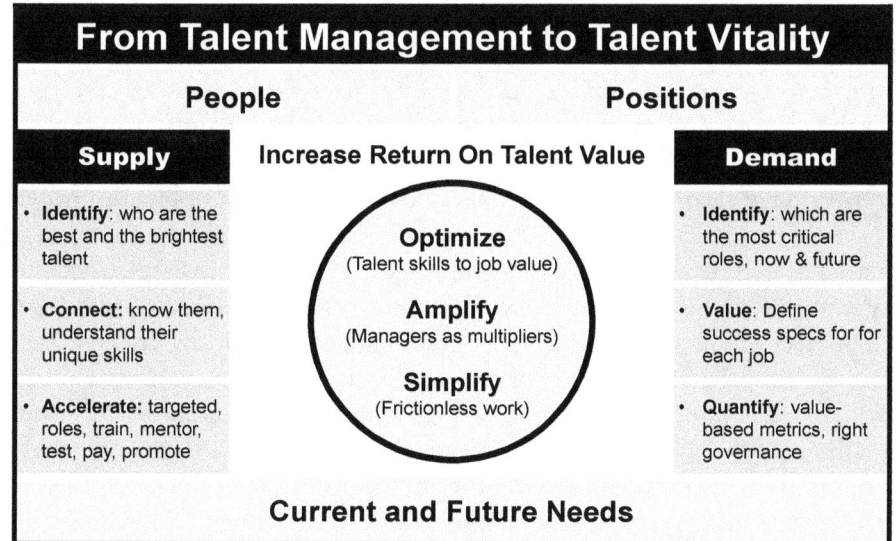

Fig. 11.4 Framework for the Vital Talent Economy implementation

positions on the field and she/he knows deeply the players and their capabilities and therefore can design lineups in the best way for team success; 2) The coach understands the importance of her/his role as performance advisor, source of insight for improvement, prioritizes the right culture, and ensures the team plays in cooperation, collaboration, and 3) the coach works to simplify the complexities of the work so players can concentrate on scoring, not the uniforms, the equipment or the dressing rooms.

Mastering the Return of Talent Value

The first action at the center of Fig. 11.4, *Optimize,* is about finding the optimal skills matching for each person to fit the position's value to transformation. The analysis begins with a definition of what success (economic value) means to critical roles. In the Talent Economy approach we do not optimize skills against job *content*, but against job *success*. This is, what does the role must *achieve as outcomes*—not just what is required to do as *responsibilities or duties as inputs*. For example, it is not enough to say we need to fill the job of VP of Product Design and offer a list of qualifications and duties. In addition, we need to define what success looks like for the role. In this case, an example would be to say that 'in two years the VP of Product Design will lead the organization to ensure we launch a new category of products that will grow revenue by 10% and that will capture 30% of the addressable market within five years, using digital platforms'. This description is not about activities, responsibilities of 'the job'. It is about how will we know that the role accomplished what was needed for the company's evolution and performance—this is, for *success*. That specific definition of success is what we must have clear, at least for the most consequential jobs, but in time, for the whole company. With this language it is easier for the recruitment team, internal or external, to differentiate among candidates to increase our chances of getting the right talent for success, not to just fill the job as fast as possible.

The second element *Amplify*, is the manager factor in the equation. Increasing return on talent value is about finding ways to maximize performance, create opportunity to accelerate change and results, beat the odds of failure, and solve problems. Managers will need to understand what is going on in the field, with their people and intervene as necessary to facilitate success. This means connecting people and teams, accelerating decisions, and removing barriers for people to use more of their time in productive work. When managers are absent from the operation and from decisions, their teams follow and soon the team realizes everyone is on their own. The most visible action of an amplifying manager is *presence*. Not only physical presence, but presence of mind and being there for their people in times of need. Finally, managers increase value when they amplify the culture of the larger teams above, this is, they must fulfill their role as 'meaning maker' to their teams constantly, and for newly hired or promoted people, that becomes an indispensable task.

The third action to increase return on talent value is *Simplification*. No matter who you hire, if the company's process makes the work harder, slower, you will end up neutralizing the most capable, innovative, motivated people you can find. Different from regulation, which imposes unique work needs that we do not control, internal processes are fully in our control and also have significant impositions in the organization. Typical examples include how many approvers are needed to release something—a report, a product, a customer email; how many steps it takes to go from proposal to manufacturing; who is meant to make a decision versus how many people think they are. How effective is the organization on making decisions. Organization design, simplification, and decision-making are profound drivers of liberation and vitality in companies, and we will discuss more deeply on methodologies and implications for simplification in the Organization segment ahead.

Talent Economy Roadmap Milestone 3

Redesign People Processes to Make Them a *Signature* of Our Culture

People processes require a broad discussion that must be appropriately framed for simplification of analysis and redesign. The best way to address it is to consider first the *employee life cycle* on its entirety. This is, to map the journey employees follow from start to finish in the organization. From that reference point, people process can be understood in terms of their value and outcomes, not merely by their descriptions.

Employee Lifecycle for Value Creation

No different than product design, the journey of an employee through our company is something that must be designed, then packaged, marketed, and… bought!—more than 'sold', companies are 'bought'; they are a buyer's decision highly dependent on the company's reputation. Companies will always have a reputation, but we want to manage what that is, and design for it. Therefore, it will be necessary to develop a point of view of 'what is like to work for us' to present to potential employees or buyers. That particular point of view, as we discussed earlier, is called the Employee Value Proposition (EVP), consistent with our culture, transformation, and aspirations. Once the EVP articulation is completed, the whole journey from hiring to exit can be analyzed and improved accordingly.

Three stages: A simple way to breakdown the employee lifecycle is to consider three segments: *Join*, *Succeed*, and *Further*, each with a couple of major elements of employee experience, as follows:

- **Join**—to include *Recruit* and *On board*
- **Succeed**—to include *Year-Cycle* and *Emerging events*
- **Further**—to include *Culture* and *Team*

Join: Joining a company is similar to a life event. It changes significantly how people spend their day, define their routines, socialize, and define their lives. Below is a reflection on how the stages of the life cycle contribute to value creation for the transformation:

- **Recruitment**. The recruitment experience can be better designed and implemented when it is centrally designed and performed consistently across the company and reflect the company values very clearly. This is, making it a signature process. Candidates must see the company as a place with a masterpiece in the making, art in construction that needs *them* to be completed or continued. In general, we hire for future culture and capability; we will need builders who and architect, and architects who can build. Our candidates must feel comfortable in both modes, adapt, and disrupt.

- **Onboarding**. Remove any flavor of a transactional experience. Onboarding is not a half-day deal. It should extend for at least ninety days, but truly it will be over at the first year's anniversary; once a whole performance cycle is complete. People should feel they are arriving as 'writers' not just 'readers' of the company's history. Above all, this is a *conversation to create commitment*. Our goal is to ensure new hires feel they belong, understand the company intellectually and emotionally, and have access to personalized support until the first performance cycle is completed. Managers can leverage, but never delegate this step entirely to HR.

Succeed: Being in the company has one single purpose: to succeed. This second stage covers the entire productive life of the employee at work and it is repetitive in steps, but different in content every year. This is how we use both Life Cycle and Emerging events to bring value to our transformation:

- **Transformative Year Cycle**. The year cycle is the ritual process from goals to performance that encapsulates the contribution—and the development—of our people. The performance year cycle will be analyzed in detail shortly ahead.
- **Emerging events**. The life cycle of an employee will be touched by a number of events that are rather unpredictable but inevitable. They include organization, employee, and life events.

    a. **Organization events**. These are broad changes that affect everyone in the organization. Being acquired by another company, going public or going private, filing for bankruptcy. The hiring of a new CEO is an organization event as well. Value is created with timely and clear communication, no surprises. There are tight rules on all of these circumstances and should be respected; however, there are ways to stay connected to employees and to listen to their concerns.
    b. **Employee events**. These are changes of employee status in terms of salary, job level, meaningful assignments, or promotions. Value is created by avoiding waste of time and energy of the candidate and the

team. If someone is promoted, assume that a new employee has been hired and conduct an orientation and onboarding. Everyone has a level of uncertainty that should not linger unnecessarily.
  c. **Life events.** These are significant events in the life of employees. They include illnesses, caring for a relative, the birth of a child, leaves of absence, graduation, marriage, divorce, and even death. Value is created by ensuring care is provided according to policy—the very existence of a policy in the first place—and gestures of support, compassion, and flexibility as the case demands.

Further. Leading success focuses on exits as a 'furthering' stage. This is, when employees complete their journey either because they chose to, or because they are asked to leave. That exit however, is never the end of the story. People's influence survives their physical absence. The larger the role, and the longer the tenure, the bigger the imprint the organization will experience after an employee's departure. Two main legacy factors are the most consequential: culture left behind in the group of influence and quality of the team. Value is created by working on managers' long-term expectations on amplify the right culture and build robust teams. We will address this particular aspect in Chapter Fifteen: Expectation.

The question now is, how does a Vital Talent approach gets embedded, permanently coded inside our processes? That is the content of our next section: people processes.

Optimizing People Processes for Vitality and Success

Making vitality happen comes down to how processes, policies, decisions, and the executive speech materialize the company's culture in the way people, our employees—and, by extension, our customers—experience the company and its products and services. In this section we will identify the key aspects of Leading Success that we need to embed in the design of the processes and policies. If we follow the logic of the Employee Value Proposition, in our example, we will now identify key processes and policies that would have influence on how the organization operates.

The illustration on Fig. 11.5 presents a selection of people processes consistent with the employee life cycle that represents the largest opportunity to impact the employee experience. Depending on how a design team breaks down the pieces we can have anything between ten to fifteen components. The table in Fig. 11.6 offers a breakdown of the above thirteen people processes which are strong candidates to become signature processes in our companies. That number may not be too large, but it is significant when it comes to vitality redesign; we need to focus on the processes that have the largest and most direct impact on employee experience based on our specific gaps and areas that need attention. The people process list can be seen in different ways to prioritize the work for talent value for vitality.

Essential people processes represent the totality of process necessary to operate the organization consistently for the long run. This should be the target for redesign in a lapse of about three years.

Critical people processes represent the people experiences most directly related with the Future of Work. Those processes address expectations around increased flexibility, autonomy, agency, and belonging.

Pivotal people processes represent capabilities that will solidify new cultures and materialize the transformation in concrete operational ways. Performance, Rewards, talent assessments, promotions that reflect culture and performance.

Managers. While managers is not a column, it is the only process that is both critical and pivotal and will be analyzed separately here and in the Expectations section.

Fig. 11.5 Example of critical people processes for success

Most leveraged components of Talent Infrastructure

#	Talent Processes & Policies	Essential *Talent Imperatives*	Critical *Future of Work*	Pivotal *Sustainability*	EVP *Employees feeling*
1	Recruit and Hire	X			Success
2	Onboard	X			Success
3	Manage Performance & Development	X		X	Success
4	Review Talent and Organization	X		X	Growth
5	Develop Managers to Lead Success	X	X	X	Liberated
6	Employee Learning and Development	X			Growth
7	Mentor key talent	X			Growth
8	Define a Flexible Work Policy	X	X		Whole Life
9	Define a Pay and Rewards policy	X		X	Whole Life
10	Prioritize Wellness and Mental Health	X			Whole Life
11	Accelerate inclusive progression programs	X			Belong
12	Accelerate Culture Implementation	X	X		Belong
13	Define an ESG and DEIB Policy	X	X		Belong

Fig. 11.6 Classification of People Processes based on Talent Economy priorities

Critical Processes for the Future of Work

- **#8—Define a flexible work policy.** This is, decide and promulgate to what extend the company's leadership will allow for remote work, flexible configuration of schedules, and the use of technology for meetings. This also includes vacation and discretionary leaves of absence—not health related. The big danger to avoid here is going with what executives 'believe'—as opposed to data—as the right answer, the approach that works *for them.* And what I mean here is not what works for what they need to do as executives, but instead, what they think, based on their experience and perhaps, biases, should be the right answer for the company on degrees of flexibility for their people. Companies must feel vital for the target profile of employees you will need in order to effectively execute and sustain your transformation. Do not forget who you are designing for; it is not top management and long-term employees only. Some concessions on flexibility will go a long way in the journey to the balanced design.
- **#12—Accelerate Culture Implementation.** Whether you just announced a renewed culture, values, purpose, or you have one already in place, you will need a couple of important steps for acceleration of your culture. One is to be sure everyone truly understands and embraces the aspirations, expectations, values, and purpose. This is not only a communication process; it has to be a conversation. More detail will be provided in the Expression mindset, however, in short this means that we will need to

set up *conversations* (the ones that create commitment), not *presentations* (one-way corporate language and curated visuals) to get the culture and its meaning out to people. Dialogue leads to deeper understanding; after understanding comes behavior. We now need to translate what those expectations and aspirations look like as behavioral expectations, appropriate for multiple layers in the organization. For example, if we identify 'innovation' as a corporate value or principle, we now have to describe what that means in a day-to-day language for employees at lower, middle, and higher levels in the organization. Similarly, we will have to audit how our product development process is culturally compliant, or consistent with those aspirations. For example, if a company is committed to 'accessibility', the product audit will focus on identifying and confirming in which verifiable ways the value of 'accessible' is present in concrete features in our products and services. So, culture acceleration means three big components: (1) a companywide mobilization to coordinate small team conversations about culture and its implications; (2) a behavioral translation for employees to describe how the values are lived everyday; and (3) a product process audit.

- **#13—Define a DEIB and ESG Policy.** As discussed, the post-pandemic workforce has developed a higher expectation on how the company they chose to work for follows their commitments on diversity, equality, inclusion, as well as their commitments to the environment and social responsibility. Somewhere in the culture articulation, perhaps in values or in principles, but somewhere prominent, not in a footnote, it has to be clearly stated what the company stands for in terms of no-discrimination, and very specifically, calling it by name, the LGBTQ community. Potential employees look for those important company statements as they research for your company. We have a dedicated chapter for Diversity ahead, and we will unpack more of this critical aspect in that segment.

Pivotal Processes for Transformation and Culture

- **#3—Manage Performance and Development.** If there was room for only ONE process to change, I would start here for 90% of organizations. No other process comes close to performance and development management (PMD) on its impact on the 'real' culture of a company. A common, consistent approach to Performance Management and Development applies universally for companies of almost every type. Either concentrated on a single location or those highly disaggregated. The PMD process is the great equalizer, the one piece that can be the same for everyone regardless of how different they are in their geography, industry, operation, employee base, and revenue. Our Leading Success PMD process has to clear a few standards that will be desirable in order to pivot our transformation on this process.

The twelve principles for a vital PMD Process that increase talent value.

a. **Established, documented, known.** This should be table stakes, however, over the last three decades scholars and practitioners shared a growing sentiment to question the very existence of a Performance Year-Cycle[8]. Proponents of this approach argued that the process was causing too much distress and waste of time for very little value. Over time, the consensus is that a process is needed, but it must be improved[9]. Moreover, the value was never meant to be the process but the quality of conversations—to create commitment—between employees and managers.
b. **Universal, Equitable, Standard**. Everyone, no exceptions. No privileged groups. Understandably, the complexity of goals at the top may require additional tools and a different documentation, but the key dates, key outcomes, and decisions should follow the same principles that apply to everyone else.
c. **Transformational**. Transformational ambitions must be present in the form of granular goals and priorities for specific—or for all—people across the organization. Those are added on top of the usual goals to sustain the operation.
d. **Standardized and simple**. Adopt and formalize a standard template and protocol for performance on two areas: success goals and success behaviors. In the first case by adopting OKRs, MBO's, or a similar goal structured methodology. In the second case, a formal competencies library should be acquired and implemented. PMD process can be unimaginably complicated, extensive, unrealistic. In the end, simplicity wins. You should take your time to design this process. The impact of a good or a bad design will be felt for years.
e. **Focused**. Avoid proliferation of goals; this is a creeping problem in organizations and often feels necessary due to the immense responsibilities some positions have. Leading Success focuses on relevance. Target the value expected in the position to articulate goals that matter. Three to eight goals maximum. Sweet spot on five goals.
f. **Centered on Contribution**. Goals are succinct, crisp, clear, and articulated in terms of key operational outcomes and hard metrics. Eliminate

goals that are generic, desires, good intentions. Every goal is operational, with a YES or NO answer (with something tangible, material, measurable to deliver or accomplish) and connected to the transformation (linked to a workstream or strategic priority).

g. **Leveraged for Development**. Goals will include employee development. Ideally, responding to growth areas, or aspirational plans identified in the previous PMD review, using language from common tools—competencies—aligned to EVP and values. Development can be the assignment—the goal—itself, but may include other, more traditional aspects like certifications, coaching, or mentoring. Employees must feel the company places comparable importance to their development than they do to their revenue.

h. **Committed**. Planning, feedback, and action language is the result of a dialogue between manager and employee, a conversation to create commitment as defined earlier in this book. For many companies the PMD process is broken; it may be defined but is not followed, not used for people decisions and therefore it is perceived as a waste of time. The ultimate measure of quality of a PMD process is the quality of the conversations to create commitment, not the systems or templates.

i. **Resourced**. If there are no tools or resources to work, then there are no realistic goals. Goals can be fluid in organizations due to market changes, competitors, regulation, natural events. Some goals will become irrelevant, and others will come to the fore. In every case, good managers will see that resources are provided for the goals to be accomplished. This is a significant cultural dimension that contaminates cultures rapidly: when everyone knows we can't do something because there is no people, no budget, no time, and yet, our manager still commits to it, it signals to our teams that we are not prioritizing well, that we are not rooted in reality. Trust in management erodes. If no resources are available, goals need to be canceled or postponed.

j. **Assessed and differentiating**. Our PMD must provide ways to differentiate levels of greatness in performance. No so much to identify the low, but to highlight the top performers. Highest potential employees will get things done brilliantly and will expect that those extraordinary results will not go unnoticed for managers and the executive layers above.

k. **Consequential**. The PMD process becomes the path for growth, development, accomplishment, pay, progression, and growth for employees. In the same way, it becomes a source of predictable execution, performance, and transformation for the company. What happens in the PMD process should change professional lives. PMDs should not have parallel

processes, augmented or simplified versions anywhere, unless that alteration is an exception for ultimate circumstances, sanctioned by the CEO and the CHRO.
l. **Liberating**. People come out of each conversation with a perspective that connects the dots into a picture of success for customers, team, and self.

Redesigning a PMD process is not a light endeavor. It normally is a multi-year project, even more demanding if the system of record is also changing. Every effort made to fulfill the key points identified above will pay off in a more vital experience for our employees.

- **#4—Review Talent and Organization—PART 1—TALENT.**

(Part 2, Organization Review is explained in Chapter Twelve).

The year cycle is the engine for both the company and employees to guide action and prioritization, the way to move collectively in the right direction. But there are larger questions about every employee. In the same way we have year plans and multi-year strategies for products and businesses, a vitality approach to talent should be able to answer the same questions for every employee.

What is inside a vital Talent Review? Governance, Processes, Outcomes, and Experience.

a. **Vital governance**. The CEO is the customer. Talent belongs to the organization, no to the hosting business unit. Governance is not only about formality: meetings, participants, and schedules; it is about process integrity, decision-making, accountability, and outcomes. Common approaches to Talent Management disproportionately focus on the *discussion* about talent, including calibration, designations, strengths, weaknesses, resulting in a considerable investment of time, preparation, analytics. This is important, but it should not be done at the expense of the time, effort, and executive interest left for the *outcomes* side of the process: actions, development, new assignments. The right governance will frame a complete end-to-end journey with a balanced approach.
b. **Vital process**. The Talent Review process creates the culture for talent. Here are the five vital components to make the Talent Review a vital process:
   i. End-to-end view. Comprehensive and inclusive to identify the whole spectrum of commitment talent planning requires. Managers need to understand this is managing the business, not an HR process. All the

way from standards, scheduling, any assessments, data processing, and the several meetings this will require are part of the plan.

ii. Standards, definitions, protocols. Discussions on talent are very intense and can go on tangents very quickly for many reasons. Facilitation, rules of engagement matter, but the most critical point is to make sure language does not get on the way… the right language will simplify and focus the conversation. Sometimes leaders are not clear what we really mean by terms like 'potential, pivotal, critical, bold, edge'. The best way to focus and lead to actions is to use good definitions with straightforward language to describe in two lines what we are and what we are NOT looking for. Talent identification means classification, segmentation, separation between the good, the great, and the greatest. Therefore, a classification framework will be needed. For the most part, companies use a version of a model called "the nine-box performance and potential matrix". Whatever construct a company utilizes, it is foundational to define in positive ways those segmentations, so leaders do not avoid them, and attach constructive actions to each of the designations.

iii. Clear path to outcomes. There are four main outcomes in a vital process for Talent Review: (1) Talent identification and categorization; (2) decision on key positions and individuals—promote, accelerate, keep, exit; (3) decision on succession, agreements on assignments and development, and (4) Strategic approach going forward.

iv. Readiness acceleration journeys. Once the conversation is completed leaders will need orientation on what are the choices to accelerate, support the leaders they just identified. Pre-defined paths for development with choices that allow for adaptations, adjustments will help move the executive team forward to action and visible outcomes. One part of the Talent Review must be dedicated to formalized action planning.

v. Manager roadmaps. Talent Reviews are always important and strategic, but they can be much more than that; they can be vital. The source of vitality will depend on the degree the talent review translates into actions that include the individuals being assessed and their managers. In other words, work on how managers get involved in the development of their people. We will need manager journeys; simple follow-up steps to provide insight to managers on the actions to be pursued for their people and ways to support them.

c. **Vital outcomes.** The dynamics of business reality, unexpected competitive conditions, and market variations can derail our business plans and therefore our talent plans. While successions and promotions may not happen at the pace we would like, the talent process must be followed, regardless. The vitality of a talent plan lies in the commitment companies put into it, the investments, and the pursuit of the plans, regardless of the specific opportunities. In other words, employees and particularly superstars will see the leader's intent, disposition, and investment. As they continue to grow, there is a business case for them to stay with us. It is liberating for them as their 'readiness still grows, and they know opportunities will come to them. There is a bold business proposition that we continue to create leaders that we may be unable to leverage internally. But the fact that we are committed in that way will not go unnoticed by the very best people. We make the company vital and liberating for them.

d. **Vital experience**. As talent reviews cascade into defined actions, employees will understand two very important things: (1) the company has a process that works; there is attention to it, follow up, and inclusion—this is, the process includes employees and provides assurance that someone is looking and searching for greatness. It pays off to do great work; (2) there is a path to improve. It pays off to stay in the company and demonstrate growth. For the best of the best talent, these are great news. They want someone to notice their great work, and they want a system of (positive) consequence for those who excel. Noting makes a place more vital than a place that is 'listening' and seeing what I do, noticing great work, and making bold bets on people to grow. All of those are symbols of a liberating, vital company where the best talent can express their selves through masterpieces and making the company, and others around them better.

- **#9—Define a Pay and Rewards policy**. Given the singular importance of pay and all forms of rewards, this area is normally well documented and observant of all regulations that apply locally in a global company. A vital redesign for Pay will center on performance-based Pay equity, equity in promotion, advancement of all types of employees per ethnic or other categories of grouping. While all companies will strive for equity, it is better for credibility and operational consistency that the company develops a Pay Equity Policy. This is, a statement that will create process and metrics to ensure certain metrics are produced and actions are taken to keep within policy expectations. A strategic Pay policy, with nuance and consideration for competitive factors, velocity for transformation, and cost structure, is crucial for the future of work, otherwise, finding out about misalignments too far down the road will make it very difficult to correct without infusing large amounts of money and most importantly, to change the perception in the employment market that your company pays low.

The Manager; A Critical and Pivotal Factor for Leading Success

#5—The manager. In the same table on Fig. 11.6 there is one process that cuts across both, critical and pivotal priorities, and that is our wild card: *the manager*. Earlier in our introduction and later in the definition of culture we mentioned just how important managers are for any organization. A vital place to work may lack a number of tools, processes, and definitions but if they have good managers, there is light at the end of the tunnel and our people will be fine. That does not mean we will be ready for a major transformation, but the company will not implode. That is the importance of great managers. Leading Success, aspiring to build an environment for liberation, vitality, and authentic expression requires managers to play a conscious role in this construction project. The liberating and vital environment that will allow for employee expression to elevate performance with depth and duration, making success sustainable.

In Conclusion: Writing History with Talent Vitality

Some years ago, I was the head of executive and leadership development at Motorola, and at the time we were working to apply the principles and insights from researchers from the Center For Creative Leadership, most notably, from Dr. Morgan McCall Jr. He had just released a book called *High Flyers*[10] about strategies organizations implement to develop leaders and find people who distinguished themselves as high-potential talent. Early in the book he references a remarkable metaphor of leadership based on the first American astronauts, said to have *the right stuff*—as memorialized in Tom Wolfe's book with the same name[11] and subsequent movie—a truly inspirational story. I have wondered over the years to what degree the challenge itself became a contributor for 'the right stuff' to show up, to emerge. Think about it for a minute—the opportunity to become one of the first astronauts to go into space for America, bring the country back from the difficult circumstance of falling to second place in the space race with the Soviet Union; and rewrite history in the process, set a new standard.

Few challenges bring a higher value proposition, or feel more vital and liberating than that. Few position names have the power of 'astronaut' to define excellence at its highest level and expectation. The Mercury and subsequently the Apollo Programs had the perfect mix for history-making environment. The mission, the moment, the elite talent; individuals who would have been *only* 'excellent' in history, if not for the unique mission and project at stake by which they became 'immortal'. In other words, the mission allowed for the talent (and the organization) to shine in its full glory.

In smaller ways, we tend to raise to the occasion when the opportunity is there. So many stories of unsuspected heroes populate out folklore and storytelling. The point here is that a liberating purpose matters more than just a literary, feel-good narrative. Some goals are a lot more than 'just goals' in your organization. Sometimes the story becomes the catalyst of ultimate high performance. As a liberating leader it is your responsibility to point to the North Star in its most meaningful and liberating expression to create something that only organizational 'astronauts' can achieve. Release the astronaut that lives inside your people.

But there is an additional reflection to be made about this remarkable story that illuminates the path to an organic, authentic, diverse, and inclusive organization. These astronauts were remarkable individuals, the elite among the elite. And yet, notably, parallel stories show that women[12] and minorities[13] were marginalized from the opportunity to compete for an astronaut seat and show their mettle, presumably, also with the right stuff. Even the mythical Chuck Yeager, a former General Brigadier of the United States Air Force, considered by many the best pilot who ever lived, and who, according to his official website[14] was.

> … the man who best epitomizes the unique blend of qualities that writer Tom Wolfe captured in the title of his 1979 best seller, The Right Stuff. For Wolfe, Yeager stood at the apex of "the ziggurat pyramid of flying" and was "the most righteous of all the possessors of the right stuff."

But Chuck Yeager, the pilot whose skills defined the right stuff, did not have an opportunity either. Yeager was excluded due to a lack of a formal degree, a very important and rigid filter at the time. From the perspective of talent, the story of the selection process for our first astronauts was also a story of selective opportunity, for multiple reasons consistent to their time, but selective opportunity nonetheless. The mission went on to be an epoch-defining success, and at the same time, a great opportunity was missed to recognize the best pilot who ever lived and to include *everyone who truly embodied the right stuff* on the opportunity to compete for the glory to belong in the lore of immortality; a distinction that could have been inspirational and life-changing for millions of people for decades to come.

The vital working place is one with great talent, but also one with a great challenge and the sense of a historical opportunity to have a legacy, the place where opportunity is available for everyone who demonstrates to have *the right stuff*. That sense of opportunity is what motivates those who separate themselves from the rest. As a liberating manager, never forget the power of a liberating North Star to build the capacity to succeed. Never underestimate the motivation power for the highest performers to know that no matter how they look, where they are from, how old they are, or who they love, they have a shot at 'immortality' in the scale of your company and mission. Hope matters—that is how your company grows naturally diverse, with equality of opportunity, not shortcuts and fast tracks, as many people misunderstand equality of opportunity to be.

If your ambition and transformation are akin to 'going to the moon' in your industry, you need to realize this is not something you can buy, no talent in the market will just show up and perform, you still have to create the environment, set a stage for success, and signal that the opportunity for greatness is open.

The above is not only for big projects. The Right Stuff is an illustration of how regular managers can impact performance by presenting their aspirations in bold ways, history-writing challenges, legend-building aspirations, and create spaces for greatness to show, defining the liberating value you expect, and opening opportunity for the company to do better. Everyday, in every way, talent vitality can be present in every manager, in every team, and for everyone. The emergence of talent success and the naturally diverse organization are therefore *organic* to the way the company operates.

Notes

1. Maslow, Abraham H. (1943). A Theory of Human Motivation. Psychological Review, 50, 370–396. 1943.
2. Clifton, J., & Harter, J. (2023). Culture shock: An unstoppable force is changing how we work and live. Gallup's solution to the biggest leadership issue of our time. Gallup Press.
3. Gartner. (2018). Playbook for the future of work: The CHRO Global Leadership Board. Gartner Inc.
4. De Smet, A., Dowling, B., Mugayar-Baldocchi, M., & Schaninger, B. (2022). The great attrition is making hiring harder: Are you searching the right talent pools? McKinsey Quarterly, July 2022.

5. Kowalski, G., & Ślebarska, K. (2022). Remote working and work effectiveness: A leader perspective. International Journal of Environmental Research and Public Health, 19(22), 15326. https://doi.org/10.3390/ijerph192215326.
6. Venkataramani, Swetha. (2021). Make way for a more human-centric Employee Value Proposition. Gartner, Human Resources Insights, digital article May 13, 2021. Retrieved from: https://www.gartner.com/smarterwithgartner/make-way-for-a-more-human-centric-employee-value-proposition.
7. Lewis, M. (2003). Moneyball: The art of winning an unfair game. W. W. Norton & Company. New York, NY.
8. Buckingham, M., & Goodall, A. (2015). Reinventing performance management: How one company is rethinking peer feedback and the annual review, and trying to design a system to fuel improvement. Harvard Business Review, April 2015.
9. Cappelli, P., & Tavis, A. (2016). The performance management revolution: The focus is shifting from accountability to learning. Harvard Business Review, October 2016.
10. McCall, M. W. (1998). High flyers: Developing the next generation of leaders. Harvard Business Review. Boston, MA.
11. Wolfe, T. (1979). The right stuff. Farrar, Straus and Giroux.
12. Ackmann, M. (2003). The Mercury 13: The true story of thirteen women and the dream of space flight. Random House.
13. Jackson, S. (2020, February 18). Ed Dwight was going to be the first African American in space. Until he wasn't: The Kennedy administration sought a diverse face for the space program, but for reasons unknown, the pilot was kept from reaching the stars. Smithsonian Magazine. https://www.smithsonianmag.com.
14. Chuck Yeager. General Brigadier Chuck Yaeger Official Website (2024). Retrieved from: https://chuckyeager.com.

12

Organization: Winning with Signature Processes

We arrive to the third discipline under the vitality mindset—Organization. The question we intend to answer is: how do we connect the organizational components in the best way possible to unleash the maximum yield for the organization? This is, sustained performance, people engagement, business innovation, and change capability.

In order to achieve this maximum potential, the disciplines of Talent and Organization are intricately related. As you look at the combined set of work streams in Fig. 9.2—back in Chapter Nine, we have five main components for vitality design:

Business Processes. The main ways in which the company creates the products and services customers pay for. Vitality requires these processes to adapt and evolve in order to achieve the necessary capabilities for customer success, consistent with our values, thus becoming Signature Processes.

People and Business Processes integration. In addition to the examination of People Processes as part of the Talent Discipline, a vital organization requires a purposeful connection at the business processes to ensure the transformational value is created.

Organization Empowerment. Commonly known as organization structure—or organization chart—is a critical design for the organization to facilitate agility, effective decision-making, accountability, and empowerment.

Business Metrics. All companies have business metrics, some required by investors and regulators. For a vital organization, metrics must reflect the critical capabilities required for transformation success, in particular those capabilities directly connected to the vision becoming the experience.

Governance. Vital governance will focus on decision effectiveness, risk response, and coordination. Good governance preserves the vitality of the organization by consistently focusing on how the vision becomes the customer and employee experience, through Signature Processes.

Taken as a whole, a good organization design plays a significant role in employee experience and productivity. This is one of the reasons why Japanese automakers disrupted the US market so decisively back in the seventies and eighties. The way their workers were involved in the manufacturing process, with real power to alter its design, gave them enormous speed to operation improvements and feedback to product design. Clear goals, clear tasks, elimination of waste at both operational and administrative levels,[1] enabled the creation of new frontiers of productivity inspired by ambitious ideals like 'zero defects', 'total quality', and their relentless focus on customers before finances. Their organization design was not only about reporting lines, but processes, roles, protocols of communication, and the common understanding of improvement to reach zero defects. But that is an exception. The scope of what is commonly understood as 'organization design' is reduced to its interpretation as the *organization chart*. Rarely we see all the five components described above in the design documents, project plans, and implementation. Modifying the DNA of the organization, however, does require us to unpack every aspect of the organization to redesign it consistent to transformation goals and vitality. In this section we will discuss how each of these five organization design components are designed for vitality and a liberating experience.

Business Processes

The more radical and ambitious the transformation, the more adjustment and change will have to occur in our processes to make it real. A great example is provided by the movies industry. In the mid-nineties production studios increasingly moved their technology from film-based to digital recording, impacting processes for every aspect in the value chain: storage, equipment, editing, and distribution, even requiring new investments in movie theaters. However, the new technology allowed for faster editing and opened door for multiple sources of revenue as the digital product was transferable to a variety of platforms, not only movie theaters or tape rentals. Automation in manufacturing had a similar effect in how materials are procured, fed into machines, transported, and measured, which had to be modified to exploit the new capacities and flexibilities of the new process and technology. It is always important to improve business processes, but some transformations need more than that, and sometimes the new process *is* the transformation that brings the value, like it was the case in the video and music digital production. Transformation, therefore, will require leaders to determine how success looks like in the new ways processes must operate in the desired future.

There are multiple ways to classify business processes in organizations. The illustration in Fig. 12.1 shows two broad categories: Differentiation and Acceleration. Differentiation processes focus on the conversion cycle for customer value, including the entire customer processes from market research to product development all the way to customer experience, sales, revenue operations, and service. This conversion category of processes is the center of gravitation for the business: the ways in which an organization connects with, understands the needs from, and creates value for their customers, sharpening the company's differentiation from competitors.

The second category includes all the related—and essential—enabling infrastructure necessary for the conversion to be possible, efficient, profitable. This is, activities centered on supplying all the necessary materials, IP and components, transportation, information systems, data, reporting, analytics, as well as an effective order to cash cycle and the management of all financial assets, both physical and intangibles. This category of processes is subordinated to the conversion in the sense that it should adapt itself to maximize the value potential for customers and do its best to stay out of the way, be invisible and yet, provide guidelines for maximum velocity and effectiveness, that is why I call this cluster *Acceleration.*

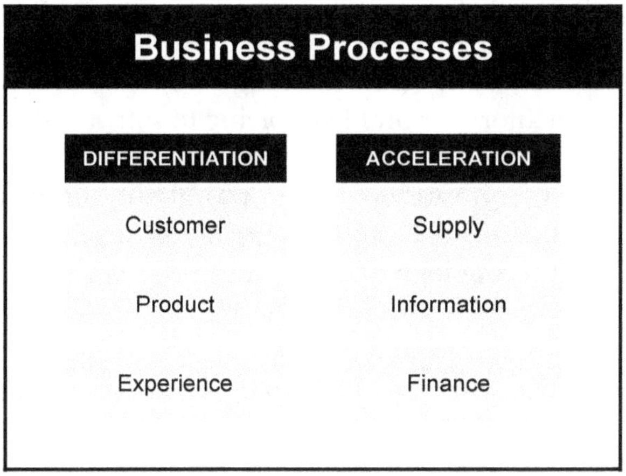

Business Processes

DIFFERENTIATION	ACCELERATION
Customer	Supply
Product	Information
Experience	Finance

Fig. 12.1 The signature business process inventory

The Anatomy of a Differentiating Business Process

The reality of any business is that no matter what we offer, there are always constraints of space, time, logistics, supply chains, and capacity of partners and infrastructures to evolve their operations according to our transformation, or evolving them fast enough. Consider the software industry and its evolution over the last fifty years. In the early days of computing programming the instructions to process data, accomplish the tasks for large computers to crank financial, scientific, or administrative data in large programs, had to be performed by experts, using large, sophisticated equipment called mainframes. This programming was accomplished by feeding perforated cards to run the programs. Every change to the program had to be punched in new cards to be reinserted for a re-run. As technology evolved, with direct interface via terminals instead of perforated cards, computers could be shared, they became easier to use, expanding the benefits of computer processing to new areas of application in industry and businesses, but still outside of homes and the common person. With the arrival of the personal computer people had the chance to experiment and be part of the digital era. Three factors gave rise to the digital era as we know it today: first, large amounts of people experiencing personal computers, using software at home solving daily problems, giving everyone a level of familiarity with common programs and games; second, the arrival of the cellular telephony giving birth to mobile devices, ever more capable and powerful, and increasingly being designed for a digital experience, not just as a "phone"; and third, telecommunications technology for mobility, data security, and e-commerce, with a global infrastructure to handle the convergence of the three factors above, in real time, globally. Computing, software, coding, evolved from problem solving to comprehensive, modular, scalable, solutions and personalization, causing a shift on the differentiating value from computing capacity, processing power, memory for problem solving to software development, vast amounts of it, to leverage all the flexibility and possibilities such universe brings. For business, software no longer was about automation, administration, but instead, it evolved into an engine of business growth. Process requirements forced technology to evolve to a point where this combination of technology and process moved from being an enabling infrastructure to become a differentiating capability.

You have to wonder, what was the human process to sustain the backbone of this software revolution?

The convergence of computer capacity, memory, processing speed, the new demand in consumers and industry applications created an astronomical demand in IT departments. The work could no longer be done in the traditional ways—a new operational model was required. The complexity of these software and hardware combinations is such that a whole new way to manage and operate processes to produce software had to be invented. First, in the shape of maturity progression to understand design and the evolving capability of software; this was the *Capability Maturity Model*, developed at Carnegie Mellon University in the mid-nineties.[2] But the growing complexity and interoperability necessary to deliver on a mobile, ubiquitous experience required to also look at the production approach utilized to write, test, and launch code to production. This led to a complete rethinking of the business processes to follow radically new approaches moving away from a predictable waterfall approach to an adaptive *agile* approach, first described formally in *The Agile Manifesto*,[3] leading to the formalization of the Agile Methodology. For anybody not familiar with the term, Agile is a broad term to include a series of techniques and methodologies with the purpose of adapting to rapid change in user's needs. In its core, it is a work classification and prioritization mechanism to coordinate resources dynamically as needs arise and change, making the most capacity out of scarce resources and the most flexibility out of a software team. Without Agile, the rapid growth of software solutions in your phones, TVs, and their links to all sorts of services would not be possible.

The Agile example serves to illustrate that the design—or adoption—of the right business processes is paramount on both the ability to achieve goals and how people will experience being successful in their work. In a different example, a college may start offering online classes for their students. That opens the market to students from other geographies, possibly different time zones. The traditional planning and set up for success on virtual modalities will require new technology, new policies, and new ways of working, possibly including how we evaluate the students. A manufacturing company may be seeking to offer customers a large array of options of features in their products and decide the best way to do that is to adapt their process to manufacture to specific orders, instead of creating large inventories. The traditional resource planning, supply chain, the accounting, and materials flow will have to change to accommodate for this new vision.

But there is more. Process innovation implies new methods and, in most cases, new technology. Therefore, process innovation inevitably creates organizational capability gaps in your transformation, like all technology transfer processes do. People needs to learn the new ways of work or at least the ways to operate the new equipment, software, materials. The experts in your operation will be the reliable guides to map the sequence of steps this learning and adapting should include. There is never a solution in a box on process improvement, this will be a discovery process. What is liberating for your transformation is to recognize there is a real need to plan for the adaptation, it is not something to be left to chance, for 'people to figure out'. There is planning, there is training, investment, and therefore, a new definition of success and performance. That is ultimately how this transfer will be complete and productive.

From 'Support Areas' to *Business Acceleration*

Business acceleration covers an important array of infrastructure for the conversion process to function properly. Those areas are called the "support areas", a term consistent with the Industrial and Financial eras—see Fig. 4.1. In the Customer and Purpose eras—where we are today—the enabling infrastructure is about *business acceleration*, not just support. This is because the adaptation to transformative processes requires constant improvement and innovation within that infrastructure: how we procure, measure, supply materials, manage data, use software, computer power, align workflows, optimize facilities, and tools to mention a few. Each one of those points of contact with the conversion process becomes either a factor of delay or a factor of acceleration, making those areas agents of value creation.

To better understand the migration from support areas to business acceleration it is illuminating to examine a little closer the software story. In the early days, the 1950s to 1970s, software applications were called 'programs' and were single focused on solving particular problems for companies. In most cases those problems were administrative—payroll, inventory management—not core customer or consumer orientated. For those companies, software (coding, programming) was a *support area*. Within a couple of decades software became part of the core business of companies driving digital enterprise connectivity, e-commerce, personalization, telecommunications, directly linked to customer acquisition and revenue. In other words, *business acceleration*.

While not every function can replicate the scale of what the software capability did, functions like HR are not fundamentally different. In the industrial era companies needed employee services and workforce availability—a *support* value proposition. But today, in the Customer and Purpose era with business imperatives and enterprise success highly dependent on exceptional talent and people intangibles—customer relations, innovation, design, leadership—we see a comparable migration for the People Function toward business acceleration; as it should be the case for every infrastructure area.

Where Does Accelerating Value Come from?

The enterprise value from the business acceleration areas comes in several key enablers:

- **Information**, including all forms of data, measurements, control, automation, product and process parameters, as well as qualified decision-making protocols for operational productivity. There is significant potential for value and for waste in the management of information. There is no coincidence that we need CIOs and CTOs with large teams to address this huge enabler.
- **Simplification**, to examine and determine how to reduce or eliminate the steps necessary to accomplish the conversion. In simplification, the approach matters significantly. Consider the question 'How do we simplify this process?', compared to 'how do we make this process unnecessary altogether?', and then compared to 'what needs to be true for this entire array of steps to be completed in seconds, not in hours?'. Each question has a growing potential of value, and vitality to it.
- **Design**. The enabling infrastructure must be appropriately configured to function properly. However, higher value will require us to go beyond a 'lay-out' of components, it requires the adoption of a perspective the consulting firm IDEO called *Human-Centered Design*[4]. This perspective is much broader than just process design, it is an entire design philosophy that puts human needs at the center—in this case, the need to be in a vital environment for productivity and self-expression. The right human design facilitates extraordinary performance, reduces cost, makes it simpler, inclusive, comfortable, harmonious, and aesthetic.

Information, simplification, and design are dimensions inextricably related to human activity and performance. There is therefore a need to connect the business processes to People Processes as we described those processes earlier in Chapter Ten.

People and Business Processes Integration

People processes, such as hiring, managing performance, payment, training are closely connected, and well integrated with business processes. But there are levels of integration between people and business that raises the bar in terms of impact. On one layer is the supply of necessary elements for conversion, in this case the people to do the work. The common company will be satisfied with this layer of impact. However, in the presence of an accelerated curve of innovation, growth, and complexity, we are interested on value above supply; this is, the creation of new capability, not just more capacity. What does this mean?

In every job, the work people do creates more than just the output of the job itself: it creates *capability*—new abilities and capacities for the organization that are permanent and replicable. This is what people learn, understanding of how the processes flow better, and operational innovation. Creating capability is a surplus of a vital design. In a higher level of integration, deliberate actions and steps are used to leverage the opportunity provided by the task or the project being performed to learn in the way learning organizations do: experiencing, analyzing, codifying, documenting, and sharing. New methods, new technologies, new problems to solve are extraordinary grounds for people development and should not be wasted. Transformations bring along learning environments that open a self-reinforcing loop: productivity-learning-innovation which is the vital integration of work and people. In practice, some of these integration opportunities include:

- Build transformation teams with people from different areas and different experience, tenure, backgrounds.
- Include people in teams for the main reason to be a learner.
- Perform 'post-mortem' sessions focused on what was learned in the process or project.
- Give leadership roles in the project to people who normally does not have managerial responsibilities.
- Formalize and communicate process improvements or innovations resulting from the lessons learned.
- Use the above opportunities for recognition.

A third layer of integration is the very act of knowing better about the demand side of the Talent Economy model. This is, how the new technologies, or new processes alter the skills necessary to accomplish the goals? For example, in the last few years the expertise in social media, digital analytics, experience design exploded across companies, industries, and countries, including governments and non-for-profit organizations. A good understanding on how the work people do will change as new methods are implemented, informs the People Function how to model skill demand, enrich the position profiles, and prepare better to address the talent market. The same happened with software development skills after the pandemic. Every company discovered how urgent it was to become digital, to have an offering consumable through interactive, mobile experiences. The explosion of software engineers demand made it even worse for a market that was already small. Business process, transformation requirements have an impact that must be quantified and planned for in organization design. The next big wave is going to be related to Artificial Intelligence in the workplace. We will discuss this further in Chapter Nineteen, People Outcomes.

Organization Empowerment

Everyone is familiar with organization designs, perhaps even more familiar with redesigns, usually called *reorganizations*. Some companies have been forced to go on multiple rounds of organizational changes year over year in order to adapt to extreme changing conditions; in some places it has become a common occurrence, to the dismay of managers and employees who constantly have to adapt.

Where do organization changes come from? It is almost inevitable that at some point in the transformation every company will be forced to align the organization to be more consistent to its renewed purpose and goals. It may be a need to create new areas, integrate departments, separate groups, or simply adjust cost structure. In every case, organization design should be concerned with four distinct outcomes: functional structure, clear accountability, power distribution, and agile connectedness. We can think of organization design the way architects design living spaces, after all, that is a great analog for organizations. Architects design functional space for people who needs to accomplish something, fulfill a goal. Different goals will call for different space solutions: houses, schools, warehouses, banks, etc. Architects work to understand the needs for the space before they can recommend specifics such as how many rooms, halls, corridors, stairways the space will have. They take into account a number of parameters like how many people will live or visit, what unique facilities, tools, or installations will be required—swimming pool? Larger parking lot? Architects take all that information, visit the site, understand the context of weather, terrain, materials available, and learn about the client's vision for the space—style, look, and feel, intangibles, the culture the space should project. Only then it is possible to 'architect' a *solution*, blueprints, materials, specifications.

Now imagine an architectural design that only tells you how many rooms the building will have and that there will be hallways and stairs to connect them but does not indicate how they connect, where the doors and windows must be; it does not say either where the halls will be, how deep and how wide they are. It also says there are bathrooms, kitchen, garage, but fails to explain how the rooms and the common areas build the functionality required for the use of the building. In short, we know what *is* in the building, but we don't know how the pieces *connect to operate*. Maybe top leaders don't think that is important at this stage, and therefore delegate to the crews to figure it out during construction. There is clarity on components but no clarity on how they become a solution for *success*.

Well, that level of undefinition is what you get if you see organization design as a structure organization chart. Valuable, but insufficient. Your builders—business units, functional leaders—will do their best to come up with the specific answers on their own. The electrician and the plumber will do their best, but you can't expect alignment, high performance.

The Five Risks that Erode Vitality in Organization Structure Design:

If you are architecting an organizational design, it is important to consider a handful of common aspects known to negatively affect organization designs.

- **Oversimplification.** Thinking that organization design is about defining the organization chart.
- **Wrong focus.** Missing success definition for roles. Focus on job's description, not transformation.
- **Past orientation.** Designing disproportionately for the present, instead of the future. Using past projections instead of future-back methods.
- **Personal, emotional.** Designing disproportionately to accommodate for people you like (or dislike!).
- **Transactional implementation.** Confusing one-way communication with commitment.

The above reveals important risks to avoid for a vital design of the organization. An organization design should not be a dozen of slides in a presentation, but it should not be a PhD dissertation either. There are proven methodologies[5] that help follow the common steps to get you to a good place. Failure, as I have witnessed, comes from the impatience of leaders rushing toward implementation, but also from their beliefs of what success looks like. Let's look at the five risks to elaborate on this point.

Mitigating Oversimplification: Design for power balance and conflict reduction. Every organization design has imperfections; it will not solve for everything. The representation of a hierarchical model such as an org chart, implies that the people on top will have the power to define the 'last mile'. Some of that is true, for example, several regional sales leaders come under a larger region and under one single leader. How the accounts get distributed is certainly something the head of that new larger region can resolve. However, when competing features to product design create conflict, the resolution of the conflict should not be delegated to the lower ranks. Local, special agreements can be achieved to alleviate design pressures but—typically, they come with great friction and time investment to land on a solution that may not work for everyone or that contradicts a larger policy. Not all conflicts are easy to resolve down below the ranks where players have less visibility to the broader picture and to the strategic decisions to sub-optimize areas for the larger good. In the most unsuccessful cases I have seen, teams are left to their own devices to find a solution. Leaders commonly advocate for their own needs and they reorient their work to "win" the negotiations, "defend" their functions and territories. Quickly your organization turns 'political', leaders become lobbyists for their points of view with the CEO, adversaries are created, and the culture rapidly erodes. Leadership must own enterprise design conflict resolution. A crack at the top means a canyon at the bottom.

A good starting point is to ensure tradition and comfort are not the driving values on design. In many places this will require a conscious effort. Historically, organization structures are considered the 'birth certificate' of the new era and the only document that truly matters for leaders because it provides the answers for silos definition and power distribution, not organization effectiveness. Most leaders are eager to see who they will be reporting to, who is reporting to who, for ultimate understanding of who won, who lost, where the power center is.

Our guiding light is the outcomes we are looking for: to architect ownership, decision-making, and accountability. Defined scopes, clarity on what is in and out, particularly if the scope is changing. Identification of new metrics and ways of work.

Mitigating the wrong focus: Center on success. Beyond tiles and Job Descriptions, define *success* and value. The next second risk I have identified is understating what success means when defining a role for a transformation. The Talent Economy perspective requires us to discuss, identify, and articulate what value each job is intending to create, not only what activities or duties the job needs to perform. The illustration in Fig. 12.2 highlights the main differences between the two. The amount of effort and detail will be proportional to the role; some critical roles will be more detailed, some others will be more numerical, but no job should be defined by describing the candidate we need. And that is, unfortunately, what happens most of the times. Under the pressure of time, hiring managers merge in their minds job needs and candidate profile in one single step and immediately start talking about the person they need. The discipline of Talent, under a talent economy perspective, is based on two differentiated steps: role profile, and candidate profile. Finding the value to the role may take only ten minutes, it does not have to be a whole new meeting, although sometimes it should be, for example, when hiring for a C-level job, or a GM in a new territory, a new division, etc. in those cases, yes, we should take our time. That is why every serious search firm will force client companies to define what are the needs of the job before they describe the ideal candidate.

Vital Design of Organization – Positions	
Common Job Description	**Position Profile for Value**
WHAT THE POSITION DOES	WHAT PROBLEM THE POSITION SOLVES
Defines **parameters of the role** for HR classification, valuation and hiring teams	Defines what **success** looks like in the position's **outcomes** after 2-3 years
• Title, Reporting line • Business context, culture, purpose • Duties, Responsibilities • Scope, Team, Budgets • Competencies, desirable experience • Candidate profile • Goals of Position in general	• Outcomes relevant to transformation • New capabilities to be created • What changes, what stays the same • Team, culture, organization outcomes • Problem or limitation to eradicate • All of the above in OKR format: quantifiable, specific, yes/no verifiable

Fig. 12.2 Difference between job description and position profile

12 Organization: Winning with Signature Processes

Requirements should be written answering the question: what does success look like for this role, today and tomorrow, based on our aspirations, our transformation, and our values? Leading Success starts becoming real in this exact point in the journey. It is not about what activities and responsibilities the role has, that is important context and baseline, particularly for compensation analysis, but the critical value-creation question is how we will look back after one or two years after the hiring and determine if the person has been successful in the role. That is the new standard, and the reason why we will need *Position Profiles* (Fig. 12.3) with two distinctive segments. Outcomes for success (not just results) and transformation expectations. For example, a role may have a revenue of $1.5 M a year, market share above 18% after year two. In addition, an economy-based talent discipline will indicate, that the job is also about building a collaborative team with diverse skills and backgrounds that relates to its wide customer base, build the next generation of product, the next generation of customer support capable to sustain these results over time. In terms of transformation, how the role contributes to the larger goals in the organization.

In other words, we need to get clarity on the parameters of success of a position (the value to be created in the position), and not just its activity. Position value is a better differentiator to help the Talent Acquisition teams judge candidates' experience, either internal or external. Here is an example of the Talent Profile focused on Talent Value (Fig. 12.3).

Lets explore a few important elements in the Position profile. First, the core focus of the position in the immediate future, indicates what needs

Position Profile	VP, New Business Unit					
Core focus now	• Build the new XYZ business unit to diversify sources of revenue and growth • Create a new business model *ecology* with existing business units • Collect disperse capabilities and resources to create a baseline operation • Establish a new team with clear focus and a strong culture of innovation					
Success Criteria 2-3 years	• Reach 45 M revenue at end of year 1 • Achieve NPS above 25 at end of year 2 • Reach market share of 10% or above at end of year 3 • Produce a product pipeline with at least 3 certified, approved products by end of year 1 • 30% of our company income come from this business unit at end of year 3					
Change Expectation						
Sustain	Improve		Accelerate	Turn around		Reinvent
Sustain success, strong focus on execution, not as much on changing the business	Continuity, Drive Improvement. Deploy performance improvement initiatives on same business model		Evolve the business under growing uncertainty, win hearts and minds, innovate and differentiate	Turn Around – Radical change in results. Dramatic improvement to realize ROI		Create or Redefine business model, reinvent the business, cultural evolution

Fig. 12.3 Example of a position profile

to be done most urgently. And the second section, describing the success criteria, indicates the parameters to be used within two or three years to assess if the role has accomplished its main purpose in the transformation journey. A success criteria is a set of longer-term goals, but broad enough to be accomplished in several cycles. This is how a position contributes to the larger purpose and goals of the company. The third section is a very important point we often miss in organization design and in the way we intend to fill the position with the right candidate. This is, setting expectations for the level of change expected. Not all positions require the same level of change, but if they do, we must ensure the candidate not only can perform the duties described in the job description, but just as important, that she or he can accomplish the change expectations set forth for the position. This is important in both directions: bringing a stability candidate to a job that needs a turnaround would be a misalignment. But the opposite is equally problematic; a leader that only can change but can't lead stability. Here are the definitions of those five categories of change.

- Sustain. Success on this role is largely (70–80%) about the execution of a pre-determined or already committed plan. The leader is not expected to radically modify or deviate from the established direction.
- Improve. Success on this role—in addition to executing on a plan—is about a radical improvement on critical business areas that most be corrected or addressed in the operations and customer experience. It is also about stabilizing the operation after significant changes.
- Accelerate. Success on this role is about innovation to accelerate growth, higher revenue, expanding customer share and base, new geographies, get to new markets, increase share, and secure the revenue budget and profitability through both organic and M&A strategies
- Turn Around. Success on this role is about an aggressive and significant change in the way the business is conducted, re-prioritization, reorganization, building new capabilities, addressing needs and opportunities in radical new ways.
- Reinvent. Success on this role is about business model innovation, redefining the basis for our revenue generation, product or brand differentiation to produce a quantum leap on the company's competitive positioning. Success will lead our access to emerging business opportunities or secure our relevance/permanence in the segment or geography.

Once success is defined, we can turn to candidates to have the people conversation.

12 Organization: Winning with Signature Processes

Hiring and promotions are the fastest ways to alter a culture and change the fortunes of a team or company. But companies run very fast, and the pressure to fill the jobs quickly escalates. While some jobs really can't wait, particularly in operations, distribution, call centers, we will raise the speed to hire in order to respond to the urgency; we can spend less time on value analysis because those urgent operational roles are mostly defined in terms of process output, production quota, less on transformation nuances. For every other job, Leading Success will require us to do our best on predicting how likely is that a candidate will match the value and success description in the position profile; both in skills and mindsets. While this is essential for every role, it is even more critical for people manager roles. Managers have a disproportionate weight on employee experience, in the company's results and its transformation, and therefore, any candidate for a manager position has to be carefully vetted in terms of Leading Success parameters: liberation, vitality, and expression, as defined in the position profile. Finding the right manager means that after the data and interview analysis, the candidate *trends* as a liberating leader, energy contributor, vital, and open minded—granted that she or he has the technical abilities required for the job. Mindsets and beliefs are not very easy to find in resumes and interviews, some people master the art of interviewing while disclosing as little as possible about themselves, that is why we will need additional tools, reference checks, and assessments. We can never be sure we will have all the information we need to guarantee we are getting the leader we need, but we will be able to identify markers, tendencies, preferences to give us a clue.

Mitigating past-orientation. There are two risks on bringing the past to limit the future. One is designing the organization to sustain the old structures of relevance or power, and the second is to hire people to preserve existing strengths at the expense of those we need for the future. In the first case companies run into hard decisions. You may have the largest revenue segment, destined to decline considering technology and other trends and then you also have the new business unit that is projected by industry, not just your estimations, to grow significantly in years to come. You also know that nothing is completely certain and the last thing CEOs want to do is to increase the level of risk in the operation that is currently bringing the bulk of revenue into the organization. There is no equation or mathematical certainty that things will play out as expected. This means that a degree of uncertainty has to be accepted in the calculus, but bold moves have proven successful if we follow some notable cases. In his excellent book Creativity Inc, about the creation of Pixar, the author Ed Catmull[6], shares a great story about George Lucas, who having just released Star Wars in 1977, decided to create a whole new Computers Division in his Lucas Films studio, something visionary and substantially ahead of the industry at that time. This gave George Lucas a long head start in a nascent technology that would completely change the industry for decades to come. Another masterful example of past-to-future orientation is provided by Bryce Hoffman in his book *American Icon*[7], about Allan Mulally's tenure as CEO of Ford Motor Company, describing how divided Ford was at the time he became CEO and how their biggest risk was to stay that way. Innovations and even market insights were not shared among its car divisions, causing duplication, delay, cost, and most importantly, lack of organizational capacity to learn from their own experience, at the time others were running away with market share. The future-enabling decision was—as simple as it sounds—to unite Ford as ONE FORD. The extraordinary story dives into the nuanced difficulties of how such a simple strategy may include so many hurdles and challenges and serves to illustrate that future orientation's worst enemies are the perceived success of the past and the perceived comfort of the present. Future orientation can take multiple forms, not all of them have to be about technology, sometimes a single identity is the biggest obstacle to collaboration, innovation, and success. If a company indicates something is the most important area or capacity for the future but fails to indicate who is in charge of that, we have an inconsistency. Leaders want to say that 'we all' in the management team have that priority in our goals and that is how we ensure things will happen, but some capabilities will require someone 24 × 7 thinking on that exact agenda, and a resourced, credible roadmap.

The moral of this story is—go bold. Waiting too long may prove more disruptive than the potential internal disruption at risk.

In the second case, hiring people for the present, the risk is higher because while structural decisions for total organization, its segments, divisions, departments fall in the purview of CEOs and possibly Board Members, the decision to hire employees sits under every manager in the organization, and the variation can be significant. It is not uncommon that managers see candidates rationally, understanding they need certain profile to move faster into the future and yet, end up selecting someone different, someone friendlier to the status quo, less disruption. Hiring for the past in those jobs situated in the middle to lower levels in the organization are a huge invisible risk for companies. Although, the problem is not exclusive of those levels, when it happens at the top it is easier to detect because there are more checks and balances, not always the same across the layers. If a company is not culturally committed to hire for the future—what we would call higher potential people with the skills, we need to break into new markets and constant innovation—we are slowing down the engine for generations ahead.

Finally, another common trap on past orientation is the salary structure. New skills trending on the market will drive higher salary expectations, creating the dilemma of the *internal justice problem*. Bringing differentiating talent means people on similar levels in organization, with superior skills and experience, will have different salaries creating an internal equity disruption. It is quite unfortunate but there is no way around it, unless hiring managers abdicate and choose salary consistency over high-potential talent. I have seen managers under-hire on talent quality just to stay away from dealing with salary differences. If a company is trying to become something different, it will be inevitable breaking the mold in several places, including compensation practices, judiciously and selectively. Equally important in this regard, are the fears some managers have for not being able to master the future bringing talent that possess those out of the box skills the manager may not possess her/himself.

Mitigating a personal, emotional design. Vital organization designs work deliberately to avoid biases toward people. But that requires conscious effort because we are emotional beings, and we are innately inclined to *listen* to our reactions and feelings; after all, that is also part of the managerial instinct. There are a few ways to work to limit such influence on the design of an organization:

- **Performance vs culture.** Once a leader proves to be exceptionally valuable, it is not uncommon to see a strong bias toward giving this people more responsibility. In most cases all works well, but a few risks should be verified before decisions are made. In addition to performance and results it is imperative to look at the culture beneath their people; understand what culture each leader is creating as legacy for the organization. Some extraordinary business results come at a very high cultural cost. Most of us have seen that before; great performance comes from an empire-building leader who creates concession spaces from leaders above and rewards loyalty from leaders below. These are hard conversations for CEOs but the ones Jack Welch was most concerned about: those leaders who perform well but in the wrong ways.
- **Rewarding with scope.** While giving more responsibility to high performers is consistent with a developmental and financial approach, a line of demarcation will be necessary to avoid overdoing it. Disproportionate amount of operation under a leader creates unbalance of resources, weighted decision-making, and uneven power dynamics. Beyond the sheer

size or organizations is the issue of potentially gluing things that do not belong together or creating conflicts of interest. For example, giving a regional leader an additional global role focused on distributing resources to regions. Giving leaders smaller versions of global functions to have their own 'shadow team' on functional or design work. These are very confusing arrangements for the operation and should be carefully considered, perhaps on a temporary basis in case of legitimate emergency.

- **Pleasing performers.** A related, but different problem appears when leaders do not agree with the organization. In other words, they do not like what they got in the redesign. Some threaten the company with leaving creating pressure on top management to agree on concessions, others make unreasonable demands. It is a very human process, and CEOs will be tested. Once a decision is made, it works in everyone's best interest to hold the line and stay on course with the design unchanged. It may be necessary to make adjustments, but those have to be harmonized with the interest of the business, or they will come at a high cost on consistency and leadership equity.
- **Too much subjectivity?** In my experience I rarely see emotionality absent in organization design—although, nobody will admit it. Leaders like some people more than others and their final decisions are affected by it. Certainly, at some levels everyone is competent, but the distribution of work—and thus, power—tends to include a not unsignificant portion of emotion. It is on these cases that consultants can add significant value to organizations, by bringing a more objective criteria to at least make it transparent for leaders to what degree they may be overstating their personal preferences.

Should we expect objectivity, rationality on decisions over power distribution? Yes, but it will demand a conscious effort from the leaders to eliminate biases. Organization design should be about the commitment to the vision. But in reality, we see all sorts of situations and we must be careful not to fall on these non-rational traps. Typical problems that come with these decisions include CEOs or c-suite leaders who understand someone to be the best talent for a role but feel uncomfortable with the person. It could be as simple as old disagreements, clash of personalities, feeling threatened, or it could be a case of diversity, language, style, being uncomfortable with someone who thinks very different from them.

As mentioned before, methodologies will help, but the real reasons organization designs stall is not as much the methodology or the rational part of it, but the human side of things, see the list below.

12 Organization: Winning with Signature Processes

Common examples of emotionality in organization design.

- Bringing someone you know for a job that is not a fit—but you like the person.
- Half-way decisions. Unable to determine a leader for a certain area you split work in unnatural ways, undermining one or the two people in the process.
- Trying to 'signal' to someone you no longer trust her/him, hoping the person will just quit, and work to diminish the roles artificially, creating conflicts.
- Stop believing on a leader and instead of firing the person, you act on the organization, by diminishing it, creating a cultural crisis.
- Mixing areas only because someone you value wants it.
- Not shielding future revenue enough—per Leading from the Future.
- Creating unnecessary roles only because a loyal leader needs a job.

This is one of those reserved spaces for the head of Human Resources to advise and guide. Even if the CEO or the leader of the group is not ready to concede on her/his beliefs, triggering a thinking process is a necessary step in the right direction.

Mitigating transactional implementation. Organization designs are not simple constructs to absorb. It will be necessary to stage a strategic introduction with deep dives. Every design will still require people to complete tasks and make decisions not contemplated in documents, procedures, and policies. People, therefore, must understand the principles of the newly architected space. No matter how hard you try, your design will have areas less defined, and other areas only visible from a different level. Nuanced design makes competitive differentiation possible, therefore it will be important that the interactions are clear, by defining the 'handshakes', borrowing the term from Gregory Kesler and Amy Kates[8], which take into account the 'last mile' of interactions to design for coordination and velocity. In very simple terms, what is changing at any level needs to make sense and be explicit to be implemented. If for example, we will no longer have customization in some product lines, how will that modify everything and everyone who are involved: from what salespeople say to customers, all the way to inventories, systems of record, pricing, etc. Other changes may be less complex, but still important, like the implementation of a new policy for remote work. How is that going to be implemented, what managers can and cannot do, how we run the administration of choices and logistics for people to have desks, participate in meetings. All these changes in the organization have the five components of Talent and Organization and align with Culture and the EVP.

A good design does not leave unresolved those open-ended questions that will undermine its effectiveness. Successful companies do not leave to chance how they implement important changes.

Business Metrics

A well-known quality principle leading to the Japanese manufacturing revolution from the sixties to the end of the Century was 'measure to manage'. Metrics are revolutionary and fly under the radar on big transformations. The truth is that if you want anything to happen, just measure it. The competitive nature of your organization will take over and march toward it. Sometimes too literally, so you have to be careful. Some managers are so committed to the metric that in their unwavering pursue of the rating or score—and the corresponding incentive—they may try forcing the issue. That may carry consequences if we did not think well about the ramifications. In setting sales goals, with mixed products we should be clear if we care only for the sales numbers or if we care for the mix. Sometimes sales can be achieved with an unfavorable mix for the broader company. People matters may ger complicated too; diversity goals cannot be stated as numbers alone or we will get quota-making behaviors with all the complications we know. Therefore, as important as they are, we need to keep in mind that *metrics are not the goal*, they describe it, but metrics are not reality, and some leaders need to be reminded that it is never about the metric but the reality that produces it. For a process to improve, metrics cannot do the job alone, we will need intelligent conversations about cause and effect, considerations of history, culture that need to be addressed for a metric to reveal our process is indeed moving in the right direction. We will call that *governance*, as we will see in the next section.

Metrics bring a wealth of opportunity for culture affirmation and simplification. Based on common transformation needs here are five focus areas to ensure vitality in your metrics:

1. **Measure what matters.** Quantifiable outcomes. In his book *Measure What Matters*, author John Doerr[9] makes the point that there are few metrics that really matter to run a business. His perspective on metrics fully connects with a vitality designed organization. Measurements are costly, time-consuming activities, they multiply very easily, and almost never die.

They linger for long time even if they are not used. It could be that a report is someone's job, or that they are automated, but mostly because after some time, goals and incentives are attached to certain metrics, over time organizations finally master the metrics and refuse to let them go. But what if it is the wrong metric? The first priority for metrics is to pick the right one. Second priority is to define it in ways that it can be quantifiable, with independent numbers coming from the field or the process, or in ways that they can be evaluated with a yes/no answer. For vitality to flourish, we must concentrate in few metrics that are reliable to assess success. In that sense a metric is evidence of success.

2. **Choose transparency**. Metrics that matter should be known by the organization. That is how people gets to understand and believe in the path we are following, appreciate small wins, and make adjustments. It brings an equalitarian culture to bear, as everyone can see where we all stand. This is not to say we will flood the teams with everything we measure. We live in a world where we must protect some information. A vital culture will require to choose what is public and be as transparent as practically possible, even if it gets to a place of initial discomfort. There are ways to publish results, using dashboards with the key results data, some relevant statistics, trends, and other important referential information such as benchmarks, or competitors' public data. The point is, metrics not shared are a wasted opportunity for change and the acceleration of the transformation.

3. **Design metrics with customer and culture in mind**. The golden rule of metric selection is to make sure we are paying attention to things that matter to our customers and to the company's competitive positioning. An important decision is to balance how much we measure internally versus externally. Net Promoter Score, customer satisfaction, market share are examples of external metrics, while productivity, efficiency, cost to produce goods are examples of internal metrics. This balance is important also for cultural reasons, companies should not be too inwardly focused, only measuring things they can control inside their organizations. People must be affirmed that they belong to a competitive place that sets its eyes high, competing with the best of the best.

4. **Design metrics about your EVP, liberation, and vitality**. While you cannot measure 'liberation' directly, there will be questions that will have a close approximation to the concept of liberation by looking at employee experience, particularly as it relates to the company's values. The best way to do that is by creating metrics that reflect the dimensions of your Employee Value Proposition.

5. **Keep a separate dashboard for DEIB and ESG.** As discussed earlier in this book, diversity is an important feature of successful organizations and an imperative to survival in most industries. While not everyone thinks that way, for the purposes of Leading Success and the furthering of a liberating, vital work environment, we need a place where everyone feels they can belong, be their best selves, and enjoy the same opportunities as everyone else regardless of any personal characteristics, preferences, or choices they make in their lives. We will elaborate on Diversity in Chapter Eighteen. What we will say now is that wanted or not, recognized or not, diversity is a huge deal for our employees and for our productivity, and something that companies should not ignore.

Governance

Our final component for organization design is Governance for Vitality. Most leaders have clear understanding of what corporate governance means, including aspects of accountability, transparency, risk management, strategic oversight, performance, investors, and succession, some variations exist depending on industry and country.

A governance model serves to concentrate multi-layered input, gain insight from different perspectives, and improve decision-making to ensure the interests of all stakeholders are taken into account in the strategic direction of the

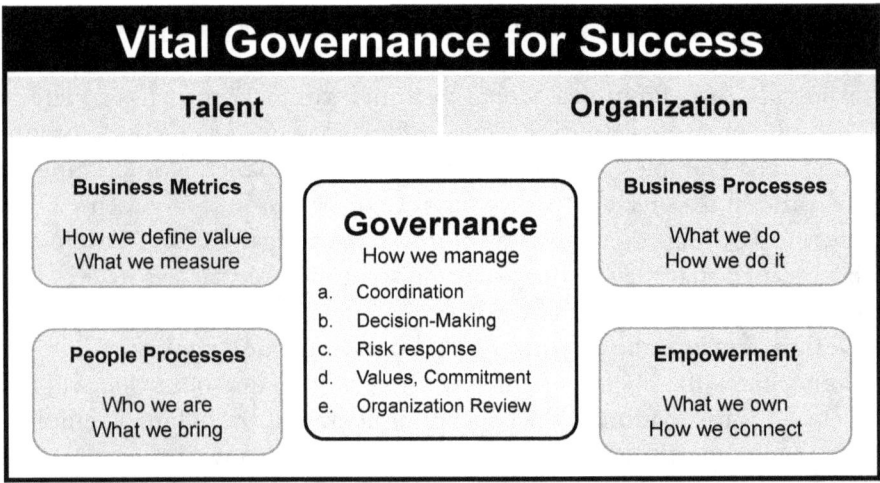

Fig. 12.4 The vital governance for leading success

company. It is the same intent for governance at board of directors' level or at the management level inside the company. This this company level, the more operational focus of governance must include aspects beyond pure decision-making. The illustration in Fig. 12.4 shows a list of Governance priorities relevant to a vital organization design, consistent with the definition below:

> **Governance for vitality** is a *collective direction body* that brings augmentation to five capabilities in business management:
> 1. **Coordination** of priorities for transformation.
> 2. Collective analysis for **decision-making** (not collective decision-making).
> 3. Vital **risk response** to assess trends and plan for emerging disruptions.
> 4. Stewardship on adherence to **values.** Enterprise monitoring of **commitment.**
> 5. **Organization Review** to know if the transformation is becoming more or less vital.

Here are the main aspects to consider on governance design for each of the five capabilities mentioned above.

1. **Coordination of priorities for transformation.** Ambitious transformations take life on their own if left unchecked. Metrics and plans only go so far and may create a negative value when unexpected events occur. Existing priorities may need to change but not at the division level. The interpretation of what matters most at every important change in direction going forward is a collective outcome. Leaders can't have isolated new directions particularly because some decisions may imply choices leaders may not like or favor. Therefore, it is imperative to have a centralized decision-making venue well established and—respect it. This may be a challenge for entrepreneurial CEOs, who have made their fortunes in agile decision-making, but as complexity increases, the company's edge, its competitive capability will depend more on the interactions between the parts than the isolated performance of the silos. Horizontal optimization is priority over vertical optimization. Segmentation of decision-making creates risks that will slow down the next big dream. Collective analysis does not mean collective decision-making, but ensures the big picture is considered, the data is reviewed, and the implications—including business risk, financials, values, people processes, impact on all areas—are properly discussed.

2. **Collective analysis for decision-making (not collective decision-making)**. Governance sits at the center of the entire vitality design because it is the designed space for conflict resolution and strategic decision-making. Directing a transformation is not hard only because of the changes it inevitably requires, including cost reductions, mergers, acquisitions, divestitures, opening and closing areas, elevating and demoting leaders, it is also hard because the floor does not stay flat. External forces will intrude in your plans forcing changes of direction to some degree, and those changes cannot be discussed in small chambers with singular perspectives. We will need the data, the voice of the process, the voice of the customer, and the voice of the people. CEOs will continue to have the final decision-making rights in almost all cases, other than regulation or the Board of Directors, but Leading Success intends to augment the quality and context for the decision, ensuring that the very process followed to analyze and decide reinforces the culture. Nothing erodes trust faster than the perception of a favored decision at the expense of others. That does not mean people will like all the decisions, or that all the people will like a decision, it means that the process is defensible in the cultural and values analysis for the common employee. This is a critical battleground for companies as they must ensure the highest levels of engagement in order to beat the odds of a grand plan that will fail if people only do what they are supposed to do. Everyone will have to raise the bar above the norm to achieve the most ambitious outcomes.
3. **Vital risk response**. Transformations fail, get delayed, or underperform because of internal integration issues but also because of external factors that are unavoidable. Most recent point in case is the pandemic. But other, less dramatic global issues can create enough disruption to cause a redirection, a change in tactical response to sustain continuity for the business. Good examples include the supply chain disruption caused by a massive cargo ship stuck on the Suez Canal in 2021[10], or the lack of semiconductors for automotive controls resulting in minimal supply of cars to the market for nearly three years. These environmental influences must have a process to land and protocols to discuss and define the right response, instead of the immediate reaction. These challenges are cross-functional, impact multiple areas and their solutions are also cross-functional. The augmented capacity to analyze, sort through data, look at competitors, having a finger in the pulse of the people, and understanding what customers and employees need enables the governance team to look at the challenge through multiple lenses before concluding too soon what the response should look like.

4. **Stewardship on adherence to values.** What exactly is the right thing to do? There are times when companies find themselves, even if for no cause of their own, at a crossroads of difficult choices in order to address an issue. It could be an emergency situation with employees at risk or the change of a policy that may affect some people while benefiting others. In every case, the common denominator is a choice with no absolute *right* answer, only a *better* answer, which often involves ethics or values deliberations. In many circumstances, protocols, and policies dictate what we should do, but some unique situations require nuance, discussion to calibrate the right response with cross examination from multiple angles and perspectives. In these cases, an appropriate response from the company both internally and externally can be best served if we have a governance team who has a process to conduct quick benchmark, gather data to inform the discussion. The point is however very clear, contrast the choices against the company values and universal human rights before making any decision. Governance allows for these conversations to occur collectively and in a culturally consistent way.

5. **Organization Review.** An organization review responds to one simple question: in the way we are organized today, are we moving closer to, or further away from the intended transformation's outcomes? This level of aggregation for an answer comes as a result of a systematic review of factors and metrics about the organization with consistency over time. We call that an Organization Review, and it is the Part 2 of the Talent and Organization Review discussed in the Talent Economy section of Chapter Eleven. These reviews intend to reveal to what degree the existing capacities, ways to operate, workflows, segmentation, metrics, incentives, partnerships, are helping or hindering the acceleration to our stated Success. Including the identification of the best set of metrics to determine such assessment. We are interested on both, status and trends showing systemic obstacles. Organization reviews are the best antidote for non-liberating environments as they are focused on finding areas where time is wasted, old architectures are in the way, the wrong metrics are sending contradictory messages, poor decision-making is creating friction for vitality and expression. While the numbers on the indicators are important, the most critical aspect of this review is the discussion about 'why' the numbers are either good or bad, and second, the identification and agreement on what actions can modify—or sustain—the trend. Numerous consulting firms have Organizational Health models with validated metrics to illuminate this aspect. If you are a large corporation, you may already be using one of the big consulting firms or have hired one of the best-selling authors to help you

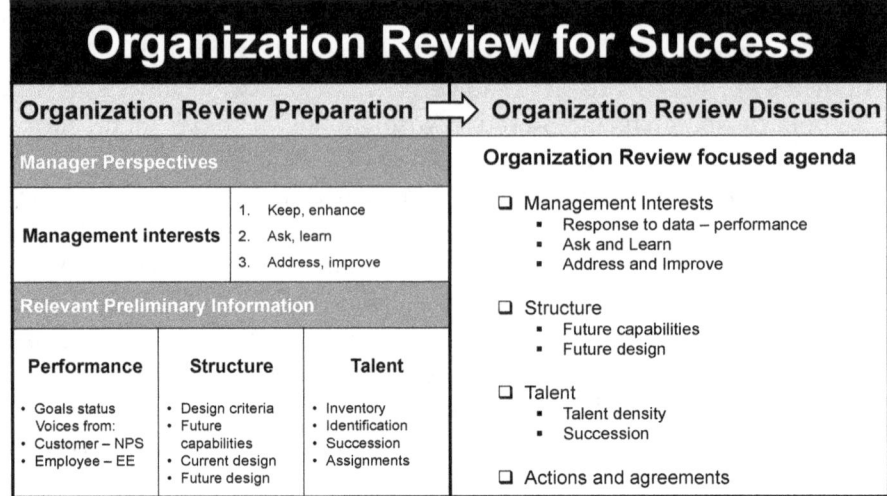

Fig. 12.5 Generic organization review design for vitality

in the process. If you are not, there are a few things you can do to approximate the best practices. Here are a few key lessons from experience on Organization reviews(Fig. 12.5).

- The Organization Review must be a highly prepared discussion; therefore, it is time demanding.
- It should be performed for every larger segment of the business and selectively with teams below.
- The session is best performed when it does not become a data review, but a true discussion about effectiveness and improvement.
- The agenda must be highly responsive to the manager's concerns.
- The minimal outcomes to achieve are manager concerns, future capabilities, structure design, and succession.
- This is the right place to connect people processes with business processes. Future capabilities and future organization discussions are best when you also discuss the people you have in mind for those future opportunities.
- For a complete analysis of risk, the agenda should include positive or negative trends on employee engagement and feedback.

Governance in Action for Signature Processes

The operational implementation of all the governance components above is the formalization of a space and time reserved in all the management or executive teams to have those conversations. In other words, the implementation of a structured calendar with defined areas of focus responding to the different needs management teams have. Governance therefore is implemented via unrelenting discipline. The best organizations put themselves through a governance schedule that is tight and meaningful, however, the very best make those to be *conversations to create commitment*, not PowerPoint downloads. It is through this process that we listen—and stay connected—to the pulse of the organization, and are able to course correct, collectively, following our values; this is by living our *signature processes in action*.

The illustration in Fig. 12.6 offers a point of view of a typical governance cadence for a company with a management team, a board of directors, and investors.

The best teams can seldom achieve championship status based on culture or talent alone. They need coordination that adds up, multiplies, elevates. The right organization design is like driving in a modern city, with signals, traffic flows for speed and safety. The city is prepared for rain and snow and is prepared for emergency response when it is needed. Your best talent will spend less time fighting, litigating, competing, and more time working, collaborating, creating outcomes. They will choose to stay because they can

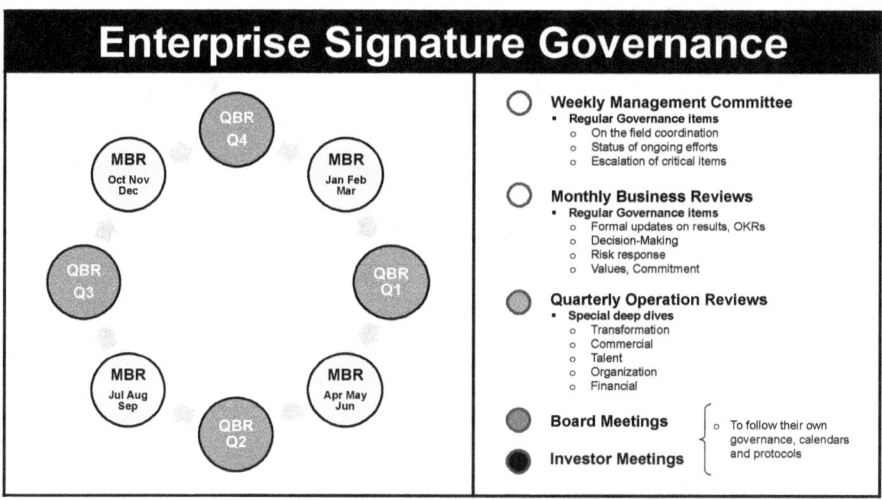

Fig. 12.6 Components of a vital enterprise governance model

be successful, they grow, they can have a life, and because they belong. They realize their expectations with us better than with anybody else.

That is the power of the vital organization.

A Vision of Vitality, Working on The Trilogy for Execution

We have now concluded the second mindset: Infrastructure Vitality Design. We have covered Culture, Talent, and Organization as disciplines that hold the key to a more enduring and successful company. The Trilogy, as a metaphor to articulate the three necessary steps to adapt the organization to a renewed DNA, marked the steps for design, and in a way, will also be relevant in the next mindset, execution. The vitality design will come alive in forms of expression in real life, no more drawing board. Every manager gets to live their own Trilogy be the source of culture, create a talent economy that connects with the enterprise, and live the signature processes defined for a signature experience.

With this in mind, we now move to our next and final Mindset: Expression.

Notes

1. Ohno, T. (1988). Toyota production system: Beyond large scale production. CRC Press.
2. Paulk, M. C., Weber, C. V., Curtis, B., & Chrissis, M. B. (1995). The capability maturity model: Guidelines for improving the software process (1st ed.). Carnegie Mellon University, Software Engineering Institute. Addison Wesley.
3. Beck, K., Beedle, M., van Bennekum, A., Cockburn, A., Cunningham, W., Fowler, M., Grenning, J., Highsmith, J., Hunt, A., Jeffries, R., Kern, J., Marick, B., Martin, R. C., Mellor, S., Schwaber, K., Sutherland, J., & Thomas, D. (2001). Manifesto for agile software development. Agile Alliance. https://agilemanifesto.org.
4. IDEO. (2015). The field guide to human-centered design. IDEO.org.
5. Galbraith, J. R. (2002). Designing organizations: An executive guide to strategy, structure, and process. Jossey-Bass. San Francisco.

6. Catmull, E., & Wallace, A. (2014). Creativity, Inc.: Overcoming the unseen forces that stand in the way of true inspiration (Expanded ed.). Random House.
7. Hoffman, B. G. (2012). American icon: Alan Mulally and the fight to save Ford Motor Company. Crown Business.
8. Kesler, G., & Kates, A. (2016). Bridging organization design and performance: 5 ways to activate a global operating model. Wiley. New Jersey.
9. Doerr, J. (2018). Measure what matters: How Google, Bono, and the Gates Foundation rock the world with OKRs. Portfolio Penguin.
10. Yee, V., & Glanz, J. (2024). How one of the world's biggest ships jammed the Suez Canal. The New York Times. https://www.nytimes.com/2021/07/17/world/middleeast/suez-canal-stuck-ship-ever-given.html.

13

The Expression Mindset: Becoming Your Purpose

The View at a Glance

What is it?	Continued action, with a voice, in line with our values. Expression is the way to achieve superior performance. Organizationally, it is the capacity to mobilize the organization at scale to become your vision. It is through expression that people perform and excel above and beyond the norm.
Why do I need it?	To mobilize for execution in order to achieve the transformation, produce the changes necessary to succeed, and make that capacity to change sustainable.
So what?	We deliver on revenue, profitability, transformation, leadership, and resilience. Solid results against the unexpected: be prepared to learn and adapt fast. Survive disruption.
What's in it?	The disciplines of: Engagement, Expectation, Experience.

The Elevator Speech

It is time for execution. Having completed the discussion of the first two mindsets for Leading Success, Liberation, and Vitality, we go now to the last mindset: Expression, which is focused on addressing execution and performance. We will see how the next three disciplines will help us get exceptional business results that are organization-wide, scalable, implemented in a way that makes the company resilient for future disruption. We have called that capacity the *Liberating, Vital, Expression*.

At this point in the transformation, we are concerned with an implementation that delivers on its goals, aligns with our vitality design, and that looks consistent across teams, layers, and geographies; this is, consistently scalable. Three important questions come to mind:

- What does it take to achieve scalable, sustained high performance?
- Where does the capacity to change, innovate, create differentiation comes from?
- How do we execute for sustainable Success?

The usual top-down change planning and coordination of actions is not going to be enough as a new culture, a different way to operate necessitates the commitment from many more people than just the top of the pyramid. The only way to execute is to find a way for everyone in the organization to choose to be *in it*, not just a few, not just the top. In Leading Success terminology, we need a committed workforce that follows our vital design, leveraging our primary infrastructure for success. We need three disciplines to get us there: *Engagement*, to ensure everyone is in the game, *Expectation*, to translate the strategy and plan to everyone's role, with specific goals and personalized descriptions of success. And finally, we close the circle by making the *Experience* for both customers and employees match our vision as described in the first discipline. These three disciplines create the space for the liberating expression that moves people to go beyond and overachieve. But this mindset also brings to us a fresh perspective on managing execution: the realization that the transformation is not an award, or a step at the end of the journey—instead, the transformation is happening at every moment, inside every opportunity of work. We are in some sort of flux of execution that brings results to bear making us close the gap between vision and experience. This is to say that, at every moment, we are *becoming* our purpose.

Why Are Execution and Performance Forms of Expression?

Execution is a well-defined concept, and most people understand what we are talking about when we mention that word: getting things done, complete a task, hands on to convert something into an outcome, to perform. However, it is possible to conceive a spectrum of execution from the necessary, sufficient, in one end, to the elevated, superior types of execution in the other. A good way to illustrate the difference would be to drive a car in a highway safely and effectively, as compared to drive a car on a racetrack, in an elite competition such as Formula One. While in both cases the driver is in execution mode, there is a significant distance in terms of skills at play, and outcomes on each situation. In their excellent book *Execution, the discipline of getting things done*,[1] Larry Bossidy and Ram Charan establish, very convincingly, that execution is a *discipline*, directly connected with leadership, culture, and people management. Leading Success, as a management model, embraces that perspective. As a point of view about leadership and transformation however, execution is considered more than getting things done. Leading Success considers Execution as a mindset responsible of building an organization where ambitious change is possible and transformations are enduring by means of extraordinary performance that comes from the highest potential expressions of their people. The belief behind that rationale is that extraordinary execution requires ownership and agency, both facilitated by a liberating, vital workplace.

Companies live in environments where execution quickly faces the customer, not just the process. We need, in our car driving example, competitive driving, with superior skills, exceedingly above the norm levels of performance to sustain our journey to reach the stated ambition. We need the totality, the full reservoir of talent and personal excellence in everyone, the one hundred percent of the person, including experience, emotional stability, passion, personal mission; in short, the full person. This is more than just 'driving the highway' performance, this is a form of personal expression of excellence and the self, channeled through our contribution, through our work.[2] Therefore, exceptional, elite competition performance and execution can only be achieved as forms of superior, authentic self-expression.

Earlier in this book we briefly introduced the concept of Expression, indicating that performance and execution are forms of expression, as we can see everyday in sports and the arts. We mentioned that those artists and sportsmen and women are called 'performers' and that we celebrate their uniqueness, their stories, their backgrounds, everything that makes them special is a contribution to their performance. Performer and performance are blended, making the experience personal and more transcendent. However, when we think on work at the office, we as managers very consistently expect the *performance*, but we do not show the same level of consistency on interest, or appreciation for the *performer*. Her/his story, background, heritage, interests, aspirations. We may unconsciously, or not, separate the person from the action in our own minds, invested on maximizing only the performance, not realizing that such separation is merely an illusion, a simplification of the mind that creates mixed messages and significant belonging problems.

People at work lead with and lean to their personalities and their stories as much as singers and sculptors do. And it happens at all levels—and at all ages. The underlying psychological mechanisms that make children love and enjoy sharing their drawings with mom and dad—their little masterpieces—are the same mechanisms behind executives' love and joy for sharing their business strategies, their life achievements, mastermind plans to their managers, the board, and investors. Both are, fundamentally, forms of personal expression, and at those moments both the children and the executive are *performers in a stage*, and they use their full selves to do that. It is no different for the accountant, the salesperson, the product designer.

Everyone is permanently in a form of expression and yet, some feel like there is a need to separate those two worlds. The amount of energy wasted by a great employee who happens to be different, perhaps they are part of the LGBTQ community, or a person of color, or has a disability, feeling pressure to conceal, to adjust, compensate, to fight stereotypes is immense, subtracting from the freedom to be themselves and only focus on the work, on innovation, and be confident they do not have to demonstrate they belong to their work environments every single day. Instead, they should feel affirmed, included, and that they belong. An employee feeling that way feeds from that environment to deliver masterpieces of work. They are *liberated*. With this important context we can offer a definition of Signature Expression:

> **Signature Expression** is the exceptional performance that results from the authentic self-expression of liberated and committed employees, whose actions, interactions, and outcomes are directly connected and relevant to the transformation, consistent to the company's values and purpose. Signature Expression needs both, the *performance (action)*, and the *performer (expression)*, and is predicated on managers who can create a belonging environment to achieve these superior results.

Leadership of Liberation does not separate performer from performance, actively works on building a climate of inclusion and belonging where employees do not have to waste time worrying about who they are; nothing is holding them back. These leaders see people as possibility and potential, they consider their teams vital partners, they have opened their minds to see and appreciate the performer, creating a culture that feeds from it. While there are examples of great performances in business against all odds, in spite of many obstacles, we need to realize that defeating extraordinary odds, should not be the norm. We need to create vital organizations for people to channel their absolute best performance, and that can only happen the way it does in sports and the arts, by being able to be yourself, your best, feeling you are included and that you belong.

Expression is the next big revolution waiting for you to unleash. The fate of great leaders is to become liberators of exceptional performance, and leaders of extraordinary performers through vital, signature expression.

Becoming Your Purpose

Expression begets a new outcome, a new world. What you do—your expression—is who you are, and it defines what you *become*. This is a powerful concept that transformational leaders intuitively understand, and something that can be learned. Becoming is the outcome of expression. As we walk through these last three disciplines, we will consistently conclude that the team, and the leaders transform the business by transforming what they do (their work), the way they do it (new behaviors), and how they think about their work (reframing actions and connections), even in those cases where the work itself remains the same. Those are the changes driving the larger transformation that ultimately translates into *customer and employee experience*, and therefore, an improved business. In that sense, we become the actions we perform and by doing that, *we become our Purpose*.

Our third mindset, EXPRESSION, is best understood as a process of BECOMING, measured operationally through engagement, performance, customer, and employee experience. At the phase of execution, transformations can easily derail because real life takes over and people gets busy. In colloquial words, stuff happens. It could be anything: components are delayed, software is not ready, accelerated changes in regulation, a global pandemic forces everyone to work remotely, significant cultural and social events that alter everyone's perceptions and mindsets. As a consequence, defining and launching actions, goals, and metrics will not be enough for success.

Actions alone can remain unconnected as teams and people get focused on their priorities, with their heads down to accomplish *their* goals, responding to events in the best ways they can. When the unexpected emerges people will find themselves facing odd choices that will require new decision-making, judgment, appropriate adjustment, and reaction. The most sense-making course of action for someone or some group may deviate from the bigger picture of what is good for the company. This is a common occurrence in companies, and it's called *local optimization*. One area pursues its goals at the expense of other areas, even if unknowingly. For example, a sales team signing contracts for products decommitted in design, arguing that the customer wants it, that it was urgent to keep that account; they make the budget numbers and their commission, while everyone else suffers to fulfill the order. This is contrary to *system optimization* where the outcomes of a unit or a team will get de-prioritized, 'sub-optimized' for the greater good.

The question to ask in these circumstances is, *what kind of organization are we becoming with our decisions?* The same way we presented culture as a phenomenon that emerges inevitably, as product of human interaction, organizations inevitably 'become' something new, constantly. This may sound rather complicated, but it is not. When you think about it, transformations and big goals are created to help organizations change who they are: *become* leaders in certain technology, *become* the first choice for their customers, *become* a great place to work, *become* a digital enterprise, innovative, diverse, or resilient. The WORD articulates the potential to BECOME the WORLD, as we noted earlier in Chapter Four (Fig. 13.1).

What we do in our everyday work, our decision-making, the choices we make have the effect of converting the organization closer to—or further away from—its goals at *every moment*, not just every quarter, or every fiscal year. Realizing this inevitability makes leaders (managers) transformational, as they can consciously affect what the company becomes everyday. Coincidentally, they will also affect who they become, what their teams become. The absence of this monumental realization makes leaders think their decisions are just instances of operational direction toward the accomplishment of a goal. While that is tactically true, it is not the kind of awareness that creates liberation, sustained transformation, and a new WORLD.

13 The Expression Mindset: Becoming Your Purpose

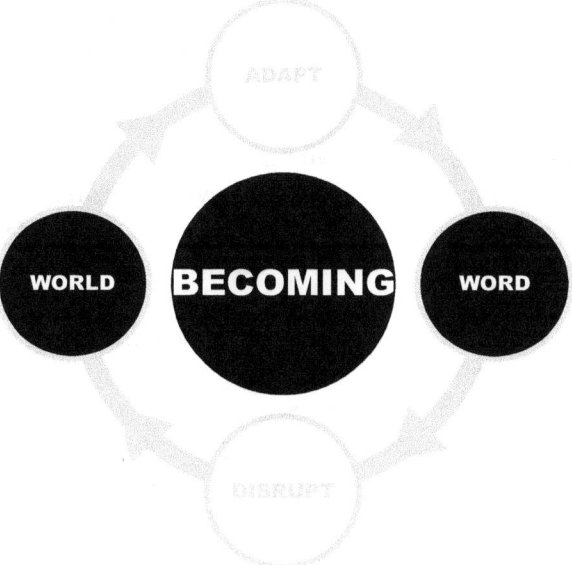

Fig. 13.1 Becoming our transformation is how the WORD changes the WORLD

> **Becoming, a definition**
> Operationally, becoming is a dynamic process through which entities (whether they be physical, conceptual, or biological) undergo change, development, or evolution. In philosophy, becoming is a process by which something achieves a new essence from its potential state. There is no static reality, but instead a state of flux defines reality, permanence is just an illusion.

Becoming, implication: There is no moment in the life of a company when the company *is* something, or stays the same, it is always *becoming* something. It is always in a process of getting closer—or further away—to its goals and purpose, that is, bringing the vision into existence.

Companies become their Purpose by executing their transformation. This transformation, FROM a current state TO a future state is predicated on clarity on big goals as a first condition—this is covered on disciplines 1, 2, and 3—Aspiration, Transformation, Commitment. This clarity of direction must sit on top a vital infrastructure that powers great talent to consistently perform with high standards. Such infrastructure includes a vital organization design including an accurate operational translation to business and people processes, right empowerment of positions, right metrics and governance.

These areas are covered on disciplines 4, 5, and 6—Culture, Talent, Organization. Then comes execution, a form of expression that is about becoming our purpose. Becoming is both a *process*[3] and a guiding thought, a philosophy. Every plan and goal in our work is just *potential* success until execution makes it real, a material success—just as Michelangelo said of liberation: the potential 'angel' lies in the marble, but it is not real yet, until an exceptional sculptor starts working (execution), with the right tools and the right environment to bring the angel to life, changing the world with it.

Leading Success' Execution mindset achieves the art and process of becoming, at scale, through its three final disciplines: Engagement, Expectation, and Experience.

The implication of this perspective is that organizations are never in a steady state, in a place, as much as our perception may suggest. Instead, organizations are always in flux, *becoming* something. A great leading success leader will always reflect, what does this decision makes us become? Closer to our purpose and our goals, or further away from them? The process and art of becoming is therefore the framework for this latest mindset of EXPRESSION. It is through expression that leaders articulate their visions, declare how the future will be, thus altering the company, instantly influencing minds to initiate motion in that direction, to ultimately change the world. In that sense, we become our vision by connecting and engaging with our people, helping them see things differently, think differently, and including them, helping everyone see themselves in the picture of success.

We move now to discuss our final three disciplines: Engagement, Expectation, and Experience.

Notes

1. Bossidy, L., & Charan, R. (2002). Execution: The discipline of getting things done. Crown Business.
2. Kreuzbauer, R., & King, D. (2015). The mind in the object—Psychological valuation of materialized human expression. Journal of Experimental Psychology: General, 144(4), 764–787. https://doi.org/10.1037/xge0000096.
3. Whitehead, A. N. (1978). Process and reality: Corrected edition. Free Press.

14

Engagement: Liberation, One Person at a Time

At this stage on the Leading success disciplines CEOs and executive teams have moved the ball long enough through very treacherous terrain of approvals, strategic agendas, finances, and now contemplate an open field to launch their life-changing visions to the broader company, the organization at large. It is the turn for everyone else to get on board. No one in the team at the top thinks this lightly. It is clearly a critical stage in the transformation. However, the way we chose to move forward can accelerate or significantly delay the velocity of the whole change, creating friction in the connections that matter the most; those areas merging, separating, those that are new, or those most radically reinvented.[1] We are in need of a method, a process that eliminates friction of adoption and empowers every layer of management to become owners of the changes at play. Top leadership is feeling the fatigue of months in the making of this moment, they are ready to hand off the execution to the ranks. Small organizations can do with direct conversations, even including the CEO herself/himself, but larger, global companies need a scalable solution. How do we do that?

As we worked with SYP, the consulting firm in San Francisco to help Michel Dell implement his new strategy for the company, we realized a conventional approach will not do the trick. After all, we had to mobilize more than one hundred thousand employees, in a company with seven hundred senior leaders and thousands of managers. The strategy was not to completely reinvent Dell but to substantially redefine how the business would grow and the new channels and markets that it would address. While these did not require to alter the company upside down, at the end of this journey, employees would belong to a different company, not the old Dell they signed up for. It was necessary to reengage everyone in this story, why we wanted this, why it was necessary, why now, and most importantly, what did it mean for their countries, divisions, teams, and themselves, and to each employee. This was not a typical communication effort. This had to be much more than that. It had to be a conversation; the type of conversation that creates commitment as discussed in Chapter Eight, Commitment. In a previous chapter we discussed how this team had gone through a process to get the commitment of executives, and our goal was to replicate, to the best extent possible, that discussion and experience. We created an enterprise-wide plan for all managers to engage with their people in a conversation to answer those big questions: why change is necessary, why now, what is new, what stays the same, and what is in it for us? Each manager would have a structured guide for this conversation. We launched this all over the world, in eleven languages, hundreds of conversations. We called it Leadership Imperative. The surveys before and after these dialogues revealed a substantial increase in three main areas: trust in leadership, intent to stay at Dell, and likelihood to recommend Dell to a friend or family to work here.

The open comments and discussions revealed that people loved the direction, appreciated the effort to make them partners in the transformation, and believed this was the right course of action. We left teams with much more than information; we achieved understanding and commitment to the forthcoming changes. We created a global community all across the company with the same focus and language—a team with thirty countries and one hundred thousand people were aligned.

What was more important for us was that this conversation got localized and resonant with their business, country, function, or team. It was necessary to also address the questions of, how does this change anything in what WE do and in what I do. This is a perfect illustration of a process that brings ownership of the changes to layers of management and creates velocity by increasing the understanding and the legitimate buy-in by all employees. This is what Engagement is all about.

What Are the Outcomes in the Engagement Step?

Engagement is a common metric with its corresponding process in the human resources portfolio, used to designate the status of organizational climate within a range from good to bad. It is possible however, to make a distinction between two types of engagement:

- **Employee Engagement,** in the more customary definition, is a metric to determine the degree of positive dispositions and motivations of employees toward the company and their teams. Employee Engagement is an *outcome* of the employee experience, and a critical metric to assess capacity of Expression.
- **Transformational Engagement**, focused on making employees owners of the change. A necessary condition to scale commitment and superior performance. Transformational Engagement is an *input* to employee experience in the expression mindset.

This chapter refers to *Transformational Engagement*. The process and features of Employee Engagement will be covered in Chapter Fifteen, Expectation. With that distinction being made, we can focus on a list of outcomes for the transformational engagement process, as follows:

General Transformation Engagement Outcomes

About the Larger Organization

- Understanding of the enterprise transformation: what, why, why now.
- Having my Voice heard as employee: protection to ask real, authentic questions.
- Commitment: Beyond acknowledgment or acceptance, get to ownership, to commitment.
- Belonging to ONE team across the company: we are treated equally to everyone else in the world.
- Success: what is success for the company and what does that mean for the team; what is success for the team, how will we define it operationally, and measure it.
- Liberation: how is this vision liberating for customers and for employees?

About the local team and the person.

- Get local: What does that mean for us as a team?
- Get specific: What is the journey? (schedules, phases, metrics)
- Get clear: What changes and what does not change?
- Get personal: What does it mean for me?

The Manager's Role in Transformational Engagement

If you think on your own experience at your time of entering the workforce, you will remember that it did not take long after you started to appreciate that managers come in very different types and styles. If we focus only on their different ways to react, adapt, and adopt change we can clearly see a wide spectrum of behavior. In one end, we observed those leaders who embraced the changes in unequivocal terms and were able to realistically understand the risks involved. They felt positive about the changes and convincingly articulated why they found them liberating—this is, why they personally believed in the solutions and did not hesitate to jump in the train with both feet. In the other end of the spectrum were those leaders who did not embrace the change, they were neutral at best but more often they were resisting it. They talked about "people at the top" not having the right information, or the right smarts or the right intentions. They made it clear "this is not what I would do, but they are making us", they apologize to their employees for the direction of the company; sometimes throwing a sad note "don't ask me, I did not want this". In general, below the top management of a company employees get exposed to the reactions of their local manager, and therefore the employee experience, what they hear, how they hear it, can significantly differ from one to another. Our problem in scaling is *variation*. We want consistency on the transformation story, and consistency on the experience, without resorting to full 'copy-paste' standardization—a robotic tape-like experience. An authentic buy-in is necessary to ensure that the new ways of working will not get stuck in the broader organization, slowing the change down. This fact sometimes gets lost to some CEOs. The natural inclination at that level is to trust their people to roll it out, put in place a communication plan that is mostly a financial story, a customer story but far from an engaging employee story. In the absence of a playbook for engagement, managers will try—as they always do—their best, according to their unique—and different—experiences and preferences.

Scaling requires a method that brings structure and leaves space for the manager's input and culture to contribute to enhance the engagement, locally, at the team and person level. No enterprise-wide design can close the last mile in people's hearts. That always comes down to the local manager.

But it is not always easy for managers. Circumstances play a role. It is not only that we have variation based on how managers see the world; we also have the nature of the transformation itself. Often, visionary changes will call for more radical measures to adapt the organization to the future. That may translate in some parts of the organization to be raised, gain importance and resources, while others will go in the opposite direction. Very often business simplification requires the consolidation of two areas; those who are folded into a different leader, who will see different priorities and probably skillsets being prioritized in the future compared to what they possess today; those people will feel at risk, unsettled, and angry. Other times it is outright spoken that certain areas will close down, possibly offshored to another country, or simply they will be closed or sold. How should the manager of the impacted area respond? How can she or he show any enthusiasm in such circumstances? How is this liberating after all?

In the end, all business decisions come down to personal implications, and transformations that cause any level of impact on the compensation or employment become personal really fast for the impacted people. Liberating leaders do not try to convince employees how they should feel about their organizational loses, but instead, they recognize and validate those feelings, then move ahead to prioritize time and effort to bring to light the factors weighted in the decision-making process leading to those difficult changes. While there is no guarantee of acceptance, this articulation is a necessary step to establish rationality, a sense of objectivity to avoid the perception that the company acted unintelligently or with no regard and sensitivity to consequences. In the rush of things, leaders often go over these moments rather transactionally, not appreciating how memorable and culture-making these moments really are. CEOs and leaders are not only speaking to those leaving, but primarily to those staying; these moments should be 'signature' in the way they show respect and values, regardless of how difficult and painful the changes may be. It will not be easy, and some employees will disagree, some may dislike it. If the strategy is sound, there will be a powerful 'why' for the changes that a reasonable person will intellectually understand it is in the best interest of the customers and the future of the company.

The WHY as a Path to Transformational Engagement

The solution to build engagement for larger teams is to design a powerful conversation where the 'why', the data, and the rationale are visible, get discussed, and difficult questions get asked and answered. When this happens, we can also use the opportunity to set expectations for managers on how the good and the bad news are best delivered. Scaling a transformation requires progressive alignment and consistency on the story. A communications package with a document of frequently asked questions or FAQs is an indispensable tool, but it does not replace the dialogue, the questions, and the connection with people. When difficult news have to be shared, CEOs get anxious too, they sometimes have to follow their lawyers in saying the minimum or nothing at all. Leaders must define the story that makes sense; and recognize that only direct managers can *make meaning* and connect with people to elevate the liberating aspect of the strategy going forward.

How to Build Liberating Engagement?

I will remain consistent that Leading Success is not a bunch of formulas or templates, nor a series of rigid choreographies that 'uniformize' the change. It is, however, an undeniable challenge bringing along a large group of people with very different states of mind, opinions, perspectives, and interests into the change process.[2] That is why I am offering a point of view on how a company could scale the engagement phase for their own *Trilogy*.

As shown in the illustration in Fig. 14.1, building a scalable transformational engagement is a five-step process. This design in particular, is one I have implemented multiple times with proven results. The process gravitates around *conversations*. But not just causal, spontaneous conversations; these are structured for larger audiences, adapted to include groups of people, instead of one-to-one, but designed to carry the same capacity to interact, ask questions and meaningfully discuss, surface honest disagreement and any aspects of the story that may create doubt or concern, bring it out to the surface, preventing misunderstanding to fester in the corridors. In summary, these are *conversations to create commitment*, at scale, purposefully designed to illuminate how the vision (WORD) *becomes* a better, liberating, and vital future reality (WORLD).

These five steps follow the sequence of the nine disciplines. The CEO and the CHRO define a small team that works on collecting the information from the first six disciplines and uses it to build a Story of Success, as shown in the first two steps. With those points (i to vi) been cleared and reviewed in detail for language, examples, and data to support them, the team must create a toolkit for managers as described in step 3. Small or big, physical or digital, simple or expensive, it does not matter; what matters is that there are elements of support to help managers conduct the session and understand what is expected of them as they perform the sessions. The structure of the session is one that leads the audience through the rational and the

	Building Scalable Transformational Engagement	
1	Define success	• Clarify the destination, use key outcomes metrics. • How the world changes?
2	Write the scalable story	i. **Why** are we changing? Industry context. ii. **What** IS changing, what IS NOT changing? iii. **Why is now** the time? iv. How are these changes **liberating for customers**? v. How are these changes **liberating for us**? vi. What's in it for **YOU**?
3	Create tools for managers	• Brief talking points, data, core business case. • Answers to most critical questions. • Hot line for employees to ask more questions. • Formalized schedule. • Training for managers.
4	Run Engagement Sessions	⇒ See **The Anatomy of the Engagement Session**
5	Measure outcomes	• Use industry-validated data questions when possible.

Fig. 14.1 The five steps to build the scalable transformational engagement

emotional journey that leaders experienced during the months of creation of the vision and strategy, only to be accomplished within a handful of hours. Let's examine how this session looks like.

The Anatomy of an Engagement Session

An engagement session is designed to provide context, definitions, and grounding on what was decided, why it was decided, what is next, and clarify what everyone can expect in the future. Our key outcome is to remove noise, confusion, and anxieties in the teams and provide clarity on the change plan. Unfortunately, depending on the news to share, some areas may feel less settled, but that is the nature of transformation, and we will have to manage appropriately those circumstances.

The engagement session must feel eventful, formal, and not optional. Some aspects may require unique logistics considerations for fully dispersed teams, significant variations in time zones and languages. What is most important to preserve are those elements that make it a culture-relevant experience that leaves employees with a feeling of affirmation, desire to be in the organization, and ownership for its purpose and transformational goals. Some insights from experience are shown below:

a) Everyone is invited to at least one session—no exceptions.
b) Everyone heard it from their direct manager—or area manager when appropriate.
c) It is contained within a reasonable window of time (a week or two)—not months.
d) It is 'the' priority for that window of time, all things being equal, of course—no manager can discretionarily miss it because they are 'too busy'.
e) Ideally—also include contract employees, since they are very much in the mix on crucial projects.
f) There is tracking and there is an enterprise survey before and after the session.

The illustration in Fig. 14.2 depicts the main areas and key considerations in the design of the engagement session. We follow the 3 × 3x3 rule: 3 themes, each with 3 questions, and each with 3 answers. Depending on the complexity of the business, the company's history, its geographical distribution, segments, and product lines, this may take from 2 hours to half day to deliver to a group between 5 to 25 people. Below is a succinct list of the unique aspects that make your engagement session a vital, liberating expression.

- **Centralized design.** Designed adaptations for locations are included in the global design, which accounts for the translations necessary for the global footprint. No region, country or location is allowed to tinker with content

The Anatomy of the Engagement Session

Business Case		Impact		Actions	
Why change, why now		How customers win		Clarity on action	
Who we are		How the company wins		Clarity on journey	
What we will do		What does it mean for US		What does it mean for ME	
Context	• Industry evolution • Customer preferences • Technology, competitors	Customer	• How is this liberating • How is this vital • Customer success	Change	• What is changing, • What is not changing • New definition of success
Beliefs	• Purpose, impact, values • Our strengths • Who we chose to be	Company	• Competitive differentiation • Financials, leadership • Renewed roadmap	Plan	• Plans, next steps • Schedules • Teams
Decision	• Our choices – options • Our analysis • Clear statement of decision	Team	• Impact to our team/unit • Good news • Bad news – as appropriate	YOU	• How employees win • New profile of success • Development journeys

Fig. 14.2 Content and sequence suggested for engagement sessions

or modify the design, only to fill in the spaces that correspond to local parts of the story and context.
- **Business case.** The sequence is crucial. From top to bottom, the logic of a liberating story starts with a clear case for change: context should be convincing to expose the why with clarity and urgency and how is the future likely to be. The beliefs will serve to contrast the reality (WORLD), against our purpose, values and who we are, what we stand for, and what we are here to do. The Decision is the introduction of our choice, the declaration of action (WORD) we will commit to in order to emerge victorious in that future we see changing. This decision must come across as a rational, but also bold, intelligent, and confident articulation.
- **Impact.** Once the decision is shared, it is time to describe how our customers and the company win. This is important to validate our reading of the context—industry, competitors, our strengths—to show we have a vision that works. From there the conversation evolves to the implications for the company and the team. The good and the bad.
- **Actions.** A succinct but clear articulation, in straightforward language, on what is, and what is not changing, including new expectations, and clarity on what success looks like. This is followed by a well-defined plan and it concludes with a deep dive on how employees win. This third piece completes the transformation model by making it clear how the company will ADAPT and DISRUPT.
- **Conversation to create commitment.** The structure of this session is that of a Conversation to Create Liberating Commitment—Refer to Chapter Eight, Fig. 8.2. Therefore, each one of the nine segments requires dialogue. This should not be a regular 'run of the mill' presentation and ideally is to be conducted, facilitated, by each manager with their people. It is important to recognize that actual *commitment* may not occur at the session. Commitment is the outcome of a personal journey that starts with an understanding rooted in dialogue, leading to adoption, which drives the personal motivation to join the effort, evolving to commitment, to embracing the plan; at such time employees will be ready to *own*, not just participate in the transformation.

Engagement as Input

Engagement is an investment, a critical jump start for execution. Transformational engagement moves employee engagement scores on a step-function—not gradual but having a positive 'bump'; because companies engage their people for *ownership*, not just to share information and tell everyone what is the change that will happen to them. Engagement should result on commitment and ownership, demonstrating how everyone in the organization is a protagonist, but not by top-down declarations; instead, by showing how their work, the metrics, and their expected outcomes are different and *necessary* for success.

Engagement is mostly a product and outcome of our culture in action. To that extent, managers account for a large portion of its value. It is therefore imperative to understand how managers can elevate their game not only for engagement but for the totality of the Leading Success expectations on them. The next step in our journey is the discipline of Expectation, to address how every employee connects with their managers to translate the strategy and goals of the company into their own. If we have done a good job in Transformational Engagement, we will be able to leverage its positive impact to this next phase.

Notes

1. Keller, S., & Schaninger, B. (2022). Beyond performance 2.0: A proven approach to leading large-scale change. Wiley.
2. Garcia, S., & Fisher, D. (2023). The end of leadership as we know it. Wiley.

15

Expectation: Conversations for Commitment

The Eight Discipline is designed to clarify the specific 'asks' we are going to insert in our people's goals in alignment with the transformation. At this stage, the vision, commitment, and story has been fully taken at heart by your people; they are excited, proud, and ready to go to see it through. While it may seem straightforward to ensure everyone is clear on what needs to happen next, in practice, and much to top management dismay and disbelief, is very common to see an aura of confusion across the organization. A change of an enterprise-wide magnitude needs to be explained even for those whose actual tasks may not change at all. This is necessary because of the connections, collaboration, priorities, and ways to make decisions may, and frankly some *should* change—and be explained, set as new expectations. People often feel less confident about change because they do not have clarity on what is expected going forward. The intangibles of the job are seldom discussed leaving people to 'discover' what has changed as the organization journeys through its transformation. Instead of learning from their managers, employees are left to experience the change by way of bumping into unexpected new ways other areas seem to be doing their work. You may wonder, how is it that leaders miss the mark in some clear changes they should have explained? Sometimes it is just the volume of activity coming their way and the fact that they talk in generalities or over-rely on corporate communication documents. In toxic cultures, leaders simply do not like or do not agree with some of the new ways of working and delay implementation as much as possible, making this confusion a point to illustrate why this will not work. Regardless of the reasons why some important things go unexplained, as leaders we have the obligation to predict and avoid this experience: not liberating, not vital, not engaging.

To unpack the discipline of EXPECTATION, let's explore the needs from each actor in the organization:

What's in the Employee's Mind?

In short: clarity and sincerity. What employees want and need to know is how exactly their work is changing. I can't mention how often leaders misunderstand this need. In trying to answer that question, they think first on the *content* of the work, the tasks, the deliverables. Those may or may not change, but those are normally well covered. What is not covered enough are the intangibles for success; the *connections* the job has with other areas, the nature of the interactions; for example, the way priorities change, who needs to be included as part of the design, input, or decision-making, what is no longer owned, or simply clarify ownership that was unclear before. In other words, how the flow of the work is different and what is expected in the new model. In the end, employees, like everyone else, do not like surprises. Some leaders fear that telling the truth of the changes may precipitate some people to leave, get disgruntled, create chaos, and therefore they paint controversial changes slightly friendlier, hoping that the employee will see things favorably. Unfortunately, this strategy is destined to fail, and the person feels even worse in the end. Leaders must be equipped with the tools, but also have the disposition, and be prepared to engage when people are upset, seeking to clarify exactly how things change to be able to move on. It is liberating to understand things fast, increases trust in leadership, and makes it for a more vital, real experience. These changes, all of them, must now become explicit in the "value" of the position, as we discussed in the talent economy section. Success means different things now, and people's goals should include these new distinctions. The best way to address these concerns is to conduct the engagement sessions described in Chapter Fourteen.

What's in the Manager's Mind?

Keep the team intact, preserve the capacity, and sustain the morale. Managers have two imperative needs when it comes to setting expectations: the first is to master the 'why', the story that makes the upcoming changes rational and needed, the language and tools to communicate the liberating and vital aspects of the choices made, even when those may have a negative impact on the team. The struggle comes when leaders disagree with, or do not like the implications of new direction in their departments. Perhaps they will face increased standards with less people and yet, they are expected to lead the teams to that end. The second need is the ability of managers to reimagine the work differently. Deliver the value in new ways, while making the experience one of growth, learning, and enrichment for their people. There are multiple pressures in managers during significant transformations because very often future optimization design requires short-time sacrifices; reality imposes new restrictions, adjustments to cost structure, and possibly layoffs. In those circumstances the way of work needs to change, it needs to reflect the new ambitions. If we fail to have this redesign done with a vitality mindset, we will have people feeling overwhelmed; left behind carrying the work of those who have been separated. It is just physics, if we do not change the way we work, implement viable prioritization, and set a new direction, less people will have to do more work rendering the experience to be untenable. A third element, not dependent on the manager, is the larger design of workflows that goes inter-departmental, or inter-divisional, above the local manager's authority, which may be impeding velocity, agility and creating confusion, waste of time. For example, if two areas have been told that from now on, they both are 'partially responsible' of something, but no clarity is provided on how this is accomplished, we will have people duplicating tasks, running parallel processes, and holding the governance process hostage with two versions of the truth. In many circumstances the 'how' can be delegated, but not when the transformation calls for a change that goes contrary to prevalent culture or existing disagreements and expects that things will sort themselves out down below the organization. Leaders must own the big change at the right levels.

What Is at Risk for the Company?

Missing the window of opportunity. As you look back at the transformations you have been part of, and read the best-known company reinventions, the common denominator of any strategy is to hit a market need, in an innovative way, *before everyone else does it*. Most transformations are not rocket science, they are about harnessing a capacity or a technology while others are running behind trying to do the same. Competitive differentiation is very seldom a secret, it is instead a race to get the alliances, develop the technology, possess the IP or the infrastructure. If the realization of product design, going to market, customer experience, systems readiness are delayed because the organization was not able to get in sync, be ready to move fast, the company will lose revenue it will never get back. Being out with the right product at the right time puts the company on a favorable position for multiple years, sometimes a whole decade of market leadership. So, it truly matters to gain velocity and master success. Investors normally do not think on the black box inside the businesses they fund but somehow, they count that we will figure out the internal challenges to come out successful and make the numbers. It is in our best interest to create the right culture, the right harmonization—liberating, vital expression—to leave the problems only to those coming from external sources. Companies should fear shooting themselves in the foot.

Implementing Expectation as a Discipline

Establishing the new expectations in a scalable way means getting to people's goals effectively, manage the network of coordinated actions, and the right players in a new orchestration for success. Ideally, you have been able to follow each one of the previous disciplines and you find yourself in a great position to activate your goals. The reality is that most companies will be in between the early steps of Leading Success and unfinished designs of their vital infrastructure. What to do when you are still in the journey? It will take some effort from both the company and the managers. In order to excel at this execution stage you need visible results and alignment. To that end, I offer a list for the company and for managers to jump-start the expectation process.

Company Guide

Setting liberating, vital expectations takes more than a straight talk. We need the right environment and the right management intervention. I have simplified in five points what I consider critical to set expectations for the Leading Success company, represented in Fig. 15.1.

Set expectations for top leaders. Setting expectations starts at the top. We are not going to elaborate on boards of directors setting expectations for CEOs but that is also a critical step for transformation success. With new ESG standards, boards can—and most of them do—include aspects of organizational health beyond the financial metrics as goals for CEOs. Our focus, however, is to address expectations inside of the company. The CEO is

Guide to vital expectations – Company		
Fast start:	1	Set expectations for top leaders
	2	Raise the vital infrastructure – make one liberating change
The CEO's five essential levers to set vital expectations right	3	Affirm the performance management process
	4	Choose one change to optimize rewards
	5	Establish new expectations for managers

Fig. 15.1 What companies can do to improve execution

the one center of accountability for the whole company. That accountability starts with expectation-setting at the c-suite, at the top. Transformations can go sideways easily if, in the absence of unambiguous clarification and black/while expectations about what is changing, we allow smart human beings with a lot of power and ambition to use the gray zone to outsmart each other in pursue of what they think is right, or what makes them—as individuals, or their areas, their agendas—more successful. There is no transformation that makes everyone happy as we have noted, some will have to let go of projects, segments of work they love and have nurtured for years; now those will be going to other places. None of that is easy, but it is even worse when CEOs underestimate, or oversimplify the emotional side of change, as if once you are a seasoned executive, a better paid individual, reporting to the CEO, you no longer respond like most humans do and everything turns rational and financial. In reality though, everyone responds to attachment and loss in similar ways, we all are human. There is no perfect way, or a perfect formula to keep everyone happy in organizations; but there is a principle that tends to work, and that is *respect*. From my experience, leaders in the end, will understand that certain things have to change; their reactions in those high exposition moments is less about what the change *is*, and more about *how* it was done. Everybody needs to feel respected for what they have done, recognized and be emotionally safe, keep their face intact to their own teams. Moving parts based only on business rationale is necessary but not sufficient for a liberating, vital experience.

Activating decisions without the sensitivity to the ways those decisions affect their people is one of the most common misconceptions senior leaders develop along their journeys of success. These leaders, CEOs included, know of the pain some of these changes will inflict, and many of them go out of their way to avoid or minimize those conversations, leaving it to staff meetings, or to others to make them known. But the larger risk on those inexistent or minimized conversations is the lack of clarity and decisive expectation when radical or very consequential change is at stake. If a leader will no longer own certain segment of deliverable, product line, country, anything, it has to be spelled out perfectly clear, not in half-truths, incomplete detail. So much failure comes from this simple fact. It is better to have a difficult conversation once at the top, than to condemn the entire team to months of arm wrestling and confusion. Important changes have to be talked in person, with executive determination and also with compassion—those are not mutually exclusive. That is the only way we have a chance for authentic alignment and collaboration, a chance to move on. After that step is completed, a more tactical expectation is to ensure all c-suite leaders have implemented their engagement conversations with their teams. Now we can move along with the transformation.

Raise the vital infrastructure, make one liberating change. In the Vitality Design chapter, we made the case that we cannot expect superior results by decree. We have to work on making changes to the ways we manage and operate the business in order to alter its capacity to deliver something better. Having a real shot at meeting different expectations to achieve our ambitious goals correlates with the enabling infrastructure around people. The greatest talent will not mind shooting for a higher challenge, but not for one that is contrary to the design of the work, upstream the flow of the organization, predicated on working 60 hours, weekends, and building your own capacity. Just consider this; how many times transformations call for a change that is material enough to require a complete rethinking of the process and yet, we in management simply move on and leave it to the teams to figure out? While this is in one sense an action of trust, if not well calibrated for capacity and skill it comes across as insensitive or clueless. Take for example a case in which an area will lose 40% of their people to adjust to cost structure. Leaving the work and process untouched means that people will just take more and more work. This model is known all too well in companies across the spectrum and the main source of burnout. From all the changes I have witnessed over my thirty years in business transformations, it is very rare that resources come to save the day. In 99% of the cases, leaders face the reality of less resources but leaving their goals intact. The tendency is to ask everyone to work harder, but it is not sustainable. The only way to move forward is to reset priorities and creatively look at our business process and make at least one radical change. Eliminate something that is painful, find time removing meetings or some approvals. Skip non-essential steps, make decision faster, empower people differently. Your people needs to see you are listening.

Affirm the performance management process. We elaborated on the properties of a liberating, vital Performance Management Process in Chapter Eleven. What we will highlight now is the importance of unpacking the PMP process and remove obvious pieces that no longer belong. I recall a time when I joined a leading global company as head of Talent. The PMP process called for a set of competencies that everyone—everyone with no exception, CHRO included—told me it was dated, nobody used it anymore, that the model needed to change. And yet, in order to get your performance goals in the system, the programming forced every single employee to select one or two competencies from that irrelevant set, in order to 'develop' during the year. No better example of things employees see and just shake their heads in disbelief. Not liberating, not vital. In some companies the performance process is so dysfunctional that leaders have seriously considered removing it altogether, and you should proceed with caution if that is your decision,[1] in other cases you will want to radically reengineer it. Either way, know that this one process touches every employee and it has the largest impact on the perceptions of quality of management, fairness, career advancement of all people processes. It is also one of the hardest processes to change; it normally takes one year to design, and one year to retool the systems and communicate, prepare, and launch, making it a three-year project until you regain full stability. In order to set expectations right, while you are in the middle of a transformation you will not have the time to launch a multi-year initiative. The few things you can do, however, can go a very long way to ensure expectations are set properly:

- **Remove what is not essential.** Go for the low hanging fruit to find minutes and send the right message. For example, review the number of mandatory items you currently have: a minimum number of goals that is too large—you can ask to make it three and no more than five; a minimum number of development items, make it one; a minimum number of feedback sessions, make it less and encourage constant dialogue outside of the system. Software is now trending more flexible using phones, but even in those cases the idea is to keep your process but lower the weight of the 'mandatory' side of it.
- **Simplify and focus.** Make a push for relevance. Ask managers to make it more about quality than quantity. Goals should be about success, not activity—as much as the jobs permit, recognizing some jobs are about throughput rates. Goals should be meaningful and few, measurable with

numerical metrics and YES/NO criteria of success, aligned with top and department priorities.
- **Reaffirm your existing process.** Signal that the process is alive and should be followed, particularly if you are able to make simplifications. State that PMP is a win–win for company and people and a necessary discipline for everyone's growth.
- **Elevate what matters: the conversations, not 'the system'.** Managers and employees in general are unhappy with this process for many reasons. This is a complex process that likely will not run perfectly, somehow the system, the flows, the approvals will be onerous and cumbersome. However, that IS NOT the process, that is only how it is documented. Remind everyone that the process is built out from the conversations to create commitments between managers and employees. Those are distinct and free from systems.
- **Make the CEO the chief PMP voice.** In many companies the top of the house does not follow the PMP the way everyone else is expected to do. It is understandable that some elements are different as there are other incentives programs available for some populations that require different metrics and types of work. With that said, dates, documentation, and overall discipline to follow the process should not be different. The CEO is the only voice that can make this to be understood. Companies tend to speak to PMP as an "HR" priority, it must be established, because it is, an enterprise, transformational, and liberating priority.

To close this point, the performance process is also an essential tool to keep your absolute best and highest potential people. Those individuals love it when a good performance process differentiates the few among the many, ensuring the organization will 'notice' who are the best of the best.

Choose one change to optimize rewards. Changes in compensation policy or structure are not very easy to do, but they are doable if we have an analytically sound proposal and if we are selective. The key question to ask is: what is the one compensation change you can afford to send a vitality message and get everyone noticing you are listening and doing your best? Some examples to explore may include raising the merit increase for those most left behind in the base salary range, increase differentiation bonus for top performers in most critical areas for growth, include more jobs in bonus payments even if those percentages are small.

In general, companies must ensure they do not fall too far behind market for key groups in their compensation policy. As transformations take place in modern organizations, lower levels in the company have a larger proportion of sway in the ability of companies to win, sell more, retain customers, and keep costs in check. These are reasons why incentives are trending to include lower layers in companies.

Establish new expectations for managers. It is well documented and researched that results, success, performance, culture evolution, and engagement are increasingly more dependent from good management.[2] This truth is not lost for the best of the best organziations. The greatest companies, the most admired, resilient, and enduring, they all have dedicated initiatives, programs, and investments for managers. These companies have recognized for decades now the unparalleled impact managers have in performance and change management, and they invest on it. Investment is not to be confused with management training programs alone; they certainly have them, but there is much more than that. There are rotational programs, tools, mentoring, formalized 360 assessments, peer coaching, and institutionalized metrics on management effectiveness. For those companies, key questions are not left to chance but to deliberate choice: who should be allowed to manage? What is management for us? They have curated messaging with very clear language on EXPECTATIONS for managers in terms of their obligations, comprehensively.

Along the various disciplines and mindsets covered so far, we have been calling out the pivotal role managers play in transformation and Leading Success implementation. This is not just a cultural issue for companies, it is an economic issue as well, according to Gallup's research,[3] the cost of poor management and lost productivity from not engaged or actively disengaged employees is $8.8 trillion, or 9% of global GDP. Changing how people are managed is perhaps the easiest way to boost productivity within organizations. A liberating, vital leadership style that opens the gates of creativity, innovation and truly differentiating performance has a signature. Absent a formalized academic study of leadership attributes that will be conducted in time, based on first-hand experience during these transformations, and being the head of succession and leadership development for thirty years, I can offer a preliminary list of competencies as a practical, working hypothesis in an attempt to bring more specificity to manager expectations.

The illustration on Fig. 15.2 suggests a preliminary list of skill areas or high-level competencies that would serve as orientation for managers on what behaviors accelerate a liberating, vital expression organization climate. The list is not scientific, but rather experiential; based on my broad and deep exposure to competency models and their use in talent decision-making conversations. The competencies identified can be adapted, transferred to any other model your company is using. All serious competency models[4] come from similar studies, all of them based in similar assumptions, with global and multicultural validation. A different list can be obtained for liberating leadership with essentially the same outcomes orientation. Sometimes, specific words connect better with the narratives of companies and therefore could be selected on that basis.

In a non-technical language, the narrative for manager expectations, based on the skill areas identified in Fig. 15.2, would read as follows:

- We expect our managers to lead for the liberation of the organization to demolish its limitations and unnecessary complexities in favor of simplification, customer and employee experience. Managers can achieve that expectation by improving how they deal with *Complexity*, make sense of situations and contradictions to be effective *Decision-makers* that move the organization forward using data, but without paralysis. Ultimately, every manager is a liberating manager when she/he understands what the problem we are trying to solve is, believes in, and lives our *Purpose* in ways that motivates his/her people to action.
- We expect our managers to lead for the vitality design of the organization by understanding that people must experience the workplace as a place designed for performance and success, one that affirms our company's values and purpose, that our work is done with *Signature Processes Design* that manifests who we are. We do that by understanding how to optimize

Mindset	Skill areas	Behaviors for a liberating, vital workplace
Liberation	Complexity	*Analysis, Synthesis.* Simplify complexity to create spaces that liberate action. Align competing visions, agendas, build bridges, find intersections, offer new perspectives.
	Decisions	*Courage.* Keep the organization moving by eliminating dysfunctions and misalignment. Make the necessary, courageous decisions, fast to create velocity.
	Purpose	*Envision, Communicate.* Define a compelling, liberating 'North Star' that gives direction and differentiates our company from its competitors; master the ability to tell the story.
Vitality	Collaboration	*Connect.* Engage in Conversations to Create Commitment to explore and find productive alignments for work and execution. Avoids unnecessary collaboration.
	Differences	*Value, Include.* Constantly identifies opportunities to leverage the unique backgrounds and perspectives of a diverse team. Consciously works to create a belonging workplace.
	Process design	*Operate, Design.* Leverage knowledge from multiple sources to reconfigure, simplify, and design productive processes that deliver business value and customer experience.
Expression	Accountability	*Accountable.* Focus on the right outcomes and expectations to hold himself and the team accountable for the achievement of the transformation, purpose, not just the metrics.
	Results	*Execution.* Unwavering focus on delivering the expected outcomes under changing circumstances and imperfect conditions. Finds a way to win, while consistent to our values.
	Awareness	*Self Awareness.* The liberating leader – manager or not – excels at understanding her/his own strengths, weaknesses, tendencies and biases, and works to prevent those to interfere on their own's and their teams' success.

Fig. 15.2 Skill areas to define expectations for a liberating, vital expression leadership and management practice

the work in the first place; immediately work in *Collaboration* with adjacent areas to eliminate friction, misalignments and perform with shared objectives. They also know that productive collaboration and vitality infrastructure design require them to work effectively with multiple perspectives and *Differences* to bring a broader set of capacities to the teams for the benefit of our customers.
- We expect our managers to lead for liberating, vital expression by the application of the previous six competencies to the service of a superior performance by individuals who belong, can be their best selves, have a relevant assignment, and can be successful with the tools, information, and clarity on what is expected of them. These managers will ensure *Accountability* to the commitments and goals and will engage with their teams, manage performance as expression for exceptional *Results* to ensure the success of the organization. In the end, their *Self Awareness* plays a pivotal role for them to listen, internalize, and act on feedback, learn constantly, and build an organic diverse, inclusive, and belonging environments.

Manager Guide

Companies can only do so much to facilitate liberating, vital execution. The space where management becomes a close contact, conversational interaction is the space for the manager to master. In order for the organization to achieve its highest potential, manager's contribution is irreplaceable. Similar to the five points for the company, I have simplified in five points what I consider critical to set expectations for the Leading Success manager (Fig. 15.3).

Guide to vital expectations – Manager		
Fast start:	1	Be the story: why, what, how; "WIFM", respond to engagement
	2	Redesign the most critical positions for Talent Value
Every manager's five essential levers to set vital expectations right	3	Improve talent density at every opportunity
	4	Engineer great goals for the next cycle
	5	Redefine how you run your team - reset your vital governance

Fig. 15.3 What managers can do to improve execution

1. **Be the story**. Intelligent, informed, competent employees understand the imperatives of the business and want to see their manager consistently reinforcing and role modeling those aspirations. The fundamentals include managers being able to explain why the direction of choice makes sense for the company and for their department; why it is also good for employees. For example, our strategy may dictate we must abandon a product line to focus on another, or that we are now selling to a new customer base, never addressed before, that we are acquiring three companies this year, or that we are opening three offices in other countries. These are examples of strategic business decisions supporting a new direction that may have real implications for the teams receiving the news. If you are the CEO, the Human Resources manager, or the leader of one impacted division, what do you have to do in order to answer the question: how does that impact our team?

   During transformation times managers are called to be *translators*. The first thing employees want is to hear honest answers to their questions, even if those are not great news—as long as those can be shared per timing on regulated, contractual information flows. Then they want to know in which ways does the team is affected, and what is the contribution they are expected to make to see the changes implemented. This is more than a translation; it is also about *meaning making*. This is, to be able to credibly convey to their teams the rationality of the changes, mastering the story of change to describe how customers, the company, and employees win in the new vision. Meaning making is about helping people see the larger, longer-term picture. That will not make any bad news easier, but will make them rational, not capricious or simply the result of incompetence.

   Being the story also requires managers to show listening and adaptation; as mentioned earlier in the discipline of Engagement in Chapter Fourteen, most companies conduct employee surveys to identify areas where management in general, and managers in specific receive rich sets of data to learn about their employees' perceptions. Few actions carry more immediate impact than managers openly discussing on the data and making decisions to respond to employee's feedback.

2. **Redesign the most critical positions for Talent Value**. Consistent with the Talent Economy discussion in Chapter Eleven, a relatively fast and simple action managers can implement is to define position profiles for the most important roles that are open, and those they see as furthest away from a definition of success that aligns with the future. For example, during my manufacturing years early in my career we used to have electrical technicians and mechanical technicians in the maintenance

department. But as the new equipment started to arrive with combined electro-mechanical components, ever more integrated and sophisticated, the available skills from one side or the other would not be sufficient to intervene on the machines. In other words, the new talent value, the success criteria for the role, according to a Talent Economy perspective was the ability to have combined skills that made it possible to intervene the machines with one technician, not two. Positions change constantly, and we cannot use previous position's parameters to hire and performance-manage for the new parameters.

3. **Improve talent density at every opportunity.** Take the first opportunity that comes your way to improve talent density in your team. Promote, reassign, or hire the right person for that role. Ideally, someone that will provide clarity within days of being hired because the person possesses the skills and the intangibles for the future of that role. In many cases, that person already is in your team or in your company, waiting to be discovered and given an opportunity. And if that is not the case, do not be afraid to skip the internal pipeline (if indeed is inadequate) and bring the right talent. There are few opportunities to optimize talent, do not waste them in the people you know does not have the profile for future success.

4. **Engineer great goals for the next cycle**. This point should be the most straightforward of all. It is not a big project, and is not something new for managers to do—it simply is a call to raise the personal bar on defining goals with (not for) your people. A few considerations are important in times of fluidity and transformation. Some goals are complex and will not be completed in one cycle; it is the job of the manager to break the goals in segments that make sense for the velocity needed and the capacity of the environment, skills of the person to plan for success. The goals cannot be ambiguous. Per our discussion in performance in Chapter Eleven, goals have to be measurable in a 'yes–no' answer. For example, achieve revenue of 1.5 million USD in the southeastern region by end of Dec 31st of the year of planning". This can be answered YES or NO. Instead, if we write "achieve revenues according to master plan" someone could say that the master plan changed, got modified, that the distribution of territories was uneven. Or if we say, "complete the project on product design". Completing things may not be actual outcomes. If the outcome of completing the project is to have capacity to deliver six agile team to process 10 tasks simultaneously, then that is how the goal should be written, and we can answer with a yes or no to that articulation. In the end, your goal as manager is twofold. First, to have everyone in your

team answer YES to the statement "I know what is expected of me", and second, that they are COMMITTED to it. Goal setting is a conversation to create commitment, your people should not be 'convinced' of their goals; if a Leading Success approach has been followed, the expectation is that people will be excited to own the transformation and contribute. This may not be achievable in one conversation. Some goals take longer to accept and embrace, particularly when those goals include tough decisions to disrupt aspects of their operation. It will be important to look again at the conversation to create commitment section. Finally, what happens when your people simply does not believe in the goals or the direction? Can a manager still pursue excellence? And how is that achieved? In these cases, managers need to go back to step one in this list—convey the rationality of the story and present the case for the needs going forward. Most people will comply, but managers need to understand that changes may not be for everyone long term.

5. **Redefine how you run your team reset your vital governance**. How often your team meets, for how long, what are the agenda items, and how topics are reviewed, discussed, and decided upon. How you orchestrate the overall team-management to drive the team to performance. Get a refresh on that! Simplify, use better information, and design better agendas. Three important things to keep in mind:

- Remember what your governance provides: Coordination on priorities for transformation, collective analysis for decision-making, vital risk response to assess trends and plan for emerging disruptions, stewardship on adherence to values, and organization review.
- Make governance a signature process. This means, conduct your meetings with high standards and adherence to culture and values expectations. Solve problems, make them liberating and vital spaces for expression; no judgment for ideas, and incentivize innovation.
- Make governance developmental for your people. Nothing teaches more than a regular cadence of consistent management processes where your people sees you in action and absorbs the culture in practice.

In summary, the discipline of expectation is the operational foundation for success. The main, unwavering, and most critical goal of this discipline is to ensure everyone can answer the question 'I know what is expected of me'. With that in mind, we move to our last Discipline of the Leading Success model, EXPERIENCE.

Notes

1. Cappelli, P., & Tavis, A. (2016). The performance management revolution: The focus is shifting from accountability to learning. Harvard Business Review, October 2016.
2. Clifton, J., & Harter, J. (2019). It's the manager: Gallup finds that the quality of managers and team leaders is the single biggest factor in your organization's long-term success. Gallup Press.
3. Clifton, J., & Harter, J. (2023). Culture shock: An unstoppable force is changing how we work and live. Gallup's solution to the biggest leadership issue of our time. Gallup Press.
4. Korn Ferry. (2019). Korn Ferry leadership architect: Global competency framework. Research guide and manual. Korn Ferry.

16

Experience: Mastering Expression as Performance

The ninth discipline, *Experience*, represents the landing operational outcome from our leadership and design efforts. We want our customers and our employees to have a *signature experience,* rooted in concrete, operational encounters with our processes, products, and people with one simple outcome: *everyone's success*. The final metric of Leading Success is the degree to which our people, our customers, and our investors are successful in the larger picture, not only in the immediate but in the long-term results.

> Our ultimate goal in Leading Success is to articulate the right vision (Liberation), build the necessary infrastructure (Vitality), and coordinate all aspects of the organization's performance (Expression), to produce one outcome: *success.*

Success is the result of employee's and customer's capacity to achieve goals and transformation, by expressing themselves at their highest potential; for employees, their highest potential for performance and growth; for customers, their highest potential for winning, such as the completion of significant goals, differentiation in their industries, revenue, powerful choices, and endurance. Both employee experience and customer experience can be measured. But before going there, let's explore how experience comes about and how it can be mastered as a discipline.

Experience. By definition, an *experience* is a perception that comes from exposure to anything that helps us sense reality, including what we call virtual reality. In general, these perceptions produce an effect on us—a satisfactory or unsatisfactory experience. Sources of experience can be events, actions from other people, or anything that is part of the surrounding environment. In our case the environment is built from the *expressions* from the self and from others—including real persons, material objects, or digital, virtual expressions.

Experience is created from expression. When you walk into a place, be that a hotel, a restaurant, or a first day in a new job, you are receptive to many forms of welcoming expressions, either from a host or from a manager. Those are *designed,* not accidental or random expressions, even in those cases where you see nobody, there may be a curated environment with music, clean space, details in decoration that 'expresses' care, which makes it for a positive experience. Fortunately, we all go through multiple experiences everyday, and we can compare and contrast. In the end, how anybody 'feels' at some point, or in a particular place and time, is a product of many collapsed expressions that create another expression in you. Gratitude, elation, excitement, or perhaps displeasure, frustration, or even disrespect. That is why in Leading Success we are not targeting just expressions, but *signature expressions*, those rooted in what we want our customers and employees to see, and experience based in our values, our culture.

The right signature experience creates affection and attachment to our company, our brand, and what we stand for. People wants to belong to places that 'feel right'. Those 'feelings' Gartner discovered being so foundational to employee's perception of value[1] are *experiences* lived by employees affirming that their companies see them as their whole selves and treat them with inclusivity and respect. It is the same for our customers. As they interact with our people, our products, and solutions, they will experience our 'expressions' to be liberating, inclusive, and designed for their success. In short: *experience is economic value*. Documented in multiple ways over the years,[2] employee and customer experience are represented in the bottom line.

> **More than a belief, a demonstrable fact**: Signature Expression creates Signature Experience for customers and employees, and with that, sustainable economic value, resilient cultures, superior performance, and unparalleled capacity of transformation.

Signature Experience Is Always by Design

You may wonder why bother creating a discipline for Experience. It seems straightforward that employee experience is the outcome of many, overlapping events, actions, and messages at work. Is that not a sufficient analysis? The answer to that question is yes if you are managing for results of today's world, not for tomorrow. Leading Success is not only about the present, but the future. Our goal is to be ambidextrous, as introduced by O'Reilly and Thusman in their book Lead and Disrupt.[3]; being ambidextrous means that we can manage both, ensure today's survival—ADAPT—and ensure our future implementing the transformation—DISRUPT—to bring the capacity of the organization to a raised level of performance and relevance.

Since we are building a liberating space, we are not talking about experience as something that happens on its own, but as something we design for (vitality) and create (perform toward it). For example, if you design your product, you know what customers want, what they value, with that input you mobilize design teams to produce those exact expectations as much as you can to make the experience of satisfaction happen in your customers. The very unpacking of your product should be a signature experience. If you are selling software, groceries, clothing, or even a car, how signature is your 'unpacking', set up, and first use? Altering the Experience at the point of contact—for both employees and customers—is not something that happens easily by improvisation. It could happen once or twice, but consistency and scale for a designed experience can only be obtained by a designed process. One that is specified, documented, measurable, resourced, and properly implemented. We all have heard of exceptional employees who put the extra effort to create signature experiences on their own, but that is not a sustainable strategy. That is why we need a Leading Success set of disciplines. In the rush for results, leaders in organizations tend to skip the vitality step altogether and shortcut strategy directly into planning and execution, leaving processes, policies, workflows intact in the same ways they were designed for the past. The experience we are describing as *signature* is one that nurtures a particular point of view for the team, the organization, the customer, as well as our purpose and values. That experience is different, and it is based on managers playing a role in execution that includes more than the usual governance and supervision. We need them to be connectors of intention and meaning, exhibit deliberate behaviors that will unlock and reorient the *events* and the *expressions* in the way they add up, harmonize, and multiply to create performance, resilience, success, and belonging. Designing and activating an experience can be complex. It is no accident that many more companies are creating Chief Experience Officers, reporting to CEOs to manage this emerging source of value.

Producing the Signature Experience

An experience by definition lives inside the person's mind. It is not something completely objective. It is influenced by the person's state of mind, history, cultural heritage. If this is true, how is it possible to expect a predictable response on employees and customers knowing that so much of it comes as a perception that we can't control?

In general, this is true. We can't control people's perceptions and emotions. However, our employees are not just random human beings taken out from a database. Your employees are adult human beings who have been in the professional market, with training, achievements, credentials, who chose working for you, conscious and aware of the common employment situations and environments that are to be expected as 'reasonable'. In that sense, there is a baseline of general expectation about a work experience and how it should be. You are not planning for a complete unknown. This works in our favor because we are not in need to design for wild variations of talent standards. At the same time this general expectation works against us because the pandemic and the social events raised the bar of what a 'reasonable expectation' is, and what a new 'baseline' employee value proposition should include. That is, in addition to business success and growth, aspects of employee experience consistent with the company's values, tolerance, diversity, social responsibility, and environmental causes. The experience, therefore, has to be a *signature experience* or it will fall short in the raised 'reasonable' expectations of those employees we depend most upon. For example, an employee has been skipped for promotion, and she/he is confused and likely angry. However, if the manager rationally explains the specific aspects of work that can be addressed immediately by the employee, the conversation turns into something different; it is about the project for growth and the affirmation that the company cares. It becomes a liberating experience because it frees the employee from unwarranted perceptions of disinterest, abandon, and lack of appreciation. If the reasoning is solid, the outcome is powerful. The closer the experience is to our aspirations, the more *signature* to our company the experience becomes. This leads to employee loyalty and commitment which translates into economic value. Similarly, for customers, any service interruption that is addressed quickly and resolved with the customers' interests in mind will be affirming that they have the right partner, not just the right vendor. As you can see in the illustration shown in Fig. 16.1, every time our customers or our employees get to experience the organization demonstrating their values it becomes memorable and affirming, which is exactly what the aforementioned examples illustrate. We are making the experienced "world", or what we can call 'reality' BECOME a manifestation of what we have said, and committed to or our "word", in the form of our values and our customer promises. In other words, to the eyes of customers and employees, we (and they) have become the vision.

Imagine the simplest organization. A personal tutor in front of her pupil, or a personal piano teacher with his student. A one-to-one interaction, no managers, no collateral infrastructure. In that case, whatever outcomes are in the teacher's mind, their style, their vision for that interaction, is now reality and instantly becomes the student's experience. There are no intermediaries, no distance, no narratives to fulfill. Just expression and experience flowing both ways. If the session was intended to be exciting, that is exactly what it becomes. The experience matches the vision instantly, with fidelity. The 'word' in the teacher's mind is the 'world' in the student's experience—it is 'reality'. As the sessions go, the student will improve and eventually she/he will be a competent apprentice. The 'world' is now closer to the original vision of success as discussed with the parent, or with the student in a conversation—the 'word' that got both of them into the commitment to go through the learning process.

This translation from word to world is the essence of *becoming*. The tutor, teacher is permanently listening, constantly aware of the performance and to the whole expression of the student. As it turns necessary, with

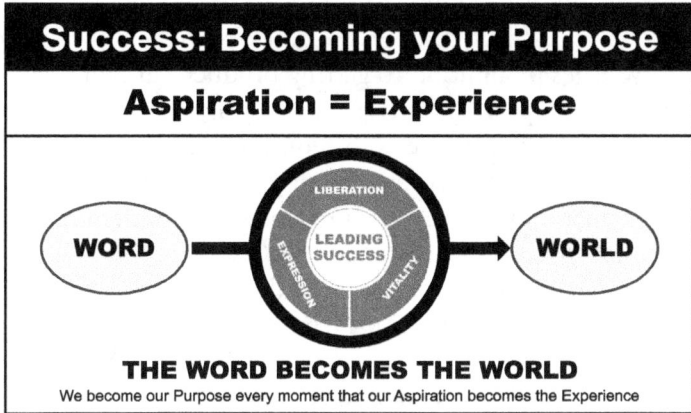

Fig. 16.1 The essence of leading success is to ensure that our vision becomes the experience, at scale

the appropriate and timely approach the tutor intervenes to adjust, correct, and sometimes, make a full stop the reset and install a new feature, a new component that will make the performance better. There is language, there is demonstration, there is examination in a dynamic of expressions interchange to generate an outcome. For generations, this was the method for learning and also for production, the artisanal way. A master of a craft passing expertise to apprentices. The performance was the expression immersed in the interchange of experiences. Performance was not separated from the performer. The master seeks to leverage every aspect of the apprentice's skills and personality. While the world has changed significantly to mass production of almost everything, and the use of automation is ever growing to achieve economies of scale, the nucleus of what a work experience *is*, remains unchanged, tied to the interaction of expressions from and with the people surrounding us. It is the need for scale, productivity, profitability that creates a new complexity on building the experience to perform, to learn, and to be successful.

The larger the enterprise the more steps we find between the 'word' and the 'world'. Startups are exciting places to be because teams—usually small—are strongly connected to the founder's vision—or to the founder herself! The noble aspirations to make an impact to the world, making lives better is visible in every conversation, in every design discussion, at every corner of the company. We are all allowed to dream big, but with success comes growth and the need to add steps between aspiration and reality; not to anybody's fault, it is the cost of success—more people, more entities, structures, layers, bureaucracy, and diverging points of view.[4] All of that is great as long as it is aligned. In growing, accelerating organizations everything scales, but it is not a certainty that the founder's management capability does. Entrepreneurs seldom are equipped to deal with the organizational acumen, acquired through years going through the ranks, to maneuver their companies across maturity stages in addition to getting product out and investors ready; and therefore, gaps appear. In very simple terms, the role of the manager in creating a signature experience is to replicate the tutor role of old, or the entrepreneur role of early—to connect with people in order to make meaning of what is going on as illuminated by our values. The modern manager creates the same personal space with each one of his/her direct employees and then, engages in the interaction to create enhanced performance, together.

Scaling brings and important consideration. The nine disciplines are not always necessary for smaller teams. A growing startup, from a one-to-one relationship, a small team with a couple of layers in between top manager and employees will require at least three elements to be in place for the creation of the experience: clarity on a liberating purpose and direction (leadership of liberation), a minimal coordination or tasks not to overlap and duplicate costs; who does what, what are the best people for us, how do we work (vitality design); and finally, a way to guide employees through the work and any possible unexpected situations to ensure success nonetheless. These are the three most fundamental components for success. Lead, design, perform, to experience success.

As the company grows, the opportunities for failure and disconnection also grow; now with hundreds or more employees, reaching the experience the way we intended in the vision includes many more people, processes, geographies, connections, different cultures through M&A and other partnerships activity. In these cases, we have to scale our capacity to make experience equal to the vision by going through the nine disciplines to reach the signature experiences and therefore success. And that is how we find ourselves in this ninth discipline.

The Process of Becoming

Becoming is not just a conceptual philosophy or a compelling theory; it is a process; it is operational. The discipline of Experience dictates that managers must live in the intersection between the WORD and the WORLD—aspiration and real experience, called *Becoming*; constantly enabling, connecting the vision with actions, decisions to produce the designed experience.

As a consequence, managers must *reframe their role*—how they use their time in meetings, conversations, decisions—as venues where they merge purpose with action. Great execution for liberating experience comes down the adoption of a fluid mindset for both manager and team. An understanding of work interactions that are meant to *modify reality through an outcome*, not only to *produce an outcome*. Here is how it looks:

- Managers help their people *see different possibilities* to address the issues, they ask different questions and bring data to help their teams appreciate an emerging risk or trend that must be addressed. Sometimes, teams or individuals—managers included—are too focused on a particular way of looking at things, perhaps a dated definition or a constraint that lives in the way people think based on past assumptions.
- These ingrained beliefs can't be just dictated away from people's minds by decree of the manager. Only the team or the individual herself/himself can do that. This is, they have to *believe something different* could be the answer. Managers use the data and new perspectives to remove those mental barriers that impede the discovery of new possibilities or solutions.

- This opens doors to consider a much broader playbook of possibilities, and in the process unfreezes teams, prompting them to *think differently*, creatively, with more tolerance for risk and bolder actions. The process continues to action, but not just any action. This is an action coming from a team that allowed themselves to think out of the box, with high ambition, purpose in mind, and no fears.
- Therefore, this is a *signature action* that expresses who they are, and what they believe. This action can be big or small, a rather punctual step on a larger project or a whole new initiative altogether, but either way, one thing has changed for sure; in the process of becoming, the bar was risen for the action to be *signature*, remarkable, ambitious, non-conventional. The kind of actions that transform reality for good. This is where managers have the space to demand very high standards and where liberation means excellence.

Three Accelerators for Signature Experience

As leaders and teams adopt a perspective to see, believe, think, and act differently, there are three critical accelerators that stimulate the process of becoming. These accelerators function the way aerodynamics works for airplanes and rockets. They smartly improve how the motion develops with less friction to gain velocity, efficiency, momentum. These three accelerators are universal and produce immediate impact: Decision Effectiveness, Prioritization, and Signature Feedback.

- **Decision Effectiveness**. In their book Decide and Deliver,[5] Marcia Bienko, Michael Mankins, and Paul Rogers make the point that

    Decision Effectiveness is … a path to a better organization, one that accomplishes what it sets out to do and that liberates, rather than oppresses the people who work for it.

    In a nutshell, according to the Decision Effectiveness model—developed at Bain & Company—being effective at decision-making is about four important dimensions in all decisions. The decision has to be *good*, made *faster than competitors*, be *implemented as intended*, and achieved with a reasonable amount of *effort*. If any of these dimensions starts to fail, the organization suffers by losing its capacity to move, to gain agility, and will slow down by bureaucratic friction. These attributes are called Quality, Speed, Yield, and

Effort in the model. Bain Consulting developed a survey to quantify these dimensions to produce the Decision Effectiveness Index, which is a significant predictor of organizational effectiveness and growth.

As leadership of liberation gets operational, very few frameworks deliver so much liberating value than this. Becoming effective at decision-making is directly correlated with being organizationally set for success. Decision effectiveness is greatly improved with the definition of *decision rights*, which are the main roles included in a decision process. To this end, Bain & Company designed the RAPID tool, a simple five step framework to identify which are these roles and how they work together to enhance Decision Effectiveness.[6] The RAPID roles are defined as follows:

Recommend: the role in charge of collecting input, understanding the content and context of the issue to be decided about, and produce a recommendation for the decision.
Agree: this role is assigned to people who must agree with the recommendation in order to proceed with the decision—can't be ignored. In other words, this role has veto power on the recommendation.
Perform: this role is for the people who will implement the decision once it is made.
Input: This role is for people who will provide input and insight for the recommender. Input can be wide or specific, or both. It may include interviews, reports, and surveys. Input can be ignored.
Decide: this is the most important role in decision effectiveness. Every role matter, but the "D" is unique in this model. There has to be one person, not a committee, to make the final decision.

RAPID is not designed for consensus, but to commit the organization to action, to increase its effectiveness and velocity. As simple as they may look in the surface, decision rights go a long way in organizations; they are essential to build consistency, add focus, and eliminate confusion. Decision Rights reinforce a culture of accountability and productivity. What are the signs to show decision effectiveness may be necessary in your organization?

- Nobody seems to have the power to make a decision. Confusion, paralysis.
- Too many people claim the power to make the decision. Power wars.
- Too many people feeling they have veto power.
- Prevalence of opinions instead of data as input.
- Every decision follows a different pattern.

- Not clear where to go with information, where to expect a decision coming from.
- Teams wonder… who is in charge?

I have personally applied RAPID for about a decade and a half with absolutely great results and great acceptance by teams at all levels.

- **Prioritization**. Prioritization is hard because leaders must choose projects to kill, and they fear upsetting people they care about, or organizations they want to support. But removing things from the list creates space, oxygen, instant liberation that translates rapidly in energy, removes excuses, and concentrates scarce resources in the vital things. Also, signals to the organization that we have courageous leadership that makes sense of what matters most. Good prioritization is not so much an art as it is science; it is a powerful byproduct of a governance that works, where leaders use data, assess the context, and adjust to the changing circumstances like a navigation system does in your car. There is a destination and the ideal route, but traffic, accidents, road closures dictate new routes should be followed. You are the navigation system for your team. Any measure of confusion is directly attributable to the manager. In difficult situations, some projects must be abandoned, postponed, and focus on the most important areas for value to customers and employees. The ability to remove obstacles in times of emergency and distress is one of the most liberating roles managers can have, and this helps the team become successful, powerful to address adversity, and unafraid of doing the same.
- **Signature Feedback**. While we normally look at feedback under the lenses of how managers help employees do a better work and grow, it is also necessary to help managers get feedback about their roles as managers. A global study conducted by Gallup worldwide,[7] shows that:

> …the majority of managers receive little feedback on how effectively they manage their team. Less than half of U.S. employees (42%) report having the opportunity to formally provide feedback to their manager, and fewer than one in four (24%) have formally rated their manager's performance. Managers are not getting much help from their peers either, with only about a third (36%) of managers saying they receive feedback from their peers as part of a formal feedback process.

Feedback is needed by everyone, including our management ranks. We have known for decades that the most direct performance improvement comes from accurate, useful, and timely feedback. However, feedback is often oversimplified, confined to a quarterly or annual ritual program. Execution, Expression, and Becoming require feedback to be a more common occurrence, a constant, trusted conversation that covers both, how the work gets done better and what behaviors help doing that. What is most interesting, this is the one thing employees want more. That same Gallup study shows "feedback" as the most common blind spot for managers and the top ranked known weakness. For anybody embarked on an effort to improve as leader of liberation, this should be a very attainable low hanging fruit that will deliver value instantly.

The Source of Signature Experience

What is at the center of a workplace that facilitates the emergence of a manager and an employee reaching their point of peak performance as a result of their most extraordinary abilities being displayed? We are interested on finding a way to raise—not to neutralize—the extraordinary, the unconventional, and the genius every person has within. To have employees' performance coming from their own interests, passion, and personal convictions, not only ours'. And how do we do the above at scale?

As noted in previous examples, it is easier to see such peak performances on elite athletes, singers, architects, who are expected to make a rendition of their best selves every time they perform, creating with it something special every time: superior quality, exceeding standards, resulting in tangible benefits for them and their organizations. Superior performance translates in superior customer experience, investor interest, engagements, followers, and a positive reputation. There is a special level of accomplishment and meaning that comes with those performances. On a different scale of celebrity and in a different stage, not much is different for people in common professional jobs with varying degrees of authority and sophistication. They too—we all—long for that meaningful legacy in our world, *and in our work*. Doctors, nurses, teachers, as well as sales representatives, finance specialists, marketing professionals, executives, bankers, and public officers in governments. Everyone aspires to being their best at what they do, creating masterpieces of their own.

The reasonable question now is, which factors in the work environment matter most for this outcome to occur?

My short answer would be to work on the implementation of the three mindsets and the nine disciplines as described in this book. But in an attempt to isolate one single behavior that gives a crisp orientation to leaders on how to create expression that drives performance I would say the following:

At the center of *expression as performance* we find the main source of employee experience—the manager—whose job is to build the environment where such expressions can be possible in the first place. This environment relates to two big factors: (1) the team as a whole, and (2) each individual on that team.

At the team level, by making sure the team acts—like *a team*. My preferred example of this condition is given by Patrick Lencioni in his book *The Advantage*.[8] He defines the concept of '*First Team*'. A first team is one where "*members of the team place higher priority to the team they are a member of, than the team they lead in their departments*". Which is extraordinarily difficult to do and sustain, but it is achievable and makes a world of difference. I have been part of such teams. It is not a natural act; these teams must be consciously and purposefully created, cultivated over time, and reinforced constantly. In my perspective however, a First Team exist not just because people opts in, but because that choice is affirmed by the way they feel by being part of the team—accepted, included, relevant, they belong, they can be successful. All of those attributes are outcomes of the leader as liberator. As a corollary, First Teams are only possible with liberating leadership.

At the individual level, the nucleus of that center is a manager that has learned to be comfortable seeing, accepting, and embracing people as they are, in their totality—not just focused on what they deliver, but also on how their unique experiences and attributes bring differentiating value to customers and to each other in the team. These managers do not intend to separate the performance from the performer. Such separation comes in the form of a manager who is making efforts to ignore, to dismiss anything that is uniquely special about a team member, signaling that any diverse issues do not belong in the workplace. For some leaders, this is the right way forward; turn a blind eye to what is different. Unfortunately, that only works for the manager, not for the employees. We must be careful as leaders not to surrender to trends and influence groups. Being accepting and inclusive is being commercially smart, robust, innovative, and sustainable; does not mean we are weak and biased.

It is also hard to define what makes someone unique. For example, neurodiversity, unique backgrounds such as military, some disabilities, multiple nationalities. None of that is part of the job but is part of the person. When those attributes are appropriately appreciated—not overstated—it creates the signature experience we are looking for. See Fig. 16.2.

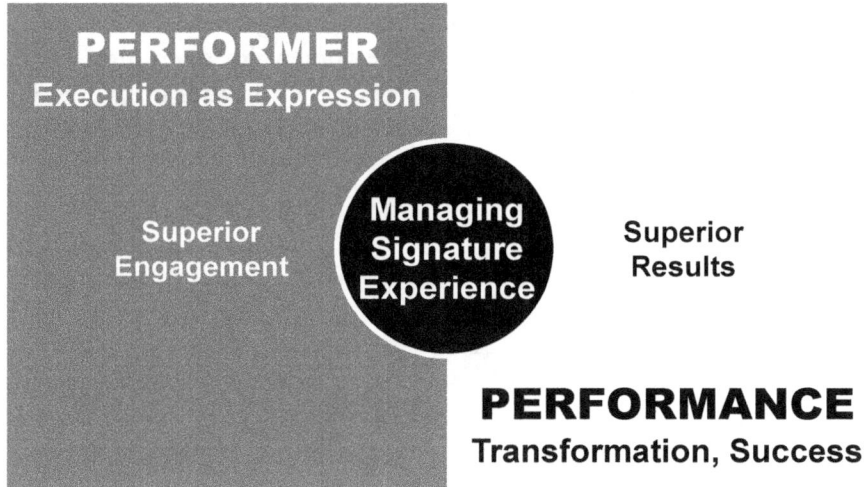

Fig. 16.2 Expression and performance as the keys for signature experience

Great leaders recognize that signature experience comes from performance that is elevated by the performer, and they find ways to bring the best output from their people by allowing their genius to show. As a consequence, a manager must become the purpose in order to inspire others to do it. Every employee must become the purpose in order to inspire our customers in their liberation journey with our products. The fate of management is to become the purpose she/he wants to create.

Nine Disciplines, Signature Experience, and Success

We have completed our journey covering the three mindsets, Liberation, Vitality, and Expression, and we have discussed every one of the nine disciplines from Discipline #1 *Aspiration* to Discipline #9 *Experience*. The philosophical and technical aspects of Leading Success are completed with abundant detail on perspectives, frameworks, and tools to bring Leading Success to operational action, not just reflection. With several global companies being the beneficiaries of these approaches, tested and refined, you will be in great company should you choose to seek inspiration or to directly implement any of the above.

With that said, the value of Leading Success is not only in the implementation of its disciplines, but in the achievement of its outcomes, designed to unleash capacities to reach a next level, a quantum leap of effectiveness in your organization to excel in the Purpose era. Leading Success, is therefore, a vehicle of unprecedented organizational development for the future.

The next section is dedicated to the exploration of the four main outcomes that emerge from Leading success: business, culture, people, and legacy. Let's now start that conversation.

Notes

1. Venkataramani, Swetha. (2021). Make way for a more human-centric Employee Value Proposition. Gartner, Human Resources Insights, digital article May 13, 2021. Retrieved from: https://www.gartner.com/smarterwithgartner/make-way-for-a-more-human-centric-employee-value-proposition
2. Metha, N., & Pickens, A. (2020). The customer success economy: Why every aspect of your business model needs a paradigm shift. Wiley. New Jersey.
3. O'Reilly, C. A. III, & Tushman, M. L. (2016). Lead and disrupt: How to solve the innovator's dilemma. Stanford Business Books. Stanford, CA.
4. Zook, C., & Allen, J. (2016). The founder's mentality: How to overcome the predictable crises of growth. Harvard Business Review Press.
5. Bienko, M. W., Mankins, M. C., & Rogers, P. (2010). Decide and deliver: 5 steps to breakthrough performance in your organization. Harvard Business Review Press.
6. Bienko, M. W., & Rogers, P. (2006). Who has the D? How clear decision roles enhance organizational performance. Harvard Business Review.
7. Clifton, J., & Harter, J. (2019). It's the manager: Gallup finds that the quality of managers and team leaders is the single biggest factor in your organization's long-term success. Gallup Press.
8. Lencioni, P. (2012). The advantage: Why organizational health trumps everything else in business. Jossey-Bass.

Part III

Outcomes

17

Business Outcomes: Transformation Success

After the rich discussion on the Nine Disciplines and the Three Mindsets, we are in a position to unpack the 'so what' of the entire approach in Leading Success. This book is not only about what needs to be done, but also about how to ensure you get the outcomes you intended to achieve from its application. The nine disciplines serve two purposes in this endeavor.

First, the Nine Disciplines are a path to follow for those companies who want to reset themselves for the future. This is normally the case when a new chief executive is hired to follow a particular direction the board of directors has considered to be necessary for the company. The new CEO will normally spend a reasonable amount of time, proportionate to the situation, learning about the particulars of the business, which are never visible from the outside, and then decide on the general concept of transformation needed. It is at this point when the Leading Success architecture is a formidable guiding framework to follow. Companies may have well developed components—disciplines—already in place. In those cases, Leading Success becomes a useful menu of components to select from, and then connect to existing capabilities. For example, an acquisition may bring new capacity that must be integrated but also create a gap to fulfill—I recall a case in which the company acquired was so significantly under pay standards that for some time we had to manage two compensation tabulators. Some misalignments can't be solved immediately. Depending on the situation you will not always need the whole nine disciplines, but you may need to use their content as a verification checklist to assess how they add up and blend in the new enhanced company.

The second way the Leading Success framework works is as a framework to compare potential external vendors or consultants on the value they bring to

Leading Success Business Roadmap
The essential disciplines to activate

Company size	Mindset	Year 1			Year 2			Year 3			
Small	Liberation	d1									**Go essential**
	Vitality		d5								• Focus on clarity, talent and expression.
	Expression			d9							• Feed from the founder's vision and energy.
Medium	Liberation	d1	d2	d3							**Go simplified**
	Vitality				d4	d5	d6				• Accelerated plan.
	Expression						d7	d8	d9		• Simplified, complete version. • Innovative, agile execution.
Large	Liberation	D1	D2	D3							**Go comprehensive**
	Vitality				D4	D5	D6				• Large, complex, global, multi-culture; move a giant.
	Expression							D7	D8	D9	• Needs buy in, steady pace. • No false starts.

d = simplified version of disciplines; D = comprehensive version of disciplines

Fig. 17.1 Recommended implementation roadmaps per company size

your transformation—a checklist of sorts. Not all consulting firms specialize on the entire spectrum of the Leading Success model (Fig. 2.3). Leading Success gives you the certainty that you know the key building blocks any transformation takes to completion; you are no longer dependent on somebody else's model, even if you chose to follow a reputed consultant, now you have a validated, neutral model to verify how the strengths and weaknesses of the different solutions your consultant brings match up with what you can supplement internally for a successful intervention. One way or the other, if you do it yourself, or if you bring external support, this framework is helpful for your success.

Another important consideration on your implementation is the size of your operation. While the Nine Disciplines hold true for any type or size of company, the implementation will look different. The implementation Business Roadmap shown in Fig. 17.1 illustrates how implementations will adjust to size.

For simplification I have identified three generic company sizes. I am considering as *small* organizations those from single digit to about a hundred employees; this will include most startups. Revenue and investment volumes are not relevant to the dynamics of success in terms of the disciplines. I am considering *medium* a broad sway of sizes ranging from one hundred to about a thousand employees. While this may look too wide, and you may think that a one hundred people company is very different from a one thousand people company, they have a couple of elements in common as transformations are concerned. First, they start adding layers, they need mid-management;

the founder or the central manager cannot possibly affect more than fifty to a hundred people with the same level of effectiveness, particularly is the company is not co-located. For must customer-centric, or software-powered businesses, the jobs will be differentiated and thus require increasing levels of coordination between them. The second similarity is that growth at this stage depends on their ability to scale effectively, not only to put product out and prove valuable against competitors, or serve a very small, unique niche. In other words, from about 100 to about 1000 employees, companies need increasing mid-management and increasing scalability of core processes to be successful. The third category, called *large*, is for companies above a thousand people. In these cases, it is to be expected a high degree of specialization, departments or multiple groups of people dedicated to serve under each of the disciplines, making it necessary to dig deep on each particular aspect of transformation.

As you look into the table, I have identified lowercase discipline designations d1–d9, and capital D designations: D1–D9. This is a way to make the point about how deep companies are suggested to go as they work on these disciplines. Particular circumstances of some medium or even small companies may require substantial work and investment on these disciplines, so we can't just completely rule out a deeper D in a small company. For example, if we are talking about a rather specialized technical component for aerospace applications, or a medical instrumentation product, we may want to go very deep on talent, or in operational design for quality and product development. Not all small, medium, or large companies are created equal.

Small Size Company Implementation

For the prototypical small company, my recommendation is to target a one-year implementation. The chief assumption here is that many cultural aspects that slow down success for larger organizations are just a natural way of being for smaller groups of people, in particular, those in early stages of their journey, like startups. The founder is the fuel and the embodiment of the nine disciplines. With that assumption in mind, I recommend CEOs to focus on only three disciplines to begin with. I call this approach, *Go Essential*, suggesting that there is no time for a lot more. In fact, there may not even be someone whose job is 100% People or Processes. But what we know is that they have clarity, or should have clarity on their North Star, their aspiration, which tends to be very present in those early years. In those cases where early writings or articulations may not be sufficient as a conceptual foundation for the future, some validation, elaboration can be done with the help of external experts. I called it 'd1', instead of 'D1', to signal this is not to be a heavy consulting engagement. On the other hand, sometimes founders get it right from the very beginning. Here is an example from Crane Company—a technology company—whose founder Richard Teller Crane, wrote this resolution in 1855, when he was still in his 20 s, and has been the foundation of the company's culture for more than 150 years[1]:

> I am resolved to conduct my business in the strictest honesty and fairness; to avoid all deception and trickery; to deal fairly with both customers and competitors; to be liberal and just toward employees and to put my whole mind upon the business.
> Richard Teller Crane, 1855

No corporate talk, it was all him, and this is the highest test of authenticity, that the original ethos comes directly from the source, the founder, with a message that is also remarkably relevant for our times. The second discipline I recommend for small companies is d5, Talent. It only comes natural at this stage that every single seat in the company is extraordinarily consequential, essential, and every person occupying it has to be 'the one'. Remember that talent is a very broad set of artifacts. It covers selection, onboarding role definition, and compensation. This is where some effort must be dedicated to defining who does what, and some basic delineations of ownership, without micromanagement or too many documents, just clarity. Leading Success' Talent Economy approach indicates that we must hire for the outcomes and value the company requires, not for activity. This, again, comes natural for early stage companies. For those not in a start-up stage but still small, talent economy is also critical because they only can afford so many people, they can't have the luxury to carry the wrong talent for growth. The third discipline I recommend is d9, Experience. At this stage the small company may opt for light mobile systems to power the essential employee services, but their focus is not there, appropriately. The focus must be on how employees create the signature customer experience envisioned in their aspiration, to secure the company's survival and growth. Experience in small operations is very close to management and to the founder. The founder becomes a source of culture in the everyday of things and supplies for the lack of written values. Founders leverage their constant connections with people, customers, and processes, and spend time experimenting to find better ways to make the vision real and fast. Founders and CEOs of these companies are many things: product development, marketing, investor relations, chef collaboration, and chef philosophy officers—and they are also learning how to succeed. That is why we do not need all nine disciplines early on. As the company grows, or as the company matures, there will be room to gain on other disciplines over the years.

Medium Size Company Implementation

Medium size companies, for the purposes of our analysis, have a wide range of size variation. In that sense, as articulated earlier, the common challenge is the necessity for middle management and the need to scale everything, not just the 'secret sauce' but the infrastructure to create it. In other words, they need to find a way to sustain growth operationally. From the distance, some may think this is a no-brainer, just keep growing; but it is not an easy task. The wrong growth strategy can create cost and complexity delaying your chances to compete effectively. Mid-size companies are in a difficult middle ground. Not too small to operate with simplicity, not too large to be able to fund sophisticated tools and solutions, not fully resourced to tackle all the challenges created by external forces. Everything is in between. The issue is exacerbated when they have multiple locations, countries, languages, and cultures. Going for a transformation involves more people and more time that it would require for a small company. We cannot depend on the founder's or the CEO's presence to bridge gaps for a liberating and vital culture because one person cannot physically be in too many places, even with extraordinary travel routines. We need to create a journey for the organization to follow. Based on these complexities I recommend applying all disciplines, as long as they are performed in their most agile and fast implementation possible—represented by lowercase d's in Fig. 17.1. These companies will start to have sufficient manpower to dedicate resources to optimize their transformation. It is no longer a one man show, the founder is concerned with leading an emerging high-level C-suite team, in need of integration.

New leaders, with fresh and stimulating perspectives bring new content, visions, and methods into the emerging complexities of the company, and now we need better *design*, coordination, and more consistency. There will be a need to think thoroughly and integrate fast. All nine disciplines will have to be implemented but we can't dedicate too much of our time. Two years will be a palatable timeframe for management and investors, unless there are special circumstances, significant M&A, or technology adoptions. However, the point is to move along as identified in the table *Go Simplified*, where simple and timely is better than perfect. The biggest value is flexibility and agility to accelerate the company's maturity. The founder will not always be as visible or even present anymore, so her/his vision has to be codified through the liberating, vital design from vision to processes in ways to discover what the signature of the company really is. The greatest advantage on this size of companies as they embark in transformational efforts is that they have sufficient mass to be able to create lasting, enduring inertia in the right direction. They are still moldable enough to define a brand of management for decades to come and truly alter their DNA within a couple of years. Leading Success is a terrific approach for these companies which can't always bring the top Dollar consultants to help them in the effort.

Large Size Company Implementation

When a company is already large, multinational, most likely publicly traded, been around for decades, with sophistication and resources to have dedicated teams for everything, a transformation is a big deal. Some of these transformations are in the news; Fortune 500 organizations reverberate in labor markets and also in city politics when layoffs are involved, offshoring, closing, or opening of massive operations. These are maneuvers of redirection similar to the ones you see in transatlantic ships; can't move too fast or you break the structure. There are significant advantages of a large company transformation implementation, namely, resources, a powerful brand behind you, and proven governance structures already in place. But there is also a number of factors that must be considered to manage risks; with very prominent sources of corporate power, influence at the top is not a given—CEOs can't just go and mandate things as they would do in smaller companies, unless they are willing to pay the price on multiple fronts and create uncertainty. In some extreme cases, that level of disruption may just be exactly what the CEO wants. For example Elon Musk's management of his acquisition Tweeter, mandating people back from homes, eliminating entire departments overnight, changing the name of the company with one of the most recognized brands ever created.

Those are risks not everyone is ready to take. These large companies must carefully consider their Public Relations strategies to preserve the company's reputation, but more operationally speaking, these companies are surrounded by experts, dedicated departments with well-paid and experienced executives, supported by reputable consultants—but not always connected, sometimes marching through the organization with their own methodologies, surveys, data, reports. Therefore, vertical alignment, horizontal integration, coordination, getting a foundational operation capacity to transform, getting a rhythm, is disproportionately important as compared to small and medium companies. The usual way transformation comes to these large companies is with a starting point at the top, with profound, well-informed conversations at the board level on the different needs and perspectives for the future of the company, then a thinking partner is brought along, usually a high-end consultant, to assist with the thinking as an objective third party. At the right time, they will start involving the operation and creating a whole schedule of projects and activities. Managing an existential transformation in this environment is what I have been able to lead multiple times, being part of the company, not the consultants, and my experience is the source of inspiration for this book. Based on the above, these transformations will consume significant infrastructure to accomplish alignment for execution and are greatly benefited from Leading success. These projects will take longer but results can be seen relatively rapidly from the various stages of the journey. This is why I have called this plan *Go Comprehensive*. Based on my experience, these are the top five recommendations on how to manage transformation for large companies using Leading Success:

- **Governance**. Once the decision is made to pursue a significant transformation, a team must be put in place. But this is not just any team. This is a very special task force in which leaders must invest the time and reflect very seriously on how to build. Large companies may have redundancies; closely related or duplicative roles with people doing very similar jobs in different divisions. Teams can't be too large, but there is a cost for exclusion, so a thoughtful balance will have to be found; no 'black or white' answers, every organization is different and must respond to its cultural needs. The typical mix includes business units, regions, corporate, and a very clear leader. If this will be a Leading Success approach, you will be better served by appointing people that can see things differently and who can remove obstacles, naturally. Particularly in the role of the leader we need someone with liberating, vital capability. And we need more than just a team with a leader. There has to be a steering committee above, which normally is the entirety or a subset of the c-suite, and the CEO. Depending on the scale of the operation, smaller teams may be necessary within divisions or regions. But make no mistake, these have to be coordinated with one single leader and follow one voice for alignment.
- **Decision rights**. The next immediate action is to define who has the 'D'. Meaning, who will have the ultimate decision-making power for the parts

and the whole process. As we discussed in Chapter 16, Experience, RAPID is the tool that will be best utilized to advance this important step. RAPID is a powerful and intuitive tool that helps identify and document the decision rights all the way from the CEO, Steering Committee, Team Leader, and team members. With a clear governance structure and decision rights, we are halfway into the tools necessary to run this endeavor.

- **Alignment at the top.** While sometimes it may seem too obvious to ask the question, what is the goal we are pursuing? You have to ask it again, and sometimes yet again, until the answer is simple and clear. What we are looking for is straightforward language to get the teams started; for example, why are we pursuing this change? Are we transforming to be able to do what kinds of things better? When do we want this to happen? how will we assess success? And how would we measure it? These questions will have to be answered clearly and tested often. As the team embarks on data gathering, new insights bring light to areas not originally contemplated that may change some of our assumptions. This is why we are constantly alert and come back to our goals to confirm their clarity as we learn more, and occasionally, clarify further. As you go connecting across the organization and through the layers, the meaning of what can be seen from the top gets significantly enhanced by the vantage point from the operation.
- **Rules of engagement.** A simple recommendation: there is *one transformation*, not many. A big change will affect subsets of the organization differently, and it may give the immediate impression that we are running different projects, and multiple transformations, each one claiming independent life on its own, but it should still be a coordinated, coherent plan. No part of the organization can afford to go solo, ignore the rest, or unilaterally decide they will do it differently or not do it at all. When very unique aspects of a division require unique considerations, the decision still is made in the governance structure, not through isolated decision-making.
- **Centralized plan and metrics.** One version of the truth is essential, the ultimate test of coordination and the ability to stay away from chaos. When someone at the core transformation team says, 'my numbers are different', we have a problem. Either, someone's math is wrong, or we have someone running its own accounting with different formulas, assumptions, or definitions. In the end, agreement on metrics comes in the front-end, with clarity on who will run the numbers and call it 'real'. In my experience, this may actually be one of the single most important roles and external consultant may have. Some organizations are so polarized in their internal differences and turf battles that will never agree on metrics they did not

create. But they will not fight the consultants. Not a small value to bring to a complex transformation.

- **Impeccable commitment above and below**. The one single value we are looking for is *trust*. In the surface, a transformation is a huge project with goals, milestones, and activities. But there is much more depth. Leaders care more about transformations because they go beyond outcomes, they are about legacy, history, what they will be remembered for. Leaders significantly care about that. Leading Success provides a framework to understand the whole journey and help leaders see the forest and the trees that build the end-to-end transformation, so they do not miss relevant chunks. It also provides context on how these segments of the journey should be led and the culture they promote. Leading for liberation also applies for the transformation team, and since their members, by definition, will have little power on their own, the governance structure becomes a big empowerment tool to remove obstacles and move along. But this capacity to connect at the top is predicated on absolute immaculate commitment and delivery, clarity, truth, and demonstration of the right perspective and pulse of the organization. It is very easy to lose credibility at the top, and teams must understand how much this matters. Much of this credibility depends on the understanding of the organization as the transformation is concerned. In other words, the team must have a sense of what is going on across the organization and have the ability to raise the issues that merit a decision at the steering committee. Too much or too little information is a problem. Team leaders must understand their audiences well to keep this balance and leverage the minutes and the opportunities to make the right consultations and the right decisions to keep the project moving. And they have to be trusted by the larger organization, by those powerful business units, regions, and centers of expertise. Those leaders may not be working for their legacies, but they are working for their people, and for the preservation of a way of working that have come to accept and live with. Any wrong interaction will create distance, density, friction, less access, less data. The office or transformation must be seen as an honest, trustworthy point in the organization, a group of people, and a way of work that brings liberation and vitality, that is welcome even if the transformation is scary and unpopular. No half-truths, condescension, sense of hiding information, hidden agendas, taking sides. It is leadership of liberation at its best, and also an art form.

The bottom line on road mapping business transformation is to be clear on destination and adapt. The same model holds true: WORD, WORLD, BECOMING.

I would like to conclude this chapter by sharing what you need to be prepared to address and resolve to ensure success of any transformation. In my journey I found repeatable patterns of behavior that significantly derail transformation. I call them the archetypes of failure.

The Five Archetypes of Failure in Transformations

These five archetypes are lessons from experience after having the opportunity to succeed and fail in multiple experiences leading change along my career. They are also validated by numerous studies about transformation and by most change methodologies. Failure is a matter of degree in organizational transformation. Rarely a change effort completely fails in absolute terms or completely succeeds in every possible way. In reality, success in transformation is a measure of how much potential was realized and how much opportunity was left on the table. As I look back from my personal journey and from numerous examples well known in the industry most transformations fail for internal reasons, not as much because of their competitors or other external factors. These archetypes point to those internal aspects, the ones we can control to make more from our effort and go further in our aspirations. Each of these archetypes has an illustration, composed of three columns for easy reading. The first column is a visual representation of how these issues impact the ability to leverage Leading success. To do that I am including a line for each pillar and a rating number from 0 to 100 to give an idea of how much that pillar is leveraged to its potential to build a liberating, vital organization; a score of 100 means the maximum positive leverage. These numbers are descriptors illustrating a proportion, not analytical, algorithmic results of any calculation. In the second column I have a small depiction of how the different tools and solutions relate to the Leading success Framework, to show the gaps being created by the archetype and how mindsets are affected, leveraged, or sometimes blocked, skipped. And the final column articulates the common consequences of such archetype.

Archetype 1: Disconnected Tools and Investments

Companies find problems and make bold decisions to address them. No CEO will just jump to a solution. They are thoughtful, analytical individuals and try to ensure these investments are used properly for years to come. However, some tools require more than just technical installation, they are built on a series of assumptions about how the organization works, how people are motivated or incentivized to properly adopt new tasks to make the tool produce the intended outcomes, and many times those requirements are found at implementation, after teams start hitting walls and unable to make the tools work. The issue is that some of those requirements remain invisible or are ignored in early conversations, or in the worst cases, not spoken by vendors, leading to disruption and failure. Great examples of these are shown in the illustration on Fig. 17.2. I will take only one example to elaborate here. Spans and Layers, a process designed to simplify organizations, accelerate decision-making, and optimize resources. The methodology includes three big phases; first, a process to gather data across the organization to identify how many people report to every manager—referred as *spans*— and how many levels of management the organization has—referred as *layers*; giving it its name. This is also a fact-finding phase to understand important organization design problems.

In the second phase, the output of the data is examined to identify opportunities, compare to benchmarks, and decide which opportunities will be pursued considering a number of factors, included how much of the

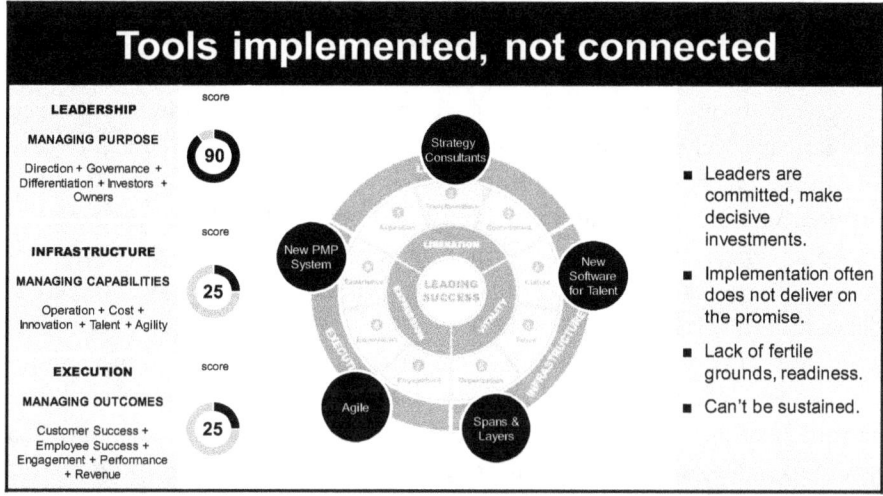

Fig. 17.2 Implementation risk: disconnected solutions

change the culture of the company can absorb. This leads to phase three, which is centered on redesigning the organization to fulfill spans and layers goals with a sound redesign. Here is where decisions are made to implement changes, typically consisting of realigning departments, promoting or demoting leaders, sometimes includes exits. In practice, this is a high friction, high heat process. Most of the readers have likely been part of a similar project. Spans and Layers is a good exercise for a company, but it is not free of consequence if its implementation is not exceptionally good. There are important ramifications because it touches power, identities of individuals and teams, and forces the amalgamation of areas into a single leader in order to make the spans index work. If not careful, the math will drive the design, and odd combinations will arise. For example, a small research team put under an operations area to ensure 'no manager has less than 5 people reporting to her/him'. A notable unintended consequence that companies discover is that they now have *less* management positions, therefore, less room to develop managers. Teams grow in complexity, increasing the skill and sophistication required to manage them, uncovering existing gaps in management depth. The choice of who is promoted and who is demoted can be problematic if any level of favoritism is perceived—within weeks and very easily the project could—and it usually does—become a culture shock for the company. After a year or two, enough 'exceptions' have been granted that the spans and layers indexes are no longer in the desired range and the promised results are not fully realized. There are important risks to any organizational intervention and Spans and Layers is no exception.[2] Does that mean Spans and Layers is a bad thing? Not at all. In fact, having a high span, low layered organization is a very important predictor of organizational health.[3] The problem is that companies very rarely are culturally prepared to the significant demand and disruption this process brings with it, and find themselves in a hole: everyone is hating the project, uncertainty is rampant, changes seem too financially centered, not customer-centered, opening a big crack of credibility in management. Finance teams see the potential savings, the CEO sees the potential on cost and agility, velocity. But very little cultural preparation is ever done. These are deep transformation and redesign projects often treated as tools, or 'studies'. If a project of this magnitude is not strongly connected to a deliberate transformation, connected to our purpose and values, approached with a liberating and vital redesign perspective, it will be nearly impossible to complete and sustain. In these projects the financial goals are often achieved, but at the expense of productivity and vitality. As a consequence, a high score is given to strategic planning, but poor scores to infrastructure and execution. Depending on the tool or solution, the outcomes may get a higher score, but only on a dimension of the goals, not in all of them. There is no vitality and no signature expression coming from this type of implementation.

How to avoid this failure? Understand the ecosystem that is necessary to build around the tool, or solution in order to raise the chances for success, not just its path to execution. With that in mind, you can recommend adjacent components to limit the risks and make the investment more effective. One of the most direct ways to do that is speaking to a counterpart of a company that implemented the same tool with these vendors. You will be able to pick up from the perspective of a real user what are some potential issues and not depend only on what the sales team tells you.

Archetype 2: Skipping Organization Redesign

In this archetype of failure, we see management doing the right thing, bringing the expertise and data, discovering sources of value, and determining what must be done for the future. The Board presentations are very successful because the rationale is fundamentally financial and future oriented. The considerations on culture and people are mentioned but there is no comparable elaboration to the detail included on the financials. In most circumstances, the CHRO is not invited to the close discussions on targets and asked about consequences. Some CEOs consider the sense of urgency the primary force of change: to reach financial stability as fast as possible because it is existential. Any mention of the criticality of organizational readiness, culture, and change management, comes across as 'not wanting' to do the hard things, or 'not understanding' the business. Speed is king and a plan is put in motion. Very often, a communication plan is confused with a change plan (Fig. 17.3).

Leaders want to tell and explain the story, no time for listening, no time for conversation. Ramifications of the changes are explored only as far as executives are involved for either more responsibility or less responsibility, promotions and demotions, or when entire departments are moved under new areas. Beyond that, it is assumed that leaders will hold the fort and make sense of the changes to their people. The next action is to start the identification of people to exit and the implementation of the changes. Why is this archetype so prevalent? Too many companies suffer from lack of efficiency, built for larger revenues in the past, with no clear strategic path to increasing the top line, therefore carrying significant overhead. In some cases, leaders go for cost cutting aiming for instant impact on profitability, show positive signs to investors. In other instances, the projects include important investments that will be funded by exits. Either way, companies jump

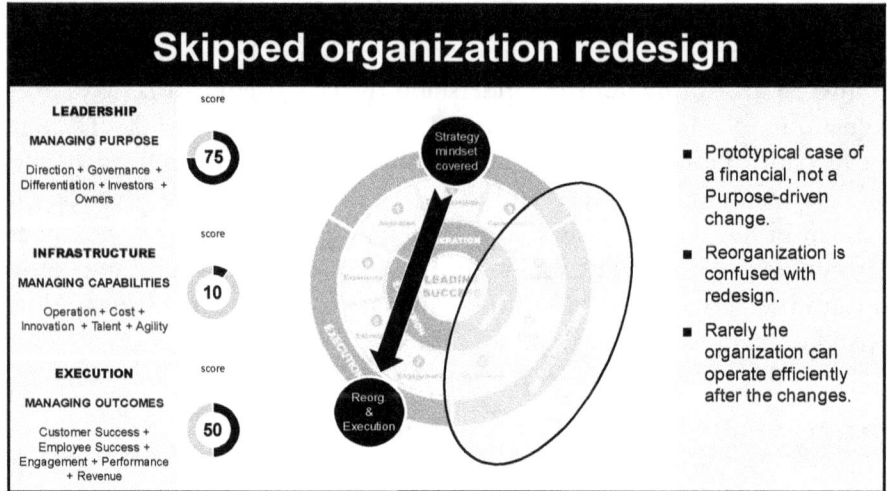

Fig. 17.3 Implementation risk: oversimplified execution of transformation

to implementation skipping redesign. To be clear, I am advocating for the changes the business needs, that is not the point; if we must do it, we better do it in a way that ensures its success, and shields the organization from rebounding back to the vicious cycles that created the original problems. This is, we need some level of redesign as indicated in the culture, organization, and engagement disciplines. The score on leadership is high but not very high as the envisioned change is not seen as a transformation that needs redesign, only adaptations. Infrastructure is extremely low, because no new infrastructure for success is being created to sustain the new ways of working. The organization will just have to cope with it, adapt in the best way they can. Therefore, the outcomes in execution will be only a portion of the expectation and certainly not sustainable.

How to avoid this failure? Identify what the situation can offer in terms of flexibility and take it. See the company and manager guidelines for Expectations in Chapter 15. While you will not be able to cover all the ideal aspects of vitality design before implementation, you may be able to cover the critical aspects to sustain morale and trust in leadership. Reference to values, engagement sessions would be essential. Everything else in the vitality design can be accomplished as you go into the journey.

Archetype 3: Commitment to Only a Part of the Journey

Transformations are energizing and exhausting at the same time. By the time all the strategic work is completed—and the list is long: analysis, fact finding, identification of the North Star, the articulation of the desired transformation, and the culture is identified, a partial victory is declared. At this point some leaders think the work is done. They want to switch gears to get busy on implementation to mobilize the transformation. What they really mean by that is that everyone goes back to their corners—be left alone—to activate the parts of the transformation that falls in their scope. But in Leading Success we know better—there are organizational, and talent designs they cannot, and perhaps should not, solve on their own corners; there is a whole vitality design work to do ahead of us which must be collective. The impetus to start, bias to action, is indeed what we need, but we also need to address what must change in the organization to make it desirable, enjoyable, sense-making—*vital*. Some c-suite leaders think that their job of 'thinking and directing' is mostly done and therefore they see themselves relieved of collective duty, the whole action is now at the execution levels. That is true in a sense, but there is more to it than just a powerful articulation. I recall completing a culture project to define purpose, mission, values. The cleanest, most energizing, and collaborative process I ever saw at the c-suite. We completed the first four disciplines: Aspiration, Transformation, Commitment, and Culture in textbook fashion. We climbed the mountain together. We were now ready to activate talent, organization redesign; and as I was getting ready to start working on it, I got a significant push back that frankly took me by surprise. It seemed the team was thinking of the next disciplines work as an addendum, something above and beyond of what they had signed up for—as if those areas did not belong in the transformation (Fig. 17.4).

They had vigorously immersed themselves in the concept creation and were ready for execution but regarded the necessary vitality design as *additional* work, something HR wanted to do, but was not really necessary—or even worse, that any next steps were the HR job, not theirs to do. It hit me at the moment they were never aware of the whole journey, and I had wrongly assumed it was clear. I owned that mistake, but not having it clear from the beginning, really broke the action to complete the cycle. I had been working on aspects of the other disciplines and with extraordinary efforts we were able to survive the journey but did not achieve a vital design. We completed the work; we got ahead but there was value left in the table. Most importantly, the c-suite stopped working as a team for the transformation. They worked from

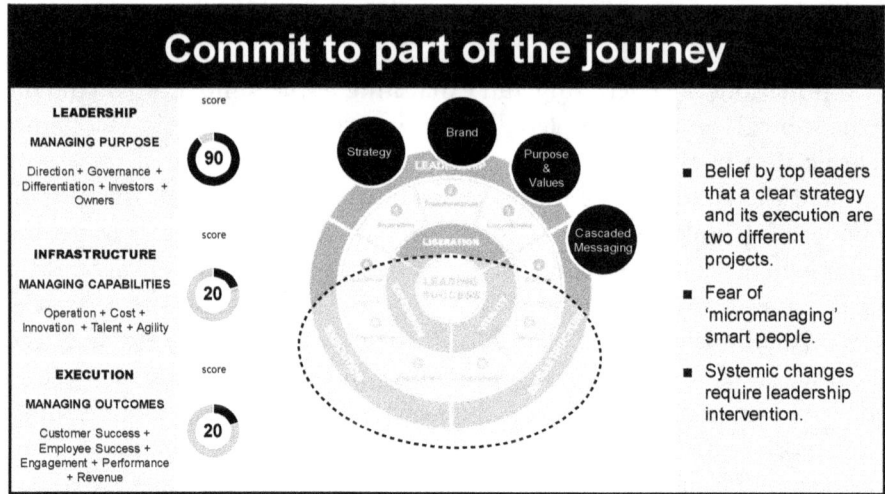

Fig. 17.4 Implementation risk: leaders unclear of whole journey of transformation

their corners to contribute, they own their pieces but delegated the whole messaging to the CEO, we all got busy and underachieved.

How to avoid this failure? Paint the full journey from the beginning and make sure the discussion at the c-suite includes all the steps of the bridge from aspiration to experience. I recommend showing the entirety of the Leading Success Framework, as illustrated in Fig. 2.3 from Chapter 2. Gaining an end to end perspective was a primary reason Leading Success is designed as a journey in three mindsets and nine disciplines. This does not mean companies have to check nine boxes, but it provides clarity on what success looks like—and what it takes—to achieve the liberated, vital organization.

Archetype 4: Investments Made with Incomplete Vision

For many readers of this book, it will be surprising to hear there are times when companies have too many resources and too much money to spend on tools and infrastructure. When I was hired at Dell in 2007, I learned the company had grown so fast that there never was a time to slow down and consider an optimized design and a coordinated infrastructure for the future. Reality was moving too fast, and the business was still too fluid to commit to a design. Companies are like cities; you have to make some decisions early and then adapt as the city grows. First you decide where the center is and a few main roads. With time you add streets, define sectors, then neighborhoods, bridges, facilities to bring power and water, and the list goes on.

Same happens with companies. Production is first, remember our evolution of effectiveness, you have to put product out first, make sure it is profitable, and care for customer success. Somewhere along the journey you need help to coordinate your success. This can be manufacturing facilities, supply chain networks, people, policies, and also information management. In search for capacity to deal with that explosive growth at Dell, its regions, countries, and divisions had to create local infrastructures to operate the increasing demand and complexity. That is how you end up having several instances of everything you may need to run a company. It was not born from a mistake, but it resulted in significant redundancies, cost, complexity. For example, I found we had thirteen LMS systems in the company, we also had four different leadership development methods and philosophies, sitting at corporate, regions, and divisions. It took a global initiative to bring those numbers down. What this case illustrates is that not having a unifying vision not always means a *lack of vision*, but the timing to have one had not arrived until then. Other cases are more extreme; for example, building entire manufacturing facilities in places that make no sense, for products we will no longer produce.

Some companies have resources in a distributed structure, allowing for punctual decisions that may or may not be connected to a core central strategy. When this happens, we add velocity in one way, but we add cost and inconsistency to the whole. It is a strategic decision determining when one is better than the other to the benefit of the company's growth, but at some point, things will need to connect to a common sense-making story that gives orientation to employees and managers about their careers and chances for personal success.

A third consideration on this archetype of failure—and moving away from Dell as an example—is that simply there may not be a vision at the top, other than revenue and profitability targets. And therefore, business units and corporate departments create their own versions of vision and push for solutions consistent with their perspectives. It happens a lot more frequently than you may think. Finance systems not talking to Human Resources systems, or to Supply Chain systems. Same case with Product Design and Procurement processes and systems, but the differences may also include different philosophies—a continuous design agile product may be incompatible with a supply chain inventory management based on long-term forecasts. Before you think I am talking about a disaster kind of organization, that may not be the case at all. There are times when companies reach a plateau on their existing business models. They still command market leadership, high revenue but a big tectonic change lies in the horizon, for which the company has yet to define its position and a strategy. There is a vision for what the company is in the existing paradigm, but not for the future; there is no clarity for what the company wants to be; the North Star is fading. Business units, segments, still have resources and ways to go solve real problems, invest in very sophisticated and important tools but there is no long-term vision to connect them to. As you can see in the illustration shown in Fig. 17.5, there are many ways to add capability. The one I would like to elaborate a little deeper is the one on remarkable talent. Of all the potential investments this one may not be the most onerous in terms of pure dollar amounts but represents the biggest loss of opportunity for the company in terms of potential for success. Over my years at these Fortune 500 companies the one aspect I was more disheartened about was the waste of talent that could have made a real difference.

In the search for answers, companies go and get top caliber, top dollar, superstar people. Those brilliant individuals are brought into a very undefined environment for which commitment to something tangible still does not exist. These leaders do well for a time fixing the issues but eventually are impeded to breakthrough with innovation and positive disruption because the culture can't support that, there are antibodies, organ rejection factors that end up neutralizing the superpowers we wanted from these people in the first place. I saw many top leaders who were successful before coming and crashing in our walls because we were expecting them to do something for which the culture and frankly, the very top of the company was not ready for. Admittedly, sometimes it goes the other way around, the leader fails to adapt to the turbulence of these times.

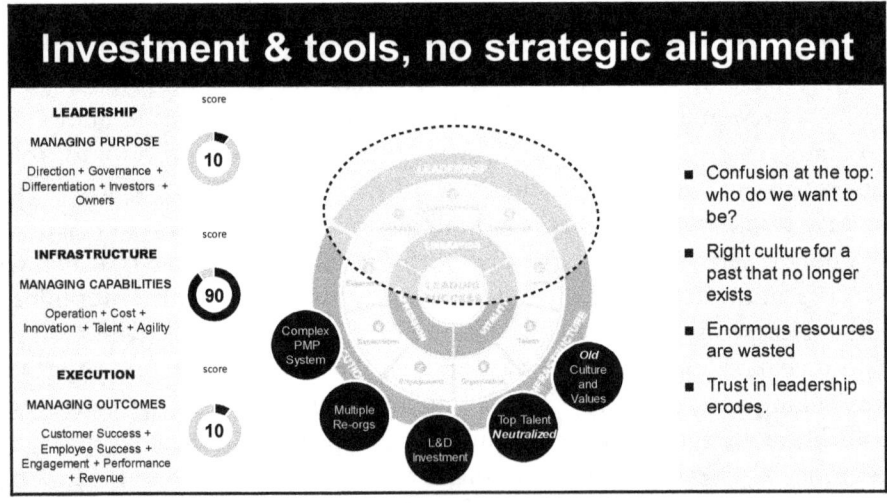

Fig. 17.5 Implementation risk: investments and solutions without strategic orientation

How to avoid this failure? It depends on who you are in the story. If you are the CEO, this is the time to regroup strategically and chart a new path for the future. It is also the time when Boards of Directors bring a new CEO to rejuvenate the story and redefine the future. No better time to gather a team to adopt a Leading success approach. Use the first mindset to identify risks on deployment. A very successful practice is to leverage your executive sponsor—or to get one—for each of these tools or initiatives. C-suite executive sponsors can help bring the message to the top executives for the need to work on a unifying message. In cases of simple proliferation of solutions and tools, you can recommend a rationalization project—again with executive sponsorship—to simplify the offering and reduce cost.

Archetype 5: Inability to Act

I have mentioned parts of this problem during the discipline's discussions. Transformation is a story everyone tries to translate into something familiar and very connected to what they do. That is always necessary for action and results, except when leaders try to preserve the status quo, even if unconsciously. Sometimes companies must be reconstituted by breaking existing sources of revenue and power, or by making strategic investments overseas, transfer assets to other divisions, no longer be in charge of something they created. All these matters require very strong commitment and also very good governance and capacity to make decisions (Fig. 17.6).

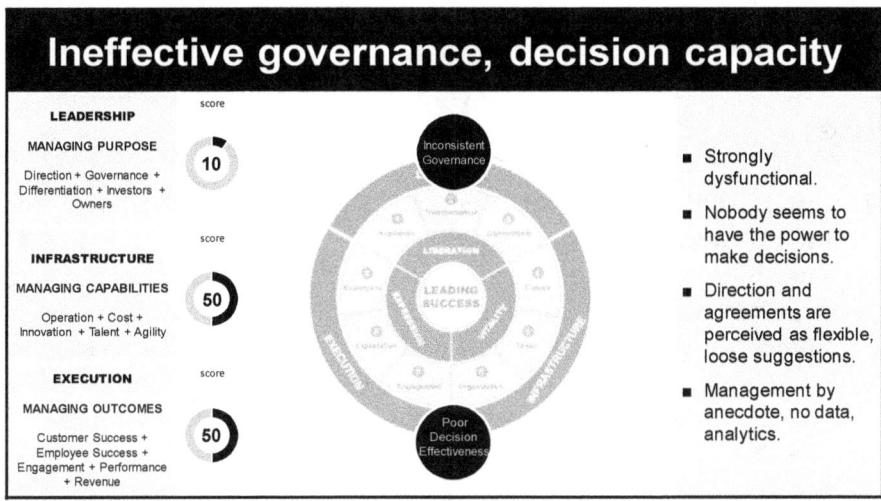

Fig. 17.6 Implementation risk: Lack of transformation management infrastructure

This particular problem is not unique at the top. In fact, permeates across all the places where change is happening. People cooperates less when they dislike the solutions. Leaders take measured approaches and try to avoid over-reacting to signals that we have deviation from the plans. When this approach does not result in alignment, we need to have the infrastructure for decision-making and a capacity to monitor execution. In the absence of a definite course of action being discussed and formally adopted, organizations run by making decisions only to change them later in private conversations, they lack the ability to stay the course or change it with effectiveness. The solution? Strengthen governance, implement RAPID, reinforce commitment, and revisit the engagement story. Those are the main failure points when this archetype appears.

In Summary

Business outcomes related to Transformation Success are indispensable to keep everyone engaged, willing to do more, know more, be part of it; all the way from employees to executives to board members and even investors—this feeling is like oxygen flowing to the transformation. The most important lesson for me on all these years of helping companies transform themselves is the following: *do not defeat yourself*. Most transformations fail because of preventable internal oversimplifications, power disputes, rushed timetables, and some levels of arrogance. As we will discuss in detail in Chapter 19, this is one of the most important values the head of HR leaders can bring. To help the executive team stay out of their own way.

Notes

1. Crane. (2024). Crane Company – Who We Are. Retrieved from: https://www.craneco.com/about/
2. Wulf, Julie. The Flattened Firm: Not as advertised. California Management Review. Vol 55, No. 1. Fall 2012.
3. Tillman, P., Toma, A., Roghé, F., Morieux, Y., Maaseide, S., Tamboto, E., & Koike, J. (2016, April). Smart design for performance: A new approach to organization design. The Boston Consulting Group.

18

Culture Outcomes: Smart, Profitable, and Inclusive

Building the Organically Diverse, Equitable, Inclusive, and Belonging (DEIB) Organization for Everyone's Success

My premise on culture outcomes is that first, the real outcome of a culture is not the environment it creates in the organization but how that environment translates in productivity and capacity of success for everyone. The second premise is that a workplace that feels great *for all the people* is significantly more effective, than a workplace that feels great for only some of the people.[1] Therefore, we are going to discuss how organizations can create such an environment as a natural outcome of the very way they operate following its signature processes, this is, *organically*, consistent to their vitality design.

As stated earlier, there are three foundational elements of culture: its articulation (what it says—written), its implementation (how embedded it is—designed), and how leaders live it (how it is demonstrated by managers). Written, embedded, and demonstrated; in the end, cultures are *experienced* as the convergence of those three dimensions. Cultures translate in multiple forms of behavior and dispositions that either accelerate or slow down the company. There is no such thing as a neutral culture, instead, cultures are elevating up, or lowering down companies, at an imperceptible but steady pace. This great capacity of cultures to affect companies is an organic outcome of the many ways in which a culture manifests itself. As we have discussed, every aspect of the organization—the policies, the practices, the metrics, the ways of working together, and attitudes of managers in their interactions with employees—play a role in, creating the resulting mental state of liberation, vitality, and expression.

But cultures also create powerful sentiments of belonging, inclusion as a result of how fair, how balanced, or *equitable* the experience overall is for an employee. The more different anyone is from what a community considers as 'the norm', the higher importance these belonging aspirations will have for those individuals. In our time of the world, this is an imperative for many employees and for almost every company. Cultures translate into organization design via Employee Value Propositions, Talent, and Organization. This is perceived in the overall design of the organization, its configuration toward customers and employees, hiring processes, onboarding, performance management, rewards, promotions, pay equity; all these components create the organic outcome of what the company *is*, conditions who is in the company, who leads, who stays and goes. In essence, anything the company is at some point in time is the result of what its design—deliberate or accidental—dictates it is constantly *becoming*.

Consequently, a diverse, equitable, inclusive, and belonging organization is not the product of one program or one initiative, and it is not the experience of one group or another, it is what the company's design makes it to be. In this way, a vital design inspired by a liberating leadership, focused to a signature expression will have the power to beget a company's employee experience that is just that: diverse, equitable, including, belonging, flexible, and exceptionally high performing.

In this sense, some companies have been chasing diversity in the wrong ways for long time. We want companies to *think* and *act* with equity and belonging in mind, but some still can't *see* and *believe* how those attributes are critical business imperatives; therefore they have not designed themselves for vitality and signature expression.

You may wonder, how does the experience of an organically DEIB organization looks like in the eyes of the main parts involved:

- **For employees.** People—all people, not only the groups we identify as 'diverse'—are able to be themselves and do their best work. Feeling that they belong and that they are included. Seeing a natural 'organic' grow, progression, and opportunity regardless of how they look, what religious beliefs, or any sexual orientation they may have. Seeing that opportunities for success respond to performance, not gender, class, or ethnicity. Experiencing comparable rewards and compensation based on the merits of their work. Observing that representation at the top is equally available for men and women, for white employees and people of color, people

with disabilities, and more. Everyone is equally rewarded according to job and responsibilities. People see others choosing to stay in good and in bad times.
- **For our customers**: Their interactions with the company are not random or based on who happens to be facing them at any point in time, instead, there is a visible, perceptible, deliberate design for a vital, liberating experience *for them*. The products, the ways to collaborate and operate with those solutions is itself liberating, inclusive and non-discriminatory, accessible, designed for everyone. Our people, product design, marketing, sales, customer service, and employees in general, including executives, look like them—our organization resembles our customers.
- **For the industry and the community**: The company is a beacon of hope for many who want to be part of it and for those peer companies who want to emulate what it does. The programs for the community are meaningful, their efforts toward environmental responsibility, even if small, are authentic and there is recognition for the impact the company is making beyond products and profits. The company has become a symbol of success for the future of work.

Leading Success, with its focus on leadership of liberation, design for vitality, and signature expression is capable of creating and sustaining such environment, not because there is a DEIB program, but because there is a culture and a design that has been translated to expectations and processes. Let's explore how.

The Diversity Ecosystem

If you have tried running diversity programs in the right way: with a champion, budgets, metrics, sponsorship, continuity, and yet, your outcomes are rather flat, not much progress is visible, and in spite of your best committed efforts at the top, most of your employees think your company is not a diverse-welcoming place, you are not alone. Leaders recognize how critical diversity is and are compelled to pour resources into it, show visible commitments, report something positive in their ERG scores, however, diversity can't be bought, it can only grow in the agricultural way: preparing the soil, planting the right seed, cultivating, and then harvesting. In other words, what you need is *an ecosystem for DEIB*, and not only a *program*. What does this mean?

For many years, actions to increase diversity in the workplace have been around with mixed results.[2] The general picture is that senior leaders recognize the importance of having a diverse workforce—intellectually—but sometimes they fall short on a couple of different ways: either they do not know how to implement it—knowledge—or they are not convinced that diversity matters—values. There are oceans of information, and misinformation, on the merits and the investment that it takes to create diversity, and there are myths about its benefits or lack thereof. In short, DEIB has not been central to business management, it often lives in the periphery.

Except for companies with a visionary leadership team constantly raising the subject to the top of the list, the average company sees diversity as one of many areas under HR, the metric for accomplishment has been compliance and 'activity', to ensure we are not breaking the law and to show something is being done, most likely in the form of a DEIB program, training, Employee Resources Groups, but not a plan focused on outcomes. As you examine real data on promotions, executive hires, and hiring in general, most companies—except for the golden stars—are behind on their diversity goals and significantly behind on equity as compared to their own internal populations. For example, having a large proportion of female talent, but the top 10% of income still is for a majority of men. Or having one third of employees of color but two thirds of promotions are still for non-diverse talent. It is rare to see diversity as a key corporate goal, most companies have it in the second page after financials, markets, products; treating it as a 'nice to have', the right thing to do, but not as an existential imperative.

While part of this problem is how we have managed DEIB projects in the past, without the resources or the senior visibility they deserve, the central problem we face in companies is not the infrastructure, or the knowledge, those can be acquired when the commitment is present. The problem can be thought as the result of three types of mindsets:

Advocates: Leaders who understand that more diversity means better results. They want to have more diverse companies but have not achieved it.
Non-believers: Leaders who don't see why diversity is necessary or relevant for the business.
Detractors: Leaders who culturally and ideologically oppose diversity.

Non-believers have one belief—at the senior-most management levels—that business results truly do not require a diverse workforce; the belief that diversity is a fashion that will eventually go, or a compliance element they will have to live with. They argue their customers are not asking for it, business has always been good, irrespective of the diversity of their customers or employees. Is not that they oppose the social importance of diversity, but they can't see a connection to business performance, or believe that the gains of a diverse organization are much too small and hard to prove to merit the effort.

Detractors include leaders who simply do not believe diversity is a good thing to pursue. In their vision DEIB is damaging to society and therefore they not only ignore it, they combat it. These leaders see diversity as a byproduct of the culture wars and disregard it as 'woke'; a liberal value that amounts to a misplaced social service. In the worst cases, a belief that diverse people are less qualified, less deserving, taking resources away from non-diverse people and therefore, it is better to manage their company with a majority of non-diverse executives.

Advocates are our direct target audience in this book. However, the right organization, with the right corporate mentoring, manager training, and job-based development programs will contribute to introduce young leaders, in both non-believers and detractor groups, to compelling perspectives on why Talent Success necessitates a DEIB environment to reach its highest potential. Many leaders who are advocates however, are leaders who have an authentic interest on building a diverse organization but have not been successful doing it. They remain unclear how the outcomes look like and are yet to see a path for success, and most are aware of the turbulence and agitation on this subject with the prevalent social polarization; and yet, they continue with their efforts. This chapter is for those leaders. There is a particular subgroup in this cluster. Leaders cornered by cultural wars; they want to have a diverse team and a product that speaks for liberating values, but a portion of their customer base rejects those notions so loudly and even violently, that these CEOs choose to stay out of trouble, secure the revenue and ring-fence DEIB internally, quietly, or even leave it for another time. Inevitably, their employees are observing, and so are their customers; both will wonder if the company is trying hard enough.

Regardless of the reasons why diversity may not have moved forward in your company, your employees are interested. They are inspired by the promises of the Future of Work and are eager to see it through, to put the work, to be agents of this change. When I talked to these employees, I found they understand the complexities of the cultural polarization in society and they are reasonable when our actions are designed to limit existential risk for the company, but they will still want to see leadership's unwavering commitment to the values of the company by doing everything possible, internally and externally, to advance conditions of equality and send a message to employees that they care.

How Do We Move Forward?

In a magnificent study conducted by Glassdoor,[3] a question about progress on diversity was asked to two groups of people in the same companies: Black or African American employees, and everyone else. For those employees outside the Black or African American demographic the DIEB program was increasingly successful, but for the people it was designed to serve it was just the opposite—increasingly unsuccessful. Most concerning in the data is that the rate of differentiation of perceptions has worsened, a growing gap of 200% between 2019 and 2021. This study resonates with my experience and that of many CHROs. It is not uncommon to hear senior management and non-diverse groups stating that the Diversity Program is doing fine, that they have made significant progress in the last few years. However, for the Black or African American employees, or for any other minority groups for that matter, the answers are very different. In fact, in spite of the efforts and investments that can be objectively observed, they are even less positive about the progress. What explains this different perspective? In simple terms, they are looking at different artifacts as they judge success. One group is looking at the *program*, the visible activity, the compliance, logos, emails, pronouncements from management. The other group—those who responded that the program was not going well—is looking for *evidence* that equality gaps were decreasing, and they could not find it. This is, rewards, progression, representation—had not changed, and sometimes were going in the opposite direction. The difference is the result of 'working on diversity' as a *program*—focused on inputs—instead of working on diversity as an *ecosystem*—focused on structural design and outcomes.

An ecosystem for DEIB is built when a company installs DEIB actions—designs for liberation, vitality, and expression—across all three cultural factors: written culture, designed culture, and manager culture—see the illustration in Fig. 18.1. A typical DEIB program only covers one or two of the factors, but very rarely covers all three of them. DEIB is the outcome of a complex array of balances—like ecosystems. It is no different than product development and customer satisfaction. You have to strategically plan for it, understand your audiences, design accordingly, and build the experience you need to deliver in order to acquire and keep your customers (in this case, employees), create or change processes, establish policies, metrics,

18 Culture Outcomes: Smart, Profitable, and Inclusive

Building the DEIB Ecosystem							
Act on culture							
Written culture		**Experienced culture**			**Designed culture**			
• Liberating Purpose • Values • Principles		• Manager expectations • Manager feedback • Team success			• Policies, Processes, Programs • Organization design • Metrics and governance			
Follow the Twelve DEIB Imperatives							
Provide Clarity		Elevate the Experience			Signature Processes			
Own	Declare	Plan	Implement	Clarify	Measure
Aim	Focus	Supplement	Engage	Baseline	Govern

Fig. 18.1 The diversity ecosystem for leading success

include your customers (employees) in the feedback and ask your managers to perform following those standards.

In this way the outcomes for DEIB emerge *organically* based on the actual work people do, as opposed to the Program approach; perceived to impose additional tasks managers and employees must perform to comply with the program. Those words are the worst enemies of BEIB in organizations: people will think of them as additional work, enforced activity, compliance. Managers will always feel good that something is being done, that good results can be achieved and shared, but nobody feels that real progress is being made if critical operational metrics do not change. In other words, managers do not want to look busy and get no results from it. And much less their employees.

Typically, DEIB Programs include employee seminars, manager training, the creation of Employee Resource Groups, events, observance of the celebration of cultures during the year. To be clear, DEIB programs have a place in the solution, they keep awareness and bring diverse voices out. But they are not transformational, they are *supplemental* to the core businesses and people processes. By definition, DEIB programs on their own, are limited, incomplete solutions to advance diversity systematically and effectively. Because they are built from activities conceived *apart* from the core functioning of the business, they live in the sidelines.

The Most Common Mistake

The Glassdoor study highlights a second dimension of the diversity perception between different groups, those affected and those unaffected by a less equitable organization. The issue is *ownership*. Who owns solving for diversity? For many non-diverse populations that is someone else's problem, someone in HR, someone above, but 'not me'. In the worst cases the belief is that it is the job of the diverse population to create the conditions for their own happiness and adaptation, that the company is what it is, and they just have to 'suck it up', get in the train. In these companies we see all the diversity work as a separate set of activities, a schedule for people to socialize in affinity groups but apart from the main core of the business. Something similar happened with the women's groups in the past couple of decades. They had sponsorship, recognition, sanctioned gatherings, discussed relevant problems but in spite of some slow improvements, very little has meaningfully changed in representation and pay as a result of those interactions. In the end, it was considered a problem only tangential to business success and ultimately, a problem for women to solve. The reality is that inclusion, equality for all types of diversity, women, people of color, disabilities, age, LGBTQ, are dimensions of social justice prevalent in society and all we can do is our best to create an environment for a better world inside our walls.[4] Any solution not advancing equity, inclusion, and belonging is—according to FIRO B terminology—a form of *exclusion*,[5] which, as the opposite of *inclusion*, is, psychologically threatening not because people are weak, but because it is a need all humans (and even social animals) have from birth. According to Schutz, inclusion is the need that appears the earliest in child development and the one that precedes the needs for control and openness/affection. Inclusion cannot be resolved by way of affection and power alone; it must start with the affirmation that *everyone is IN the group*. Operationally speaking, inclusiveness is not a one person, one department, or one level problem to solve. It requires the entire organization—or a very large critical mass to make it real. Everyone owns inclusion and belonging, everyone owns equity. When that is the case, a monumental weight is lifted from people and now they are liberated to focus on winning, achieving, and becoming our purpose.

How the Right Culture Builds the DEIB Organization

Very simply put, companies have to define their expectations in the written culture—diversity must be spelled out explicitly in the highest aspirations of the company. Then we have got to modify people processes to 'hardwire' actions to ensure the employee journey cannot happen unless there are certain aspects included—yes, this is internal compliance—a necessary step to create habit. Then, in order to make it real for employees we need to enlist our managers to amplify the reach. Compliance alone will not be sufficient and can be negative; we need managers to voice their conviction that they see the world in the ways of our culture. A very hard and delicate step, because there is no guarantee that managers will agree with diverse principles. This is where the implementation aspect of Leading Success is so critical—the Expression Mindset. If we cannot get the commitment of the managerial ranks, DEIB—and the culture for that matter—will not reach critical mass and the implementation may stall.

Finally, the right metrics and governance will keep the priority on top, messaging and elevating successes and failures in the journey to our aspirations. Those four steps are depicted in the illustration in Fig. 18.2.

Leading Success, with its liberating leadership mindset, intends to raise managers' awareness to see and appreciate their people as they are; and to

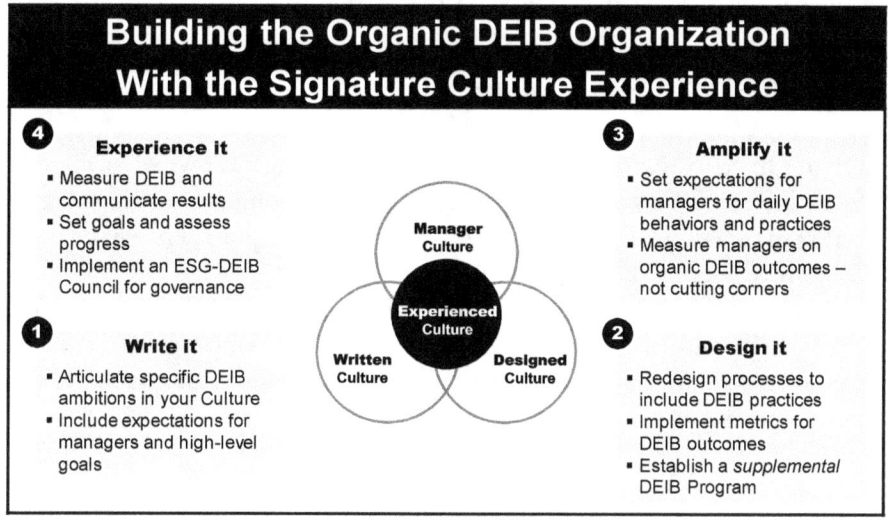

Fig. 18.2 The organic DEIB organization

focus their energy on developing their people's potential to unlock an exceptional outcome of the job and the business. Liberating leaders understand that the only way to get to that virtuoso level of performance from their employees is by helping every one of them deliver their best work, their 'opus magna' everyday; as opera singers, athletes do; although in a different stage, the challenge is the same—the *expression* of the best from our employees though their performance.

Building the DEIB Ecosystem: Diversity as an Outcome

There are numerous approaches to building diversity in organizations, CEOs can choose from a large list of qualified consultants with sound methodologies. During my almost thirty years in human resources and also being a people manager in several countries and having coached and observed successful and derailing leaders across industries and cultures, I have observed a common thread of good practices that consistently works, that can be dissected to its very essence. Based on that experience I created a checklist that brings a point of view on how DEIB is built organically and to be sustained. The list highlights how a vital design aligns the necessary people and resources in your company, the right ownership, and governance to ensure the effort is not wasted in good intentions alone. I call it *The Twelve DEIB Imperatives* and they are illustrated in the bottom part of Fig. 18.1.

The Twelve DEIB Imperatives

i. **Own**. Diversity, equality, inclusion, and belonging are owned at the CEO level, full stop. This is a priority for her/him, personally, and it must come across that way. The CEO deputizes HR to run the plan. The entire c-suite co-owns the plan and sponsors it.

ii. **Declare**. Diversity aspirations are articulated, in explicit language in the written culture statement. Purpose, and more importantly, company values, are unambiguously consistent with these aspirations. See a great example from the Sony Group[6]:

We Belong, We Create, We Grow, Together To Bring KANDO to the World. We believe that innovation happens when we embrace *the diversity in each other beyond boundaries*.

The Sony Group will continue to evolve as a place where everyone belongs and demonstrates their individuality, inspiring an inclusive society.
*KANDO = emotion

iii. **Aim**. There has to be a diversity goal, a broad statement that provides the North Star for the plan. It can be about one aspect of focus—like representation of minorities in the company or in management positions, or several areas of focus, such as Management, Representation, Progression.
iv. **Focus**. Diversity, equality, inclusion, and belonging applies to the entire organization, its people, and its customers. It will be important to classify the priority areas for the plan to orient people on what is that we are trying to achieve. For example, Google states that its diversity program focuses on three areas[7]: Workplace, Products, and Society.
v. **Clarify**. Diversity, equality, inclusion, and belonging need to be translated to behaviors or metrics terminology for everyone to understand what is the change we are looking for. The best way to do this is through a 'FROM - TO' description for the Plan. Better yet if you include what everyone, and particularly managers, are expected to do different.
vi. **Measure**. Attach hard metrics to the areas and key changes you want to see. This is the pivotal element of any plan. By choosing the right metrics you keep the focus on structural change, not on activity or 'opinion'. Measurements should be reported both, enterprise/division, team, and also by ethnicity and other categories of diversity as described in the OFCCP definitions. For global metrics, we should, at least, include women and other minorities per local regulation.
vii. **Baseline**. Crucial step—cannot be underestimated. You must measure every key metric before the plan starts. That is the only way to determine progress and eventually success, and the only way to attach goals and ownership for the processes.
viii. **Govern**. The natural organization structure is built around work affinity. Since Diversity belongs to everyone, the CEO and CPO will need to create a governance structure to ensure credibility, transparency, and participation with formality and accountability. In general, the CEO is the Chairman of the Plan, the CPO is the Plan leader, the entire C-suite become the Steering Committee. It will be necessary to create a DEIB Council with the CPO as leader, built from multi-levels of employees, middle managers and select leaders from across the business units. This will be the working group where the plan is vetted, defined, and where recommendations are created.

ix. **Plan.** The first step is to be very clear of what is *in* the Plan. This is, what is the work to do for diversity. It should not be constrained to the usual—DEIB activities, monthly celebrations, employee conversations, and ERGs—we must go further to affect structural design, what success means for managers and employees, the source of where the hard metrics are created. Everything else, as valuable as it is, lives in the Supplemental Program. What we are talking about is *vitality design* for DEIB. The identification of processes, policies, and working methods that will need to change to achieve the changes we expect (as stated in the FROM-TO and the metrics).

x. **Implement.** This is the actual work following the Plan, specifically on the areas to change, including hiring processes, systems of record, interview standards, review promotion processes, all the talent performance and talent review steps, forms and profiles, policies for rewards, recognition to achieve pay equity. In other words, to modify what is necessary to reflect the values and new standards in how the company operates. This will extend to areas of product and customers as necessary.

xi. **Supplement.** The most common areas of DEIB programs in companies are very important too, but they do not 'create' a diverse organization. They are indispensable however, to propagate the story, to keep the conversation going, and to refresh the commitment across all the company; these activities are powerful as additional elements to demonstrate action and bring everyone along as part of the solution. This will include Employee Resource Groups, Employee Conversations, Communications, and Newsletters. These activities are what we have called 'The DEIB Program' in this book. Most companies focus overly on this component failing to affect the sustainable aspect of creating a diverse environment, which is the Plan above.

xii. **Engage.** Communicate your results and discuss strengths and opportunities with employees. Diversity needs to be reinforced constantly and appropriately, but not in a way that makes managers do 'whatever it takes' to comply with the metrics. What this means, is to avoid punishment or ridicule, or overly criticize areas where goals have not been accomplished. Everybody needs to understand that creating a diverse place organically means it will take time. We do not cut corners on DEIB. An important aspect of engaging is to communicate the results of the program with transparency, as we talk about other goals in the business. Diversity is a journey, and we as leaders need to buy into a multi-year plan that will go slow sometimes. No need to overstate results, paint too rosy of a picture. People can see through the organization anyway, but they will appreciate and feel more liberated to know they belong to a mature, real, authentic organization.

The Barriers You Will Find and How to Sort Them Out

On the journey to build an organic process that creates a diverse organization there will be obstacles. Some of them you may not expect. Below is a short list of the main barriers I will recommend you keep an eye on. Note that all of them come from an incomplete Commitment to the vision for the company—as we discussed in Chapter 8, leaders must get to a place where they can consciously and practically live with the liberated, vital company we want to be. A crack on that commitment at the point of implementation reveals we did not cover that milestone.

a. **Uneven commitment**. Every person has a point of view, and it is unrealistic to expect all your c-suite leaders will feel and think the same way on issues of diversity, even if they endorse the DEIB plan out loud in meetings and events. It is not uncommon to see some leaders exceptionally committed and motivated to the Plan, and some that will demonstrate passive resistance to the initiatives. Nobody in that table will openly voice opposition to the Diversity Plan, but you will see different degrees of speed, disposition, and open doors to experiment on things from those leaders who are less inclined toward diversity.

How to neutralize this risk? A solid governance will be a starting point, but one-to-one conversations will go further. Most leaders understand they cannot fight an enterprise initiative, but they need to confirm that we are listening and giving consideration to their objections, even if we don't implement them. In most cases they will agree to act on alignment. Ultimately, this is not about convincing or converting anybody. But it is about reaching a state of motion that allows the plan to move forward. The CEO will be the ultimate place this will go for resolution, but you will want to avoid getting to that instance—the use of authority—as much as possible.

b. **Misplaced ownership**. A portion of employees, including some managers, will not believe or agree that everyone in the company owns diversity. This is not to say they will not change their minds, so it is imperative to address their questions directly, with no prejudice or lecturing attitude, and preferably in private, to have a real opportunity to explain what ownership means, and the accountability that comes with it.

How to neutralize this risk? Addressing this risk depends on the quality of commitment and clarity on expectations stated at the beginning of the implementation. This issue is prevalent when the expectation was only communicated, not discussed, or internalized. Therefore, your best opportunity at improving ownership is to have personalized conversations with these executives and employees to share the vision of our liberating, vital organization with the objective benefits for everyone's success, and re-state the criticality of their complete commitment. These new standards of ownership will be more and more visible and prevalent, more candidates will join the company looking for these kinds of environments, causing those who cannot see things differently to opt for leaving the organization as they will rather be in a place that is consistent with their beliefs.

c. **Underestimating the impact of managers**. Managers not performing their roles as amplifiers. Of all the factors at play in developing an organization to organically create diversity, equity, inclusion, and belonging, managers not living the culture is what makes or breaks the effort. Policies, speeches, methods can only go so far if managers fail to 'make sense' of why this is important, and if they fail to express their unwavering commitment to those aspirations. In the end, employees need to hear it from their managers, or they will read into it that it is NOT ok to try to live the changes because the managers will not appreciate it and will not reward it.

How to neutralize this risk? One way to mitigate this risk is by asking executives (the managers of the managers) to do the same—drive by example—and clarify for managers what is expected from them. What are the specific actions they are to perform with their teams on a regular basis, how to avoid critical mistakes and unconscious behaviors that result in microaggressions, erosion of the values, and more specifically in aspects related to talent hiring, assessing, and promoting. The second way is to create metrics that reflect the end state we want to see. For example, representation, or progression. Those should be carefully implemented to avoid the risk of appointing or hiring people to roles only because of their diversity characteristics. Ideally, a variable compensation component will be attached to the right long-term metrics.

The appetite is there. Companies are expected to show commitment, to signal DEIB is a priority for the company. Both internally and externally, even though DEIB can be debated in some circles, most companies have a dedicated team and a dedicated statement of purpose in their public websites. The temptation will be to demonstrate action, activate a communications plan to say how important diversity is, and to establish identity groups. But that cannot be the only thing you do. My recommendation is for leaders to prioritize *metrics first*. Be your own internal consultant and ask questions, gather facts, understand where you are. From my experience, there are only a handful of hard metrics that will pave the road toward a legitimately plural, DEIB workplace. Let's look at them:

Pay equity. There are two metrics to consider: *dollar to dollar men to women*, one of the most popular metrics used in industry. Typically expressed in terms of cents to the dollar. Women are in average 90 cents to the dollar as compared to men, all jobs, all levels, all industries. It is a wide metric and probably good to have as a reference but not very good to target transformational action. The second metric is *job to job using white men's compensation as reference*. With this metric you will be able to track the variance against gender and key demographics. This is a metric that will require analytics job to bob and trends over time. The effort will pay off, as you will be able to understand those areas in deeper need to adjust in order to increase equity for real. Pay equity takes years to accomplish and to keep; it is never 'achieved'. You always chase this metric as numbers change as soon as you hire someone outside of the range. That is why signature processes will keep you maintain this outcome alive.

Representation. This is the hardest metric to move. Hiring diverse people should not be about diversity first, otherwise we create a bigger problem. It is about target the right skills, experience, competence, through an inclusive process to bring equal opportunity to all people. This is not a particular to people of color. Women continue to struggle in companies to get fair representation in management positions.[8] Once diverse talent walks in, the signature organization and the right management will do the work to make it worth for them *to stay*. Retention is a challenge for companies when it comes to diverse talent. People leave managers but they also leave non-vital organizations designed to spin wheels and waste energy. A well-articulated, credible, EVP with hard metrics associated to it will be one of the strongest assets to support retention.

Progression. Stable organizations tend to have few opportunities for promotion, therefore, a signature process on progression should include a rule of always having a diverse slate of candidates and remind business leaders NOT to directly hire diverse candidates only to improve their diversity numbers (quota), but instead, to hire the most capable candidate. Progression takes time too, and sometimes you can help by defining progression programs for unique, high potential populations. At Houghton Mifflin Harcourt we implemented a very bold program: LEAD Connected. This program was a rotational program, with job changes every six months and a guaranteed promotion to director level at the end of the program. The premise was centered on the selection of a group of remarkable, diverse, and non-diverse candidates—already considered highly promotable talent—to avoid any perceptions of 'fast track' or 'affirmative action' promotions. The program was culture-affirming for the company, a sound success showing the commitment in a visible, tangible way for the company to witness real action, to accelerate the curve to get the best of the best talent a special opportunity to earn their promotions.

Engagement. Engagement is a metric for a Diverse, Equitable, and Belonging organization as long as you perform analytics on the data and not only use global averages. Overall, engagement represents a significant value for the company in the form of stability, reputation, cost savings, and retention. Engagement is affirming on the choice to stay with employees of all groups convinced they are in the right place. But the results you may want to look at are direct assessments on how people perceive you are living your values. At HMH we measured the cultural Values by assigning Gallup validated questions from the engagement survey to each of our values. These associations allowed for cross cut analytics to reveal insights beyond the first-glance averages. Taking the whole African American population as average can bring good numbers, but as you break down question by question on values new clarity comes out revealing previously invisible and powerful opportunities. Sharing these insights with employees, and the actions that will help improve the experience creates trust that the company is walking the talk.

External recognition. The right external organizations that can attest as third parties on your progress will be a very important argument toward your claim on improvement and success on the DEIB field. For example, the Diversity Impact Award sponsored by the Global ERG Network,[9] or the Corporate Equality Index, awarded by the Human Rights Campaign.[10]

A Closing Note on Diversity

As this book is written, a debate that you would think belongs to the past, is taking place in several countries in the world.[11] An orchestrated weakening of initiatives, programs, and investments on DEI efforts. In many countries, including the United States, individuals in elected political positions are working along with donors, influencers, and local authorities to ban, make illegal the training on any aspect related to diversity because they consider it contrary to what their countries stand for. We will not discuss the merits of their arguments here, but we will say that if you intend to drive transformation in an industry where talent is important, it will be in your survival list of items to have serious plan to establish your company, authentically, as a place where people of different backgrounds find they can belong,[12] and a place where they are treated fairly and equally. That is being strategic, focused on markets, and responsive to demographics analytics. My advice is to continue to get focused on your capacity for success, which directly depends on your ability to create a liberating, vital workplace. As a byproduct of its very implementation, its processes, and its management, will render a profitable and winning DEIB organization on its own. Your organization will organically become a role model, a reference point in the market for talent, and serve as a source of inspiration and evidence for leaders who are open to the future of work.

But it is not going to emerge by itself. It needs you, the liberating leader, to commit to it, to pursue it, and to achieve it.

Notes

1. Ernst & Young. (2020). How board can lead on racial diversity, equity and inclusion. Addressing the business and social demands to deliver long-term value. EY Center for Board Matters. 2020.
2. Hunt, V., Prince, S., Dixon-Fyle, S., & Dolan, K. (2020). Diversity wins: How inclusion matters. McKinsey & Company.
3. Chamberlain, A., Stansell, A., & Zhao, D. (2021). America's workplace diversity crisis: Measuring gaps in diversity & inclusion satisfaction by employee race and ethnicity. Glassdoor Economic Research.
4. Kendi, I. X. (2019). How to be an antiracist. One World.
5. Schutz, W. (1958). FIRO: A three-dimensional theory of interpersonal behavior. Holt, Rinehart and Winston.

6. Sony. (2024). Sony Group Diversity, Equity and Inclusion Statement. Sony Group Portal. Retrieved from: https://www.sony.com/en/SonyInfo/diversity/concept/
7. Google (2024). Goggle Diversity Annual Report 2023. Embedding belonging in all we do. Retrieved from: https://about.google/belonging/diversity-annual-report/2023/
8. McKinsey & Company. (2023). McKinsey and Lean In organization: Women in the workplace Study 2023.
9. Global ERG Network. (2024) Diversity Impact Awards. Retrieved from: https://globalergnet.com/conference/diversity-impact-awards/
10. Human Rights Campaign. (2024). Corporate Equality Index. Retrieved from: https://www.hrc.org/resources/corporate-equality-index
11. Iyer, A. (2021). Understanding advantaged groups' opposition to diversity, equity, and inclusion (DEI) policies: The role of perceived threat. Review Article, Wiley. Department of Psychology, University of Sheffield, Sheffield, UK. https://doi.org/10.1111/spc3.12666
12. Jacob, K., Unerman, S., & Edwards, M. (2020). Belonging: The key to transforming and maintaining diversity, inclusion, and equity at work. Bloomsbury.

19

People Outcomes: A Renewed Mandate for HR

Managing people affairs, the administration of human work, has been around our civilization for a very long time. None of the marvels we appreciate today from ancient history would be possible without a form of purposeful human coordination. The more modern version of this coordination, what we recognize today as the Human Resources function goes back to the Industrial Revolution. For the longer part of the Nineteenth Century, the function was set up as industrial welfare. At the beginnings of the Twentieth Century, the function was focused on working conditions. Personnel departments, as they were called, were dedicated to the administrative tasks of hiring, firing, and paying. These were the times of Frederick Taylor's Scientific Management and the motion-time studies, bringing attention to efficiency.[1] Large companies started to realize it was important to have employee well-being investments. Labor stability was critical for production and productivity. The New Deal in the 1930s was instrumental to grow the labor unions and collective bargaining. But it wasn't until the end of the second World War, when the global corporation became the most successful model for growth and wealth creation, that available markets became ready for regional and global scale growth. Market opportunity translated in urgent needs for skilled employees, forcing companies to dedicate larger amounts of value to people, not only to machinery, patents, and land. Personnel Departments were now focused on training, development, and workforce integration, including employee relations. During the 1950s it was necessary to formalize compensation and benefits in order to structure not only cost, but career development, incentives, and performance. After the Civil

Rights Movement in the 1960s leading to the equal employment opportunity, the people function also focused on preventing discrimination. All this history encapsulates our first paradigm of effectiveness—Industrial (refer to Chapter 4, Fig. 4.1)—for which capacity, scalability, productivity, and quality were the most important descriptors of a well-run company. Coincidental with this nomenclature, some companies called the people function 'Industrial Relations'.

HR as a strategic asset for business was initiated in the late 1970s and formalized in the 1980s, with large companies making significant investments in leadership development, workforce planning, and a more structured way to examine and execute succession, marking the beginnings of HRs contribution to our second effectiveness paradigm—Financial—Companies realized how critical was for profitability, growth and market capitals to have the right talent, leveraged in the right ways. This new sophistication in HR had a steady evolution that extended to the 1990s when the famous article 'The War for Talent' by McKinsey was published[2]. At the same time, the well-known GE practice to assess people in both performance and potential and then move out the bottom 10% of talent were innovations everyone was talking about and trying to imitate, sometimes with unwanted consequences. Human Resources consolidated its strategic position; multiple models emerged to illustrate how HR could be more business focused, use analytics, centered on performance, strategic compensation, incentives, and organizational change.[3]

With technology innovations focused on personalization, customer-centricity showed new paths to growth and differentiation, the era of our third paradigm—Tech and Customer—started. HR departments, now a c-suite level organization, focused its effort on managing global workforces, leveraging the use of technology (HRIS), and a renewed emphasis on performance management tied to strategic goals. Multiple-layered goals required new ways of thinking and organizing for alignment. In this context the *Balanced Scorecard*[4] blossomed into the global business consciousness, a consequential book written in the late nineties by Robert Kaplan and David Norton introducing a novel take on organization effectiveness, alignment between business and people goals, actions, and metrics. In this Tech-Customer era, iconic successful companies that produced world-changing products re casted themselves as management philosophies; among others we find Intel with Andy Groove's *Only the paranoid survive*,[5] the emergence of Amazon from a bookstore to the global retail powerhouse we see today with the innovative persona of Jeff Bezos, the emergence of Google as the www. dot.com poster child. HR became instrumental as it was very clear how determinant for success the right talent, and particularly, the right leadership and management demonstrated to be. But also, because ethics took a center stage following Enron's demise, making culture an essential, foundational piece for corporate effectiveness. HR as a legitimate c-suite function, beyond administrative and compliance reasons had arrived. Culture and leadership were the pillars for this emergence.

HR incorporated new tools and new technology steadily and gradually but was not forced to create any quantum leaps of innovation. The fundamentals had not changed: continuing the trends of leadership, culture, the provisioning of people, commitment to diversity, the administration of life events for employees, safety considerations, and to a growing extent, regulation. That is, until the world changed, when The Future of Work arrived.[6] Flexible location, flexible schedules took center stage, the raise of awareness about the imperatives of social justice and the role companies could and should take on the betterment of society, and certainly the largest of all, the role of Artificial Intelligence in the workplace,[7] not only for analytics but also for workforce, decision-making, and in some cases peer to peer collaboration and direction from AI.[8] These forces became instantly visible and pushed the function to resolve dilemmas it did not have before. In that challenge, the function rose to the occasion and became something different, because the CEOs, investors, and our customers changed too. We all wanted meaningful work in a place that cared for something greater than its profits, a place with a commitment to contributing to, rather than moving away from, the next world and society. This was the beginning of our latest paradigm of effectiveness—Purpose—in which companies are forced to deal with these disruptive components as a new way of living. This expanded, stretched worldview was not unique to HR professionals, it affects everyone. However, HR, as the advising voice on people for the organization, and responsible to implement new protocols, programs, and to monitor remote work, has been the frontline in the fluid realities of implementing something so radically new, with no playbook, only real-time experimentation.

Human Resources teams rose to the occasion during the pandemic, but this is only the beginning of a larger arc of evolution for the function. Where does HR go from here? With the benefit of the perspective gained a few years into the Purpose era, the framework provided by the Leading Success approach, and consistent with available research on the Future of Work, I am offering a point of view on how the HR profession may successfully adapt to the future, what are the imperatives it needs to address in order to emerge as the liberating, vital force that will create the right environment to materialize ambitious business agendas. To answer this question, I have segmented the conversation in three critical components for the future of HR:

How the *HR Organization* adapts to the future?

To examine the ways in which the Future of Work will challenge the configuration of a function that has been designed and fine-tuned for people and business needs that are changing, at the time when we transition into a world for human–machine collaboration.

How the *HR Work* realigns for a Liberation, Vitality, and Expression organization?

To examine the implications of the Nine Disciplines in the portfolio of work for the HR professional. To identify the expectations for outcomes and performance beyond the traditional HR needs.

How the *HR Talent* requirements change with the above?

To examine how the talent populating the function today needs to adapt to this changed expectation and consequently, how the next generation of HR professionals and HR leaders will develop into these higher specifications.

The Evolution of the HR Organization

As we have studied in Chapter 4, the evolution of enterprises goes from what we called the Industrial paradigm all the way to the Technology and Customer paradigm—as illustrated in Fig. 4.1. The emergence of the global pandemic, together with the events that led to the social justice movement after George Floyd's murder created an environment inside and outside organizations that redefined expectations of employees and reflected on how companies would respond to those new requirements. These raised expectations would have been significant enough for keep companies busy for years, but there was more. The arrival of new forms of Artificial Intelligence (AI) in a more consumable way to the masses, and to organizations. This is what I have called 'the trifecta of change' the aggregation of forces that translated into a new paradigm of what does it mean to be an effective organization. As you look to the illustration in Fig. 19.1, you will see the continuum from Industrial to Financial to Customer and then to the Purpose paradigm we leave today.

Consistent with this evolution, in the first column of that diagram we see a corresponding transformation of the human resources function. Starting with what was historically the beginnings of a people oriented collective set of work around *Employee Services*. This means the administrative duties required to hire employees, pay employees, move employees around the organization, and essentially walk them through their life cycles until their departure. In

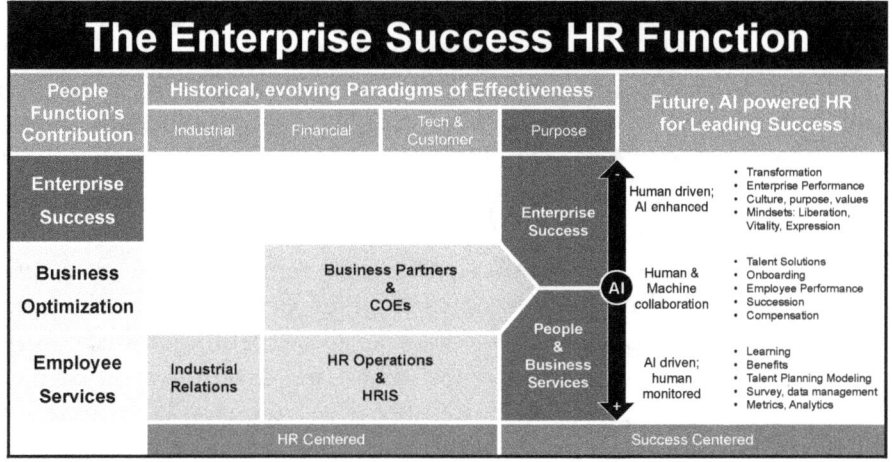

Fig. 19.1 The evolution of the people function organization

the Industrial paradigm, this set of activities were called Personnel or Industrial Relations and that is how some of us may still remember them when we entered the workforce. As organizations became more focused on consistent flows of revenue and more focused on how technology would allow to serve customers better, this approach to people in the organization proved insufficient to the emerging Financial and Customer-Tech paradigms (Fig 4.1). Now it would take more than just bringing people in the organization (the old *labor*) to be productive. Goals became more complex, and employees were required to exhibit skills beyond just operational or tactical in nature. We needed *intangibles*; capacity to relate to other people, ability to interpret a context to make business strategic decisions, the growing importance of design, and the understanding of what customer success really means to how the organization operates. The human resources function therefore moved from providing employee services to focus on *Business Optimization* and the most symbolic embodiment of this evolution was the Business Partner in HR. Business Partner positions were designed to understand the business and adapt the HR toolkit to ensure people, culture, and processes were aligned toward the complex ambitions of the business. In parallel, the employee services didn't go away but instead, evolved into human resources operations and the more pervasive use of systems and automation—also called HRIS. This model has been the dominant approach to human resources for the last two or three decades. As part of this model, the aggregation of Human Resources 'methods and science' concentrated in a few Centers of Excellence, housing critical areas to serve the business such as Talent Acquisition, Compensation, Learning, and Change.

This approach proved to be the answer for business optimization, but it comes short of the demands of the Purpose era because the subject of change is no longer behavior, it is *mindset*, which is harder to alter with the traditional tools of incentives and progression. We need inspiring reasons beyond pure business rationale to reveal the best out of our employees. This is, people working for their own convictions, and not only for ours as a company: we need liberation, vitality, and expression to move the company forward fast and *at scale*. This next evolution is shown in the same Fig. 19.1 represented as the upper row on the column People Functions' Contribution as *Enterprise Success*, pointing at what Leading Success is all about; in other words, how the HR function reframes itself to allow for a liberating vital expression environment, considering alongside the social justice expectations and the immersion of Artificial intelligence in the workplace.

Considering the function in general, and recognizing the remarkable exceptions to this rule, a secondary reason for the business optimization model of HR to be insufficient for a Leading Success environment is that HR focused too much on optimizing its tools, perfecting its delivery model, and improving itself to provide a better service at a lower cost, instead of following the migration of value for business success.[9] HR has been playing in the same space, in the same way for too long. In concrete terms, HR specialized on the disciplines 4–9 (culture, talent, organization, engagement, expectation, experience) and did not pursue with the same strength and determination its critical and necessary role on disciplines 1–3 (aspiration, transformation, commitment). Furthermore, we could argue that organization, engagement, and experience were implemented less as a design effort for success and more as instances of a formula that worked for long time.

According to this perspective, the HR organization finds itself at a point of inflection from an HR-Centered to a Success-Centered expression. The Purpose era, optimizing HR for Enterprise Success will still carry the responsibilities of business optimization and employee services, but those areas will be split in three recognizable segments of work defined around how much AI, automation, and machine-supported solutions can effectively do.[10] In this picture, the further columns on the right indicate a possible breakdown of the HR organization, not as organization structure, but as logical components of work, segmented by their ability to be more or less supported by AI.

The Evolution of the HR Work

Considering how innovative the human resources organization may look like with the arrival of the future of work it is important to reflect how the actual work of the HR professional at all levels also changes. To guide us on this analysis we are going to take as a model of reference the Nine Disciplines identified in the Leading Success framework. For each one of the disciplines, we will identify what is new in the work of the HR professional and what prevalent focus of activities will have to change if the HR teams are going to effectively implement a liberating, vital, expression environment.

In general, the leading success model is predicated on three main mindsets explained before: leadership which is about liberation, infrastructure which is about vitality, and execution which is about expression, as discussed in previous chapters. The illustration on Fig. 19.2 provides a visual representation of the insights to follow.

We start with the first mindset, *Liberation*. Human resources functions do not possess the authority to implement a style of leadership in the company, that authority is not only a prerogative, but also an inevitable consequence of the CEO's leadership style and beliefs. Notwithstanding, the People function leader has a decisive and influential role in this mindset to *reframe* the strategic conversation on the vision to express its intent in terms of liberation principles. This reframing serves to enrich the business transformation, the ambitious goals that are being pursued by reminding the executive committee—demonstrated with data and facts—that a liberating approach is

Fig. 19.2 How the work in HR changes with leading success

essential, not optional, in the post-pandemic era. This is indispensable if we are to change the company to last, not only to create a temporary cosmetic change. It is critical to eradicate the perception that the company is designing transformations to impress investors, and doing it by depleting its capacities in search for short-term gains. The People function leader builds the connection between WORD and WORLD by articulating, describing what the company must BECOME for its employees to be able to pull out the vision. Let's explore the specific work HR is expected to perform in the three disciplines under Liberation: Aspiration, Transformation, Commitment.

The work of the human resources leader on the *Aspiration* discipline or *North Star* for the company goes from *participating* in that definition as member of the executive committee to *advocating* for an aspiration that is about purpose according to post-pandemic employee expectations. This advocating however, it's not about discourse or storytelling alone, but instead is about data trends, observable social dynamics that make the case for a vision that responds to the evolution of the labor market.

For the *Transformation* discipline, HR professionals who currently *document* the change and ensure the new articulation is consistent with the new goals, now will grow their role to *assert* an explicit position, with specific language reflecting the liberating perspectives of Leading Success in the very articulation of the transformation. This is, by recommending the inclusion of concrete aspirations responding to a future-orientated Employee Value Proposition (EVP), centered on employee success, equality in the workplace, bold commitments related to women and minorities in management positions, and the creation of a climate that is inclusive and belonging. Make it clear how employees win in the transformation.

For the third discipline *Commitment* companies often oversimplify its depth by confusing commitment with discussion and agreement—not the same thing. Leading Success sees commitment as the pivot, the axis by which the entire transformation becomes authentic by inserting a discipline fully focused on the executive committee to truly endorse the transformation. Under this perspective, the HR leader with the CEO move from *expecting* leaders to commit, to *connecting* with them, to ensure there are no barriers, gaps, misunderstandings, for commitment to be achieved.

Our second mindset, *Vitality*, is dedicated to build the infrastructure for the company to feel liberating to employees. Articulating an aspiration, a clear transformation and the commitment by executives is only the starting part of the journey, and it will mean very little—or in fact it may be negative—if the workplace is not designed according to those commitments. The everyday experience for employees and consequently, for customers will be a reminder that we did—or did not—mean our vision. In that sense, the vitality mindset is not only about *engineering the processes* to get people to align with our vision. In addition, we need to think about the *design* of the organization as we think about the design of a house. It's not that we need a kitchen, a family room, three bedrooms, and two bathrooms; that is what a processes design would tell us is necessary for a house to include. But how those components connect to each other results in the creation of very different experiences for the family. That is why the role of the HR professional on the vitality mindset is to *architect*—verb—to decipher how Culture Talent and Organization come together to harmoniously beget an environment that creates high performance, facilitates collaboration and innovation. Human resources as architects for vitality are concerned not only with the great design of a culture which could be the kitchen, or talent processes which could be the bedrooms, but also they should influence the design of where the doors, the corridors, the connecting hallways, the stairs should be to ensure a particular area can be accessed in an easier way and not have to go around, create unnatural holes, ruptures, or outside the house to go to the dining room. If organizations today where representations of houses you might be surprised to find that in order to reach your bedroom, perhaps you would have to climb in through a window. It is not enough to design processes; we need to design their connections, interactions, interdependencies of how those work together as a whole. We need organizational architects.

Let's explore the specific work HR is expected to perform in the three disciplines under Vitality: Culture, Talent, Organization.

Culture articulations are one of the most extraordinary processes and consequential outcomes for human resources professionals, and one of the best documented, resourced, and well performed in general. People leaders act as agents of structure, project management, and coordination of multiple inputs across the stages of creation of narratives, but they need to be more. The are expected to *lead* the thinking process, not just the writing process. Lead the thinking with the CEO to stretch for bold possibilities on the philosophy that is embedded in the document. Human resources leaders work to ensure that culture articulations in their final versions are richer than the outcomes of the surveys and focus groups being consulted, that they have grounding in the legacy of the organization and its history, but they include words (the WORD) that have not been said before, meant to change the WORLD. Cultures must be departure points.

For the *Talent* discipline, the People function leaders will move from *replicating* very well-known practices and methodologies on selection, development, onboarding, succession, to enrich how we look at talent by *innovating* the articulation of the work in terms of talent economy principles. This includes clarification of what exactly is the employee value proposition that best represents the liberation the company is seeking to achieve, and the culture we want to express. It also includes the concept of position profile versus position description, to clearly define how the position brings value to the transformation, not just coverage to its duties.

For *Organization* we have the biggest opportunity in this mindset. In the rush of things, the term organization design has reached its most basic expression as 'organization structure', an organization chart. Human Resources commonly *recommend* design principles for leaders to embrace and implement in their teams. In the Leading Success company, the term organization design includes much more than its structure; it requires HR to *harmonize* the organization components as an ecosystem, working with business leaders to establish the vital infrastructure for effectiveness with the identification of relevant metrics, processes for business and people that are connected to the goals, distribution of power that corresponds with roles and responsibilities, in ways that the whole set reflects the purpose and values. And finally, the right governance to ensure the organization works as a living organism that has feedback to redirect its behaviors toward the results we seek.

As we move to the third mindset which is about *Expression*, the role, in general, for the HR professional has been to ensure that the right processes are followed, the standards are met, and the year-cycle works with all trains departing on time. To do that, HR teams issue instructions, reminders, job-aids, communications; they *write the script* of the motions the organization must follow to ensure compliance with goal setting, performance management, schedules and specs for compensation, and the like. Leading Success will go further, to ensure the movements become coordinated, timely, and connected, as if they are part of a stage dance. Hence the metaphor of HR as *choreographer*. Let's explore the specific work HR is expected to perform in the three disciplines under Expression: Engagement, Expectation, Experience.

For *Engagement*, HR leaders in general do a very good job by measuring engagement formally and consistently. The approach overall has been elevated from merely *measuring* and sharing engagement scores with managers (and sometimes those are not even shared) toward the implementation of actions in response to the measurements—implementing continuous improvements. Leading Success, however, differentiates two levels of engagement; the commonly used approach related to engagement surveys and action plans to help leaders and teams improve is the low hanging fruit and a practice that has reached levels of excellence in most companies. While engagement surveys are extraordinary and should continue to exist, they are a look into the mirror, not about creating a commitment for the future. Engagement scores are limited in their impact because they are about reaction, to describe how people are feeling as a result of their experience in the organization. The second level of engagement is to affect engagement proactively by changing the story and changing the experience. This is, to *create* engagement through conscious understanding and embracing of a vision that ultimately translates in an affirmation for employees about their own liberating vital visions for themselves and their aspirations. This *proactive engagement* points to higher levels of connection with the 'why'—'why is this the right company to spend my time'—which is directly connected to the Future of Work, documented in the Employee Value Proposition. That is the kind of engagement we are talking about in this discipline.

The concept of *Expectation* has been one of the most appreciated surprises I encountered during my work on performance. Imagine you own a soccer team, and you just signed an extraordinary player, a true generational talent that can change your franchise for a decade. When you place this player on the roster you set the expectation of winning every game and reaching a championship. You may be surprised that even with best rosters, teams can lose; they need more than just generic goals, they need schemes, roles to be played, unique strategies based on each opponent—those are the *expectations* that make a difference on both team and player success. It is not uncommon that managers go about creating goals by declaring, 'you know the game', 'win every game' and 'get me a championship'; this is, going back to common, obvious goals, even if challenging, they fall short on setting expectations. Data from Gallup reveals that one of the hardest areas to improve is precisely, the expectation, reflected in one of their Q12 model questions: 'I know what is expected of me'.[11] And the reason is that roles in transforming companies are less about the content of the work, than how the new culture and the new ways of work change how people prioritize the work, how people has to work with others they never had to coordinate before, and very importantly, what new outcomes matter as a result of their work and consequently what new metrics influence the assessment of their performance going forward. Therefore, setting expectations only on the content of the work will not result in an effective way to implement a transformation. The new work of the HR professional is not limited to compliance with performance management specifications, systems, and timings, but in *driving the ownership* on managers and employees to cover the space of expectation that comes with liberating, vital transformation, including how the employee plays a role in the harmonious ecology of the organization design.

We get to the 9th and final discipline *Experience*, regarded in the Leading Success framework as the ultimate evidence of success. When our customer's experience equals our vision and reflects the *North Star* we declared as a Purpose for doing business in the first place, profitably, ethically, and sustainably, we have achieved enduring success. And we know, in the Purpose era we are living, as the Future of Work unfolds, the only way to get our customers to experience this vision is by having our employees experience it first, inside our company. Customer and employee experience are important in every company and therefore we must find ways to measure precisely, regularly, and very seriously their value. Assessing is a baseline, but Leading Success will demand HR professionals to go further, to anticipate, observe, intervene, and adjust relevant deviations from the 'North Star', and thoughtfully, appropriately, go to the sources of the gap between experience and vision to address and elevate the experience. This is only possible when we are attuned to our purpose and values in a practical way, and not because we are vigilant, policing, supervising; instead, it is because we have adopted the liberating, vital, expression mindset as a way of working in the People Function. In short, our job in experience is to *realize the vision*.

The new mandate of the HR professional therefore, as illustrated in Fig. 19.3, is to embrace a perspective that creates success, by reframing, architecting, and choreographing the organization toward exceptional performance. Our existing roles are a baseline for the future of work and will move toward more liberating actions: advocate, assert, connect; to more vital actions: lead thinking, innovate, harmonize; and to more expressive actions: create, drive ownership, and realize the vision into experience. While this is no small change, most HR professionals have the full capacity and attitudes to fulfill those expectation. However, they are immersed in well-designed environments for the current experience and have been developed to solve the most urgent problems, in the fastest way possible. It is important to discuss how these skills can be fully developed in a new career development for the People Function professional.

The Evolution of the HR Talent

For long we have considered HR to be in the people business. However, I argue we really are in the mindset evolution business. That notion embraces *people* in its most complete, fulfilling, and profound concept. In his book, *The*

HR Work in Leading Success			
MINDSET / Discipline		**FROM**: Baseline work	**TO**: Leading Success Work
	LIBERATION	Affirm (WORLD)	Reframe (WORD)
1	Aspiration	Participate	Advocate
2	Transformation	Document	Assert
3	Commitment	Delegate	Connect
	VITALITY	Engineer (Processes)	Architect (Spaces)
4	Culture	Lead Writing	Lead Thinking
5	Talent	Replicate	Innovate
6	Organization	Recommend	Harmonize
	EXPRESSION	Script	Choreograph
7	Engagement	Measure	Create
8	Expectation	Drive Standards	Drive Ownership
9	Experience	Assess	Realize

Fig. 19.3 The transformation of the HR function—role perspective

Age of Spiritual Machines: When Computers Exceed Human Intelligence,[12] Ray Kurzweil —a recognized futurologist with extraordinary perspectives on artificial intelligence—established that as we move forward, the work between humans and machines will be undistinguishable from each other, that we will discover in the next few decades if and how machines become self-aware, have rights, demand respect, etc. And no less disturbing, the notion that brain implants will help people—those with the resources, not necessarily everyone—to operate in multiple languages, with vast reservoirs of data and enhanced neurological activity, potentially creating a new category of inequity. As we get there and navigate the massive transition such changes will demand from all humanity, we will be living in times of radical change, constantly. And the way to make people assimilate those turbulences will be through the mastering of the ability of think differently, believe different things, *evolving the mindset*. This is, being good at something Robert Kegan called trans-categorical thinking.[13] The ability to look beyond the forest to see the collections of forests, appreciate similarities, differences, the new whole as an entity and also to identify how multiple changing conditions are affecting the forests, anticipate how our own forest will change, and therefore adapt accordingly—even if the adaptation calls for believing something different, to revisit our convictions and certainties, while retaining the essential attributes of self and organizations. This is akin of a computer that can look at its own operating system to see where it is falling short and determine it needs to change. That is the challenge of The Next HR.

A word of caution is important to raise on this subject. The way we connect the people function with the world of AI will not be about finding the next best replacement for a tool, or how to solve a problem faster, with less people. Those are immediate steps in our journey to integrate people (not HR) with AI, but it cannot be the only path we take. Unless we want the people and business solutions being decided in other areas such as technology or strategy. It is not about which App does HR's job best. It is about how we create the organization we need and integrate humans and machines for success.

The illustration on Fig. 19.4 shows how mindset evolution responds to the fundamental need to address companies' change during our three-pronged Purpose era: post-pandemic, social justice, artificial intelligence, all three impacting organizations at the same time. Undeniably, the previous incarnations of the People Function—depicted in the first and second columns in the picture—will be needed but will no longer be sufficient to solve the CEO's problems. How we go about equipping leadership teams to evolve on their thinking is the primary value proposition for the next HR professional.

With that been said, how do we describe and most importantly, how do we develop a professional skillset that delivers on these capabilities? While conclusive research will have to be conducted as we progress into the next few years a few observations are apparent:

The evolving expectation for HR talent

Layers of Focus	People	Organization	Enterprise
Required mindset	Trajectory Consistency	Trajectory Acceleration	Trajectory Modification
What HR is here for	Solve problems fast	Implement HR Processes	Evolve the mindset
Main roles	• Compliance Custodian • Talent Recruiter	• Business Partner • Talent Supplier	• Performance Designer • Talent Economist
Relevant metrics	• Retention • Cost, speed to hire	• Engagement • Diversity as input	• Transformation success • Diversity as outcome
Sources of reference	• Behavior occurrence • Regulation	• Business results (today's) • Policy design	• Capacity, Outcomes, Growth • Environment design
What we design for	• Hiring Plan • Capacity	• HR Plan & Business Goals • Culture	• Vision becoming the Customer & Employee experience

Fig. 19.4 The people function leader for the future of work

1. **More exposure to disciplines outside the HR tradition.** Career building for the next HR professional will be enhanced by journeys outside of the function: finance, technology, sales, and with time spent across different companies and industries. Long tenures—as they are common to see—can be problematic for rapid change and innovation.
2. **The adoption of a liberating, vital expression approach at a personal level.** There is a dimension of Leading Success that is about the self. There is nothing on this approach that is not applicable to a person. We need to liberate ourselves from old perceptions, and paradigms of success on career progression, and tenure, the identity of HR as a 'support' function is a very strong belief in the function. Fortunately, Leading Success comes largely at no cost. HR Professionals can follow the Nine Disciplines and how those apply to HR to start a vital journey of their own.
3. **Balance discovery and finding.** It is hard to change a tradition. There is a very strong pull in HR to solve problems and being rewarded for it. We must break the incentive system to enterprise success, to design for vitality and expression. HR talent spends a lot of time searching to find the skills they see in their HR leaders, but there is very little room for discovery, to find the new and the next—the role of the Future of Work was pushed to us by the pandemic, but that was something already moving, just got accelerated. The next two points are opportunities to discovery in HR, to find skills nobody may have today and will be differentiating for talent in the function very soon.
4. **Full participation in the future of work dilemmas:** AI, social justice, understanding the young. HR talent can get closer to the burning dilemmas and issues of the Purpose era. Using, participating, and leveraging AI, get curious and explore ways to make it work for their jobs. Learn and understand how social issues evolve and keep a finger on the pulse of the organization via data, engagement surveys. Get close and listen to the younger employees; what do they want, what do they expect, what do they value are all clues for discovery of how our careers will evolve.
5. **Become a student of the future.** It's been said that every time is the same. Every generation sees the world through lenses of massive change and finds ways to survive it. It can be wars, natural disasters, pandemics, international conflicts, or technological innovation, but if we are to believe those who study history in long arches, there is never such a thing as a stability time. With that said, the computer, the internet, and AI don't come to every generation at the same time as the world changed with a global pandemic. The density of change is higher, because changes are instantly global, and therefore the opportunity to learn and to adapt is bigger. HR

talent—and all talent for that matter—cannot afford to be uninformed about where the future is going. Studying the future will expose HR professionals to the areas that will be less vulnerable to AI automation and those that will require better understanding and insight to design human-machine collaboration. Most certainly, companies have understood this need, and most are investing on giving people the tools to get familiar with those technologies.

The above is hardly a recipe, I see it as a list of doors to open to look at different pantries with different collections of ingredients. No recipes, only flavors. But diversity of thought and the nurturing of a trans-categorial thinking are a must. The challenge is not simple, because at the same time the next HR professionals will be looking at multiple forests they will be asked to care for their own forest, their threes, and their weeds. There is no tolerance, no excuse, and no space to fail to deliver the experience at the time we are building capacity to become our vision. I can't think of a better time to be an HR professional.

In Conclusion

The Human Resources function has been carrying significant weight in the journey from the industrial revolution to the AI revolution with remarkable success, budling the wheels for progress. And yet, no past glory guarantees success in the future. If we are going to raise above being replaced by smart AI tech, or replaced in strategic decision-making by technologists or strategists, this is the time to raise our own bar and set a new North Star for the function as a whole. Figure 19.5 shows a perspective on an enhanced identity for the HR Function, which can no longer be only about people, and the abnegation to do the impossible to serve today's needs; instead, it has to be about the emerging collaboration between people and machines, and can no longer be business optimization, but mindset modification.

A significant journey ahead and one that the CEO and the c-suite help create; this is not HR's work alone. They are the team that walks the talk first on what mindset modification is and means in practice, but the most important mindset starts in the way the CEO looks at this function; to look beyond a team that solves the next problem, not the team who brings the next strategic answer. We need a CEO—and there are many out there—who long for see the next People Function, who are impatient to have in their CHRO/CPO a co-leader for the future of work, for transformation that brings the

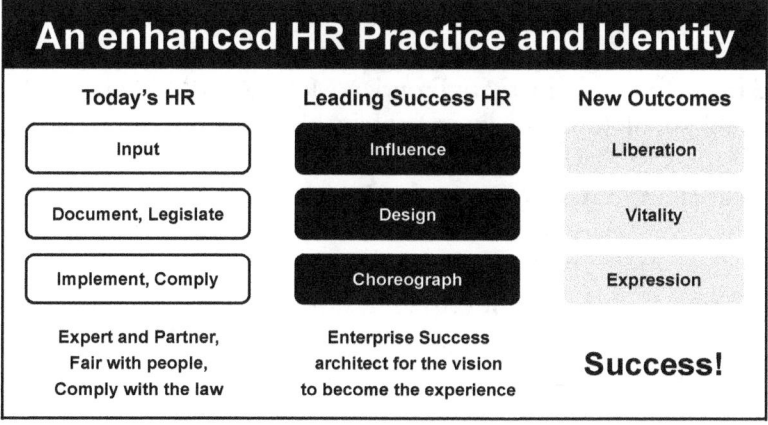

Fig. 19.5 A new identify for a liberating people function

most valuable capability to the organization: help people see, believe, think and act differently to be able to achieve the only true measure of success—the capacity to become our vision.

Notes

1. Taylor, F. W. (1911). The principles of scientific management. Harper & Brothers.
2. Chambers, E.G. & Foulon, Mark & Handfield-Jones, Helen & Hankin, Steven & Michaels, Edward. (1998). The War for Talent. The McKinsey Quarterly. 3. 44–57.
3. Ulrich, D. (1996). Human resource champions: The next agenda for adding value and delivering results. Harvard Business School Press.
4. Kaplan, R. S., & Norton, D. P. (1996). The balanced scorecard: Translating strategy into action. Harvard Business School Press. Boston, MA.
5. Grove, A. S. (1996). Only the paranoid survive: How to exploit the crisis points that challenge every company. Doubleday.
6. Malhotra, A. (2021). The post pandemic future of work. Journal of Management, 47(5), 1091–1102. https://doi.org/10.1177/01492063211000435.
7. Autor, D., Mindell, D., & Reynolds, E. (2020). The work of the future: Building better jobs in an age of intelligent machines. MIT Task Force on the Work of the Future.

8. Chui, M., Hazan, E., Roberts, R., Singla, A., Smaje, K., Sukharevsky, A., Yee, L., Zemmel, R. (2023). The Economic Potential of Generative AI. The next productivity Frontier. McKinsey & Company. 2023.
9. McCord, P. (2014, January). How Netflix reinvented HR. Harvard Business Review.
10. Jesuthasan, Ravin & Boudreau, Jonathan. (2017). Thinking Through How Automation Will Affect Your Workforce. Harvard Business Review, April 2017.
11. Clifton, J., & Harter, J. (2019). It's the manager: Gallup finds that the quality of managers and team leaders is the single biggest factor in your organization's long-term success. Gallup Press.
12. Kurzweil, R. (1999). The age of spiritual machines: When computers exceed human intelligence. Viking, Penguin Putnam. New York, NY.
13. Kegan, R. (1994). In over our heads: The mental demands of modern life. Harvard University Press. Cambridge, MA.

20

Legacy: Becoming a Liberator

In his book True North, Bill George reminds us that our lives and our leadership are all about being true to ourselves. *True North*,[1] in his words, 'is the internal compass that guides you successfully through life'. The main premise of his message is that leaders, like everyone else, are pursuing an ideal, responding to inner motivations that come from deep within. It is imperative to discover those motivations and use their inspiration to move our organizations forward with authenticity and profound determination. In my interpretation, the search is about finding the sources of your desire for liberation, to know where it comes from. So, I thought I would conclude this book providing you with a few reflections to find your sources of liberation, your personal North Star.

If You Intend to Lead, Excel as Liberator

Starting the exploration for Leading Success, or to engage in a relevant transformation, regardless of methodology or approach, will demand you to do some new things, change a few routines and habits in your managerial rituals, but at some point, it will demand you to raise new questions about your beliefs, convictions, your vision and yes, your limitations. Leadership of liberation starts with you. Dedicate time, thinking, and action to improving your liberating leadership capabilities. If you are a CEO, or a senior leader you will have plenty of opportunity to exercise your liberating behaviors and decisions. For those readers in roles concerned with operation, middle management, team leaders, project managers, you may have duties that are more about execution and less about long-term planning, but there is always room for liberation. In the end, everyone is leading something, starting with their own work and their careers.

I see leaders as owners of the entire continuum of skills and behaviors ranging from operational action to visionary persuasion. To judge their success, I don't look at their inputs—style, personality, habits, skills, competencies—instead, I prefer to focus on the outcomes of their actions.[2] That is, how close are the employee and customer experience to the aspiration the leader had for them; their capacity to liberate an organization to a destination point. In doing that, leaders make choices that connect with their sources of liberation. For example, what problems to solve and what problems to live with, what people to bring along and who to remove, which projects to fund now and which projects will have to wait, and very importantly, what important initiatives must end. All of the above creates outcomes and creates culture redirecting the organization toward the success of a particular vision. The outcomes of the leader's actions, tactical or strategic, opens and closes doors, altering positively or negatively the experience of a liberating, vital workplace.

How to get started? Make a discipline to ask these questions everyday at the end of the day: *what did I unleashed today? What important decision did I (or didn't I) make? What is the next hurdle to remove?* Find related insight and guidance in Chapter 3, Leadership of Liberation; start with the components of liberating leadership, Fig. 3.1. Look again in Chapter 15, Expectation, the list of preliminary competency areas to develop for liberating leaders, Fig. 15.2.

You Are Becoming You Next Self—Design for It

You are not static, you are permanently in motion, therefore, changing is about redirecting the motion in your actions and decisions everyday. Make you next self to be the outcome of a conscious choice, not the outcome of chance and circumstances. I heard once that we become part of every place we visit and every person we meet. That the aggregate collection of experiences we live sculpt our character and make us become who we are. Therefore, surround yourself with the extraordinary; pick the smart person over the 'yes' person, choose hard metrics that reveal authentic outcomes, instead of those that focus on inputs. There are no shortcuts to your North Star. If you listen to people who are the best achievers in their disciplines, champions in sports, the arts or science, their stories are summarized by the words 'desire' and 'work'. Desire to do something remarkable that is very clear in their minds, and to do the hard work necessary to get there. The grinding, the training, the mundane, the pleasant, and the less pleasant, all of it are the ingredients you need to become your best self.

What this means is that your design for yourself matters much more than you may think. Your personal and professional aspirations work as magnetic fields to orient and align what you do, constantly pulling and pushing actions on that direction. It is imperative to have a vision for the self, because even if you think you don't have one, you actually do, it is just random and fed by the immediate.

During my work on high-potential talent identification, there were a few questions highly correlated with extraordinary potential and capacity to grow. One of them was related to a personal North Star: 'what is you design for yourself? Who are you in the future? Where are you going?'. Some leaders would respond instantly, clearly, and were able to precisely describe that they wanted to be, as if they were watching a movie playing in front of them. It was clear they had spent time over years thinking about it. Others hesitated, trying to find words, responded with vague statements, indicating they would be ready for opportunities as those presented themselves. Over time, the first group progressed faster, more focused, and better equipped to discern which opportunities they should take; not only the most enticing, but the ones that were closer to the design they had for their future selves, making them better at decision-making, more deliberate and affirmed. Those mindsets translate in self-confidence and performance.

How to get started? Add to the end of day dialogue with yourself these questions: *who am I becoming? What beliefs about myself I should change to get to where I want to be?* Chapter 5, The Liberation Mindset, offers a great description of how the WORD and the WORLD define the ways in which leaders intend to change the world, the same can be applied to change the self.

To Be or Not to Be the Limit of the Organization

As water takes the shape of the container holding it, so organizations take on the leader's capability, and her/his limitations. It is true that teams *can* make everyone better, but in the end, what gets approved, accepted, decided upon, ultimately comes from *the leader*. Great news when the leader is able to overcome a measure of fear, tolerate the natural discomfort to trust a path otherwise unnatural for her/him. In the other way around, organizations see themselves fenced around the space of possibilities the leader is capable to embrace. There may be actions leaders will not be able to stomach or simply do not believe they are the solutions the company needs. Evidence abounds in sports, families, teams of every kind. Results follow the design of the systems that create them. We are creators of worlds and destroyers of worlds all the same.

A particular instance of *limits* takes a familiar shape in the experience of leading change: the strategic use of authority. Authority is good for change and redirection, the wise use of power liberates organizations, get things in motion. But it requires leader's self-awareness to eliminate the risk of blocking learning loops, filter customer feedback, and suppress employee innovation, necessary to reinvent and redirect the company. How can this happen? The mechanism is simple. If you over-use your authority to operate as a leader—not asking for input, not relying on data, not implementing governance processes—you risk breaking a delicate balance of judgment for your people. Giving direction excels when the actions clearly connect with the business rationale, identifying the vital principle it follows. Directive actions that are not connected to feedback, to the customer, or the North Star of the company, risk being seen as merely reflecting the way the leader—you—*wants things to be,* making *you,* not the goals, the reference point of performance. Sooner than you think, people start working less focused on the transformation and more focused on pleasing you. The lines are thin and blurred, but very real. Natural human behavior takes over and very soon people will focus on keeping you happy, filtering real data, removing bad news, anything they interpret you will not like, shielding decision-making from actual data to redirect and improve. Not to be confused here, this is not necessarily a conscious behavior by leaders; it may be simply the by product of a poor governance process, where the leader insists on being the sole decision-maker, a poor delegation process where senior leaders remove ownership from the experts and every tactical decision must be confirmed along the chain of command. It is implicit, not explicit.

The good news: limitations can be removed, frontiers can be expanded, constraints can be unlocked; *we can grow.*

How to get started? Start by seeking and listening to feedback. The key questions to ask yourself are: *what organization am I building? Is the team/ organization getting closer or further away from its top potential? Is there anything in me that can delay or can accelerate our pace?*

The concept of vitality is useful to understand how your organization has been designed over years of survival and success into what it is today and what levers can be used to change it. Chapter 9, Fig. 9.2 provides a map of the areas building the infrastructure, the roads, and avenues for your organization.

Chapters 10–12 cover the three disciplines that remove the bumps, minimize traffic lights, and create highways in your company: Culture, Talent, and Organization.

The fastest path to good management is a robust governance process. This is explained in Chapter 12, illustrated in Figs. 12.4 and 12.6.

Finally, work on yourself as a liberation project. You can find a coach, run a 360. So much value is wasted, so much talent is unleveraged, and opportunity is missed because leaders refuse to look at themselves. Without knowing it, you may be the limit of your organization, not because you don't listen to good ideas, respect other people, or follow the right values, but instead, because when a big decision moment comes, you chose to be and react in the way your past dictates, not in the way your future demands it to be.

The Leader Your North Star Needs

The place we know today as the Strait of Gibraltar, separating Europe and Africa in the edge of the Mediterranean Sea used to be known by ancient Romans as the Gates of Hercules. According to Plato and ancient mythology, the place was regarded as the limit of Earth. The Columns of Hercules, as they were also called, portrayed the inscription NON PLVS VLTRA, which means 'nothing further beyond' indicating the limits of the world, as it was known at the time, and serving as a warning to navigators that there was nothing more after that frontier. However, after the Spanish Monarchs Queen Isabella I of Castile, and King Ferdinand II of Aragon sponsored the journeys of Christopher Columbus in 1492, the world confirmed the existence of *The New World*, symbolizing a tectonic paradigm shift in the world, and cementing one of the defining symbols of the end of the Middle Ages in favor of the Renaissance. In the process, a key concept was born, *globalization*. A new world indeed.

A few years later in 1516, Charles of Habsburg, new King of Spain, adopted the inscription PLVS ULTRA—'there is more', as the motto for the kingdom of Spain, as it has been ever since (Fig. 20.1).

The way to find what was beyond, and change the world meant the risk of passing through the gates of *the end*. It may sound too trivial for the traveler of the Twentieth First Century, but crossing the Atlantic for the first time in the Fifteenth Century was a very audacious and risky endeavor.

I heard that story at a particularly perilous time in my personal journey, while visiting the City of Granada, in which the Fortress and Palace of

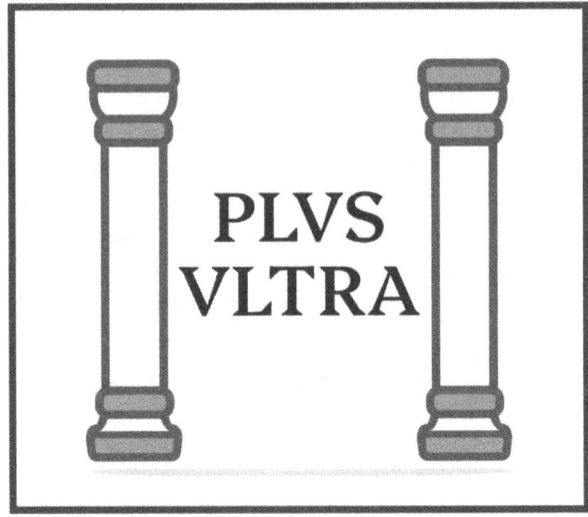

Fig. 20.1 Depiction of the Columns of Hercules, according to legend, with the inscription PLUS ULTRA, meaning 'There is More'

Alhambra holds a rich history and remarkable art depicting the monumental transition toward the modern era, recognizing that the future possibilities of Spain were in the Americas. The story changed me, as made it me realize that no matter how limited you may feel sometimes, or how certain of your limits you may be, *there is always more in you.* Enterprise work, organizational change, transformations, come with their share of defeat and compromise, and any measure of success calls for a capacity to overcome and reinvent—to find answers beyond *the known*. Either personally, or professionally, the way to a new beginning is to venture through the gates of our limitations and journey across our own gates of the unknown. A worthy challenge for the leader of liberation.

Sounds imposing, but you have done this before, and you are not alone. There is a team ready to follow your leadership and there is a vision, a map, a method, described in this book to guide your success to change the world.

May you find the passion and the inspiration. May you raise from failure and defeat to become the liberating, vital leader your North Star needs you to be.

The world needs it!

Notes

1. George, B., & Sims, P. (2007). True north. Jossey-Bass.
2. Collins, J. (2001). Good to great: Why some companies make the leap… and others don't. HarperCollins.

Brands Index

A
Aetna 113, 125
Amazon 86, 276
Apple 42, 56, 86, 89

B
Bain & Company 228, 229
BCG 50
Boston Dynamics 75, 78

C
Cannon 50
Carnegie Mellon University 161, 184
Center for Creative Leadership 152
Chat GPT 52
Cirque de Soleil 50
Cisco 50
Crane Company 240, 256
Crayola 73, 77
CVS 113, 125

D
Dana Corporation 34
Dell 73, 85, 93, 96, 97, 195, 196, 252, 253
Dupont

F
Facebook 50
Ford Motor Company 49, 172, 185

G
Gallup 47, 132, 134, 154, 213, 219, 230, 231, 234, 272, 285, 292
Gartner 132, 134, 154, 155, 222, 234
General Motors 9, 49
Gibraltar-Strait of 297
Global ERG Network 272, 274
Google 73, 77, 86, 185, 267, 274, 276
Granada-Spain 297

Brands Index

H

Hewllet Packard 50
HMH 73, 272
Houghton Mifflin Harcourt 12, 272
Human Rights Campaign 272, 274

I

IBM Corporation 77, 125
IDEO 163, 184
Intel 74, 77, 276

J

Johnson & Johnson 76, 78

K

Kodak 50

L

Lucas Films 172

M

McKinsey & Company 14, 26, 47, 60, 154, 273, 274, 291, 292
Microsoft 74, 77
Mitsubishi Electric 74, 78
Monterrey Tech 34
Motorola 56, 86, 87, 112, 113, 152

N

NASA 74
National Public Radio (NPR) 3, 7
Netflix 8, 26, 85, 124, 125, 292
Novartis 74, 77
Nvidia 50

P

P&G 75, 78
Partnership on AI 75, 78

S

Sales Force 50
Sony Group 266
Southwest Airlines 75, 78
Spain 297, 298

T

Taiwan Semiconductor Manufacturing Company (TSMC) 76, 78
Tesla 50
Tik Tok 50
Toyota 49, 117, 125, 184
Tweeter 242

W

Walmart 75, 78
Women Peacemakers Fellowship 38, 48

Name Index

A
Ackmann, Martha 155
Allen, Jim 104, 109, 234
Arc, Joan of 38
Autor, David 291
Ayres, Robert U. 25

B
Beck, K. 184
Bennis, Warren 27, 45, 47
Bhilare, Priyanka 26
Bienko, Marcia W. 125, 228, 234
Bolivar, Simon 38
Bolt, Jim 38, 48
Bossidy, Larry 189, 194
Boudreau, Jonathan 292
Buckingham, Marcus 155
Burns, James McGregor 27, 47

C
Cappelli, Peter 155, 219
Catmull, E. 171, 185
Chamberlain, Andrew 273
Chambers, E.G. 291
Champy, J. 50, 60
Charan, Ram 189, 194
Chopra, Anjali 26
Chrissis, M.B. 184
Christensen, Clayton M. 43, 48, 51, 60
Chui, Michael 292
Churchill, Winston 38
Clifton, Jim 47, 154, 219, 234, 292
Collins, J. 71, 77
Columbus, Christopher 297
Cornelius, A.M. 26
Crane, Richard 240, 256
Curie, Marie 37, 72
Curtis, B. 184

D
Dell, Michael 42, 93, 195
De Smet, Aaron 26, 154
Dixon-Fyle, Sundiatu 273
Doerr, John 176, 185
Dolan, Kevin 273
Dowling, Bonnie 26, 154

Name Index

E
Edwards, Mark 274
Ernst & Young 273

F
Ferry, Korn 219
Flemming, Alexander 37
Floyd, George 10, 14, 26, 278
Ford, Henry 37, 72
Foulon, Mark 291

G
Galbraith, Jay R. 184
Garfield, Z.H. 47
Gartner 132, 134, 154, 155, 222, 234
George, Bill 293, 299
Getz, Isaac 47
Glanz, James 185
Goldsmith, Marshall 43, 48
Goodall, Ashley 155
Gratton, Lynda 109
Grawitch, M.J. 26
Gross, Terry 3
Grove, Andy 72
Gutenberg, Johannes 37

H
Habermas, Jurgen 69, 101
Hagen, E.H. 47
Hamel, Gary 26, 101
Hammer, M. 50, 60
Handfield-Jones, Helen 291
Hankin, Steven 291
Harter, Jim 47, 154, 219, 234, 292
Hastings, Reed 125
Hazan, E. 292
Hoffman, Brice G. 172, 185
Hogan, J. 125
Hogan, R. 124, 125
Hubbard, R.L. 47

Hunt, Vivian 273

I
Iacocca, Lee 72, 77
Immelt, Jeff 51, 60
Iyer, Aarti 274

J
Jackson, Shareef 155
Jacob, Kathryn 274
Jesuthasan, Ravin 292
Johnson, Mark W. 72, 77, 80, 83, 89
Joly, Hubert 71, 77

K
Kaplan, Robert S. 276, 291
Kates, Amy 175, 185
Kegan, Robert 287, 292
Keller, Scott 204
Kendi, Ibram X. 273
Kennedy, John F. 64–66, 69, 72, 76, 84, 155
Kesler, Gregory 175, 185
Kimball, Richard 48
Kimball, Rocky 38
Kim, W. Chan 80, 82, 89
King, Dan 26, 194
King, Martin Luther (Jr) 38
Kister, A. 26
Kotter, John P. 27, 47
Kowalski, G. 26, 155
Koziel, R.J. 26
Kreuzbauer, Robert 26, 194
Kurzweil, Ray 287, 292

L
Laloux, Frederic 46, 48
Lavigne, K.N. 26
Lencioni, Patrick 232, 234

Lewis, Michael 137, 155
Lipowski, M. 26
Lopez, Juan 34–36
Lund, Susan 47, 60

Malhotra, Arvind 26, 291
Malone, Thomas 57
Martin, Roger L. 89
Maslow, Abraham, H. 132, 154
Mauborgne, Renee 80, 82, 89
McCall, Morgan W. 152, 155
McCord, Patty 8, 26, 292
Metha, Nick 90, 234
Meyer, Erin 125
Michaels, Edward 291
Michelangelo 41, 194
Mindell, David 291
Mintzberg, Henry 27, 47
Mugayar-Baldocchi, Marino 26, 154
Mulally, Allan 172, 185
Musk, Elon 242

Norton, David P. 276, 291
Novak, W. 77

O'Reilly, Charles A. III 223, 234
Ohno, Taiichi 125, 184
Olorunnipa, T. 26

Paulk, M.C. 184
Pickens, Allison 90, 234
Plato 297
Pokojski, Z. 26
Porras, J.I. 71, 77
Porter, Michael E. 79–81, 83, 89
Prince, Sarah 273

Quinn, Robert E. 60

Reynolds, Elisabeth 291
Roberts, R. 292
Rushide, Salman 3, 7, 8
Ruth, Sean 47

Samuels, R. 26
Schaninger, Bill 26, 154, 204
Schein, Edgar H. 46, 48, 112, 120, 125
Schutz, Will 31, 32, 35, 47, 264, 273
Senge, Peter 42, 48
Sims, Peter 299
Sinclair, Amanda 47
Singla, A. 292
Slater, Robert 60
Ślebarska, K. 26, 155
Slywotzky, Adrian J. 79, 81, 89
Smaje, K. 292
Stansell, Amanda 273
Sukharevsky, A. 292
Suskewicz, Josh 72, 77, 80, 83, 89

Tavis, Anna 155, 219
Taylor, Frederick W. 275, 291
Thakor, Anjan V. 60
Troussaint, John S. 125
Tushman, Michael L. 223, 234

Ulrich, Dave 291
Unerman, Sue 274

V

Venkataramani, Swetha 155, 234

W

Wallace, A. 185
Warrenfeltz, R. 125
Weber, C.V. 184
Welch, Jack 50, 51, 60, 173
Whitehead, Alfred North 194
Wolfe, Tom 152, 153, 155
Wulf, Julie 256

Y

Yeager, Chuck 153, 155
Yee, L. 292
Yee, Vivian 185
Yousafzai, Malala 38

Z

Zemmel, R. 292
Zhao, Daniel 273
Zook, Chris 104, 109, 234

Index

A

Acceleration 9, 41, 86, 145, 146, 150, 162, 177, 181
Acquisitions 113, 180
Adapt 6, 23, 46, 49, 56, 58, 66, 67, 142, 157, 159, 161, 165, 184, 187, 198, 246, 250, 252, 254, 277–279, 287, 289
Advocates 15, 122, 260, 261
Affection 35, 47, 222, 264
Affirm 211
Agile 20, 85, 97, 161, 165, 179, 184, 217, 241, 253
Agile Manifesto 161
Alignment 17, 25, 55, 68, 95, 98, 105, 113, 117, 119, 123, 124, 166, 200, 205, 208, 210, 243, 244, 256, 269, 276
Amplifiers 119, 125, 270
Amplify 17, 119, 120, 140, 143, 265
Amplifying 118, 119, 140
Apollo Program 153
Archetypes 246
Architect 4, 57, 142, 166, 167, 219, 283
Artificial Intelligence (AI) 9, 52, 56–58, 75, 76, 165, 277, 278, 280, 287–290, 292
Assert 10, 31, 282, 286
Astronauts 28, 65, 152, 153
Automation 9, 29, 37, 158, 160, 163, 226, 279, 280, 290

B

Becoming 7, 11, 16, 17, 21, 45, 55, 56, 118, 127, 157, 169, 179, 188, 191–194, 225, 227–229, 231, 246, 258, 264
Becoming your purpose 191
BHAG 71
Blue Ocean 81, 82, 89
Business acceleration 162, 163
Business optimization 279, 280, 290
Business processes 109, 157–159, 161, 163, 164, 182
Business roadmap 238

C

Cadence 51, 105, 121, 183, 218
Capability 5, 7, 11, 20, 49, 56, 81, 85, 87, 92, 95, 107, 113, 118, 130, 138, 139, 142, 144, 157, 160–162, 164, 170, 172, 179, 182, 184, 226, 237, 243, 254, 288, 291, 293, 295
Capability Maturity Model 161
Centers of Excellence 279
Change management 18, 29, 84, 100, 122, 213, 249
Choreograph 200, 286
CHRO 6, 7, 68, 127, 149, 200, 211, 249, 290
Clarity 12, 14, 21
Coaching 46, 148, 213
Commitment 12, 21, 24, 29, 41, 43, 54, 55, 63, 64, 67–69, 72, 86, 89, 91–101, 108, 111, 113, 118–120, 122, 131, 134, 136, 137, 146–149, 151, 166, 174, 179, 183, 188, 193, 196, 197, 200, 203–205, 218, 224, 225, 245, 254–256, 260, 261, 265, 268–272, 277, 280, 282, 285
Competencies 24, 27, 39, 147, 148, 211, 213, 215, 294
Complexity 64, 147, 161, 164, 179, 202, 226, 241, 248, 253
Connect 18, 51, 73, 97, 99, 105, 111, 113, 138, 157, 163, 166, 182, 200, 214, 226, 237, 245, 253, 254, 283, 286, 288, 294, 296
Control 32, 35, 45, 119, 121, 122, 140, 163, 177, 224, 246, 264
Conversation 11, 12, 24, 29, 39, 43, 92, 94–97, 99, 100, 118, 122, 142, 145, 148–150, 170, 196, 199, 203, 210, 218, 224–226, 231, 234, 249, 268, 277, 281
Conversations for commitment 97

Cost structure 17, 23, 56, 134, 151, 165, 207, 210
COVID-19 10, 15, 37, 47, 52, 60
CPO 59, 68, 123, 267, 290
Critical 5, 7, 12, 13, 35, 44, 53, 55, 56, 74, 92, 100, 108, 116, 117, 123, 132, 139, 144, 146, 150, 152, 157, 168–171, 180, 181, 195, 197, 203, 208, 212, 215, 218, 228, 240, 250, 258, 259, 263–265, 270, 275–277, 279, 280
Culture-designed 127, 257
Culture-experienced 117, 257
Culture-manager 257
Culture-written 257

D

Decision effectiveness 109, 158, 228, 229
Decision rights 118, 229, 243, 244
Demand 20, 23, 46, 56, 57, 71, 127, 128, 130, 138, 143, 161, 164, 165, 174, 228, 248, 273, 280, 286, 287, 292, 293
Designed culture 116, 117, 120, 124, 262
Detractors 260, 261
Development 5, 14, 27, 28, 34, 35, 37, 38, 43, 52, 53, 79, 86, 117, 129, 131, 138, 142, 146, 148–150, 152, 159, 160, 164, 165, 193, 211, 213, 234, 239, 240, 253, 261, 262, 264, 275, 276, 284, 286
Differentiation 52, 53, 80, 81, 112, 136, 159, 170, 175, 188, 207, 212, 221, 262, 276
Disrupt 44, 45, 67, 142, 218
Diverse, Equitable, Inclusive and Belonging (DEIB) 23, 35, 57, 146, 178, 257–263, 265–269, 271–273

Diversity 15, 23, 40, 116, 134, 146, 174, 176, 178, 224, 258–273, 277, 290
Diversity ecosystem 259, 263
DNA 18, 20, 21, 100, 104, 107, 116, 128, 136, 158, 184, 242

E

Ecosystem 86, 249, 259, 262, 266, 284
Employee life cycle 141, 143
Employee Resources Groups 260
Employee services 162, 240, 278–280
Employee Value Proposition (EVP) 32, 108, 109, 131–137, 141, 143, 148, 155, 176, 177, 224, 234, 258, 271, 282, 284, 285
Empowerment 45, 85, 193, 245
Engagement 25, 32, 54, 91, 98–100, 103, 107, 131, 132, 134, 150, 157, 180, 191, 196, 198–200, 203, 204, 210, 213, 244, 250, 256, 272, 280, 284, 285, 289
Engagement-employee 23, 24, 182, 197, 203
Engagement session 201, 202, 206, 250
Engagement-transformational 197–201, 203, 204
Engineer 138, 217
Enterprise success 162, 280, 289
Environmental, Social and Governance (ESG) 18, 38, 133, 146, 178, 208
ERG 259
Essential 5, 6, 34, 41, 53, 58, 67, 73, 74, 79, 144, 159, 171, 212, 229, 240, 244, 250, 277, 282, 287
Experienced culture 108, 109, 111, 117, 118

Expression 19–21, 23, 25, 26, 31, 38, 54, 58, 59, 73, 107, 122, 130, 133, 145, 152, 153, 171, 181, 184, 187–191, 193, 194, 197, 202, 208, 213, 215, 218, 221, 222, 225, 226, 232, 258, 262, 266, 280, 281, 284, 286, 289
Expression mindset 265

F

Fabric of connections 95, 99, 100
Fear 22, 28, 41, 44, 45, 206, 208, 230, 295
Feedback 44, 46, 105, 117, 148, 155, 158, 182, 211, 215, 216, 230, 231, 263, 284, 296
Financial 50, 51, 53, 79, 80, 85, 112, 159, 160, 173, 198, 208, 209, 248, 249, 276
Financial era 162
FIRO 31, 47, 273
First Team 232
Flexibility 11–14, 16, 17, 29, 42, 133, 143–145, 160, 161, 241, 250
Flexible 15, 42, 145, 211, 258, 277
Fortune 500 242, 254
From-To 22, 67, 79, 80, 82, 86, 98, 267, 268
Further 4, 7, 11, 21, 28, 40, 68, 86, 94, 118, 123, 138, 141, 143, 165, 181, 192–194, 244, 246, 268, 269, 280, 284, 286, 297
Future 5, 10, 11, 16, 18, 23–26, 28–30, 34, 37, 41–43, 46, 47, 49, 53, 54, 56–58, 60, 66, 71, 72, 75–77, 83, 85, 86, 88, 89, 93, 95, 97–99, 101, 112–114, 116, 118, 119, 122, 128, 133, 134, 138, 142, 151, 159, 166, 169, 171–173, 175, 182, 188, 193, 194, 198–201, 203, 207,

216, 217, 223, 234, 237, 240, 243, 249, 252, 254, 255, 259, 261, 273, 277, 281, 285, 286, 289–291, 295, 298
Future of Work 3, 13, 16, 25, 26, 30, 133, 144, 277, 285, 286, 288, 289

G

Gates of Hercules 297
Globalization 51, 297
Governance 28, 105, 109, 120, 121, 149, 178–181, 183, 193, 207, 218, 223, 230, 242–245, 255, 256, 265–267, 269, 284, 296, 297

H

Harmonize 223, 286
High Flyers 152
High potential 272
Hogan Assessment 119, 124
HR 4, 6, 8, 24, 26, 34, 39, 56, 57, 93, 118, 121, 123, 129, 142, 149, 162, 212, 251, 256, 260, 264, 266, 276–286, 288–290, 292
Human-Centered Design 163
Human resources 6, 12, 57, 175, 196, 216, 253, 266, 275–279, 281–284, 290

I

Implementation 7, 20, 21, 23, 42, 59, 91, 107, 115, 123–125, 131, 137, 145, 158, 166, 167, 175, 183, 188, 205, 213, 231, 233, 238, 239, 241, 242, 247, 249–252, 254, 255, 257, 265, 269, 270, 284
Implementation-large company 242

Implementation-medium size company 241
Implementation-small company 239
Inclusion 35, 146, 151, 191, 258, 264, 266, 267, 270
Inconsistency 124, 172, 253
Industrial 9, 27, 49–52, 132, 162, 275, 276, 278, 279, 290
Industrial era 49
Industrial Relations 276, 279
Industrial Revolution 9, 50, 275
Infrastructure 7, 17, 20, 22, 38, 59, 63, 66, 103, 106–109, 130, 131, 136, 159, 160, 162, 163, 188, 193, 207, 208, 210, 215, 221, 225, 241, 243, 248, 250, 252, 253, 255, 256, 260, 281, 282, 284, 296
Innovation 4, 9, 29, 39, 41, 51, 53, 55–57, 72, 79–83, 87, 146, 157, 161–164, 170, 172, 173, 190, 213, 218, 254, 276, 277, 283, 289, 296
Integrity 11, 12, 14–16, 18, 149

L

Leadership Imperative 93, 196
Leading Success Trilogy 107, 108, 111
Learning 13, 17, 21, 34, 45, 54, 88, 100, 131, 162, 164, 205, 207, 225, 226, 237, 241, 296
Legacy 54, 76, 80, 133, 143, 154, 173, 231, 234, 245, 283
LGBTQ 30, 146, 190, 264
Liberating commitment 93, 95, 96, 99, 203
Liberation mindset 63, 64, 67, 69, 101

M

M&A 170, 227, 241

Manager 4, 6, 13, 15, 24, 31, 32, 34, 36, 40, 44, 54, 55, 59, 63, 83, 84, 88, 93, 95, 97–101, 105, 107, 112, 113, 115–120, 123, 124, 128, 130, 137, 138, 140, 142–144, 147–150, 152, 154, 165, 168, 171–173, 175, 176, 182, 184, 190, 192, 195, 196, 198–200, 202–208, 211–219, 222–228, 230–234, 239, 247, 248, 250, 253, 257, 261, 263, 265, 267–271, 284, 285, 292, 293
Manager culture 118, 119, 262
Mercury Program 152
Metrics 18, 20, 21, 23–25, 28, 40, 42, 51, 54, 56, 84, 85, 92, 103, 105, 107, 109, 117, 123, 128, 136, 137, 147, 151, 157, 168, 176, 177, 179, 181, 192, 193, 197, 204, 208, 212, 213, 244, 257, 259, 262, 263, 265, 267, 268, 270, 271, 276, 284, 285, 294
Mindset-Expression 17, 58, 91, 184, 188, 233
Mindset-Liberation 17, 58, 68, 91, 100, 188, 233
Mindset-Vitality 17, 58, 91, 188, 233, 282
Mission 41, 55, 66, 73, 74, 77, 108, 115, 127, 153, 154, 189, 251
Moderna 37
Moneyball 137
mRNA (messenger RNA) 37

N

Nine disciplines 19, 21, 25, 53, 58, 107, 200, 226, 227, 231, 233, 237–239, 241, 252, 278, 281, 289
Non-believers 260, 261
NON PLVS VLTRA 260, 261

O

Onboarding 5, 13, 23, 117, 128, 142, 143, 240, 258, 284
Optimize 14, 55, 81, 85, 139, 162, 212, 214, 217, 241, 247
Organic 57, 153, 154, 170, 215, 257, 258, 269
Organization Review 149, 179, 181, 182, 218
Organziation empowerment 45, 109, 157, 165
Ownership 33, 91, 99, 106, 119, 121, 167, 189, 196, 201, 204, 206, 240, 264, 266, 267, 269, 270, 285, 286, 296

P

Pandemic 4, 10, 11, 14–16, 30, 33, 52, 53, 97, 134, 165, 180, 191, 224, 278, 289
Pay equity 151, 258, 268, 271
Performance management 23, 44, 155, 211, 219, 258, 276, 284, 285
Performer 190, 191, 226, 232, 233
Performer and performance 190
Philosophy 17, 27, 63, 124, 135, 163, 193, 194, 227, 241, 283
Pivotal 21, 52, 93, 108, 144, 146, 150, 152, 213, 215, 267
Plus Ultra 298
PMP 211, 212
Policies 12, 13, 16, 32, 34, 39, 40, 41, 44, 63, 87, 103–106, 111, 112, 117, 124, 136, 137, 143, 145, 151, 161, 167, 175, 181, 212, 223, 253, 257, 262, 268, 270
Position profile 130, 138, 165, 168, 169, 171, 216
Progression 14, 24, 115, 132, 148, 161, 258, 262, 267, 270–272, 280, 289

312   Index

Purpose 15, 17, 21, 24, 28, 36, 52–55, 58, 71–75, 77, 82, 83, 97–100, 108, 111, 117, 131–133, 136, 142, 145, 153, 161, 165, 170, 188, 190, 193, 194, 201, 203, 214, 223, 226–228, 233, 248, 251, 264, 266, 271, 277, 278, 282, 284, 286
Purpose era 53, 162, 234, 277, 280, 286, 288, 289

R

RAPID 229, 230, 244, 256
Recruitment 117, 140, 141
Reengineering 50, 60
Reframe 18, 24, 40, 63, 227, 281
Remote work 12, 13, 26, 145, 175, 277
Representation 38, 167, 246, 258, 262, 264, 267, 270, 271, 281, 283
Return on talent 130
Return on talent value 138, 140
Right stuff 152–155
Risk 39, 41, 43–45, 51, 52, 81, 85, 99, 123, 128, 135, 158, 168, 171, 172, 178, 179, 181, 182, 199, 210, 227, 228, 247, 250, 252, 254, 255, 261, 269, 270, 296, 297

S

Scalable 42, 96, 107, 160, 188, 195, 200, 208
Scale 7, 9, 10, 37, 44, 49, 50, 53, 54, 65, 68, 69, 84, 97, 107, 121, 154, 162, 184, 187, 194, 197, 200, 223, 225–227, 231, 239, 241, 243, 275, 280
Script 284

Signature 21, 89, 106, 109, 111, 142, 199, 213, 218, 223, 224, 228, 240, 242, 271
Signature experience 21, 131, 184, 221–224, 226–228, 231–233
Signature expression 19–21, 58, 107, 190, 191, 222, 249, 258, 259
Signature feedback 228, 230
Signature processes 24, 109, 117, 123, 143, 157, 158, 183, 184, 257, 271
Simplification 21, 24, 41, 85, 87, 88, 92, 105, 140, 141, 163, 176, 190, 199, 214, 238
Simplify 4, 40, 139, 150, 163, 211, 218, 247, 255
Sincerity 206
Social justice 10, 15, 17, 52, 264, 277, 278, 280, 288, 289
Software 37, 52, 86, 87, 134, 160–162, 165, 184, 191, 211, 223
Spans and Layers 247, 248
Strategic obstacles 85
Strategic velocity 85
Supply 15, 23, 53, 56, 127, 130, 138, 162, 164, 180, 240
Supply chain 5, 86, 160, 161, 180, 253

T

Talent density 125, 217
Talent Economy 23, 56, 108, 127, 129–131, 138, 139, 164, 168, 181, 184, 206, 216, 217, 240, 284
Talent Economy Roadmap 132, 137, 141
Talent Profile 169
Talent Review 149–151, 268
Taxonomy 33, 50, 51
Tech & Customer era 276
Trilogy 107–109, 111, 184

Trust 7, 44, 95, 99–101, 135, 136, 148, 175, 180, 196, 198, 206, 210, 245, 250, 272, 295
Twelve DEIB Imperatives 266

V

Value creation 56, 75, 130, 134, 141, 162
Vision 7, 18, 21–24, 28, 29, 35, 36, 39, 41, 54, 58, 64–69, 72, 74–76, 78–80, 83, 84, 86, 89, 97–99, 101, 107, 108, 111, 115, 119, 121, 122, 128, 157, 158, 161, 166, 174, 187, 188, 193, 194, 197, 200, 201, 203, 205, 216, 221, 225–227, 240, 242, 253, 254, 261, 269, 270, 281–283, 285, 286, 290, 291, 293–295, 298
Vital governance 23, 149, 158, 178, 218

Vitality mindset 29, 103, 157, 207, 283
Vital process 54, 149, 150
Vital risk response 179, 180, 218

W

Word 32, 34, 35, 46, 65, 77, 88, 94, 103, 135, 189, 225, 288
Word vs World 67, 97, 226, 227, 282, 295
World 4, 5, 9–11, 14–18, 21, 28–30, 36, 38, 49, 51–57, 71–77, 88, 89, 177, 185, 191, 194, 196–198, 223, 225, 226, 231, 232, 258, 264, 265, 273, 277, 278, 288, 289, 295, 297, 298
Written culture 115, 116, 120, 124, 262, 265, 266

GPSR Compliance

The European Union's (EU) General Product Safety Regulation (GPSR) is a set of rules that requires consumer products to be safe and our obligations to ensure this.

If you have any concerns about our products, you can contact us on

ProductSafety@springernature.com

In case Publisher is established outside the EU, the EU authorized representative is:

Springer Nature Customer Service Center GmbH
Europaplatz 3
69115 Heidelberg, Germany